Security and Democracy in Southern Africa

The Wits P&DM Governance Series

The Wits P&DM Governance Series explores the challenges and politics of governance and service delivery in unequal and limited resource contexts such as South and Southern Africa, by publishing relevant scholarly research. By focusing on comparative public administration, institutional economics, development and good governance issues, the series aims to contribute to the development of a knowledge base to inform governance policies and practices in Southern Africa. Titles will address neither pure political science/sociology nor mechanical old-style public administration, but rather the dynamic interfaces between public-policy analysis and decision-making, and the actual implementation and evaluation of these through a variety of institutions, organisations and social processes.

Security and Democracy in Southern Africa edited by Gavin Cawthra, Andre du Pisani and Abillah Omari, is the second book in this series. *The State of the State: Institutional Transformation, Capacity and Political Change in South Africa* was published in 2006.

Security and Democracy in Southern Africa

Edited by
Gavin Cawthra, Andre du Pisani and Abillah Omari

Wits University Press
1 Jan Smuts Avenue
Johannesburg 2001
South Africa

http://witspress.wits.ac.za

ISBN 978-1-86814-453-2

First printed 2007

The Wits P&DM Governance Series is an initiative of Wits University Press and the Graduate School of Public and Development Management, University of the Witwatersrand.

This publication has been made possible by a research grant from the International Development Research Centre (IDRC), Ottawa, Canada and a publication subsidy from the Frederich Ebert Stiftung, Maputo, Mozambique.

Typesetting and reproduction by Positive Proof, Johannesburg, South Africa
Cover design by Hybridesign, Johannesburg, South Africa
Cover photograph by Cedric Nunn, africapictures.net
Printed and bound by Paarl Print, Paarl, South Africa

Contents

Preface

This book had its genesis in two observations: that democratisation has been the major political trend in Southern Africa since the end of apartheid and the termination of the Cold War (albeit an uneven democratisation that in some cases has even been reversed); and, that like many regions or sub-regions, Southern Africa has embarked on a major project of multinational co-operation, including in the security field.

These observations led to two questions, which is what this book is all about. The first was essentially about the relationship (if any) between the dynamics of democratisation and democratic practices (or lack of them) and national security perceptions and practices in Southern African states. The second was whether this has had any effect on approaches to the regional security project.

We leave it to the reader to judge whether we have answered these questions, but a summary of the findings is attempted in the conclusion.

The research project from which this book resulted was almost as much about process as findings. It was a project of the Southern African Defence and Security Management (SADSEM) Network, a grouping of tertiary institutions in ten countries that works on common research and capacity-building programmes for the democratic management of defence and security in the region, both within and between states (see Appendix 2). The research was supported by a three-year grant from the International Development Research Centre (IDRC), Canada.

After common terms of reference had been agreed, three conceptual chapters were written: on democracy and security; on security co-operation in a comparative context; and on the background of conflict, co-operation and democratisation in the Southern African Development Centre (SADC).

Next, country studies were commissioned. We initially hoped to cover all the 14 member states of SADC, but as the project advanced this was whittled down to 11. In particular, Angola and the DRC, which at the time the research was initiated were still involved in civil wars, proved difficult to accommodate in the research framework.[1] In many Southern African countries, research into defence and security matters is still very sensitive and the researchers often had to tread delicately in seeking to knock on and open doors, but in most cases governments were co-operative.

Partly because the SADSEM Network is committed to developing indigenous capacities for researching and managing security, and partly because we are tired of being written about rather than writing about ourselves, in virtually all cases nationals of the countries concerned were commissioned to carry out the research. In some countries, small teams of researchers collaborated as part of the effort to build local capacities. A small team of international advisors also participated in the process.[2]

The team of researchers met on three occasions to peer-review the outputs and to see whether a common picture was emerging. These meetings, in Maputo and Johannesburg, were supported by the Friedrich Ebert Stiftung (FES), and were also made possible by core support to the SADSEM Network by Danida. As a further quality control measure, the project was externally evaluated in mid-term and on completion.[3]

At the final meeting, officials from governments and non-governmental organisations attended and were able to make inputs, along with the international advisory team.

Further workshops were held in Botswana, Mozambique and South Africa, where lively discussions on the findings took place between academics, government officials and civil society representatives. Some policy recommendations were derived as a result, which were written up as a policy paper and disseminated through the region (see Appendix 1).

This book is a product in a very real way of the whole SADSEM Network. The Network partners constituted a management committee and oversaw it from its beginnings as an idea to its completion. In this process many colleagues, both in Southern Africa and abroad, participated. We thank them all, as well as the main donors – IDRC which sponsored the research, Danida which provides core funding to SADSEM, and the FES which sponsored two of the formative workshops as well as the production of the book. Nevertheless, the editors alone are responsible for the final product.

Gavin Cawthra, Andre du Pisani and Abillah Omari

ENDNOTES

1 Seychelles left SADC after the research had been commissioned but the chapter has nevertheless been retained; Madagascar joined later so was not covered; and a paper was not finalised for Malawi.

2 Eboe Hutchful (Ghana), Robin Luckham (UK, and an honorary African), and Bjoern Moeller (Denmark, who participated in terms of a Danida-funded twinning agreement between the SADSEM Network and the Danish Institute for International Studies).

3 The mid-term evaluation was carried out by Francis Kornegay (South Africa) and the final one by Balefi Tsie (Botswana) and Barry Munslow (UK).

Acronyms and Abbreviations

AGOA	African Growth and Opportunity Act
AMU	Arab Maghreb Union
ANC	African National Congress
ARF	Asian Regional Forum
ASAS	Association of Southern African States
ASEAN	Association of South-East Asian Nations
ASF	African Standby Force
ASP	Afro-Shirazi Party
AU	African Union
BCP	Basutoland Congress Party
BDF	Botswana Defence Force
BDP	Botswana Democratic Party
BMATT	British Military Assistance and Training Team
BNF	Botswana National Forum
BNP	Basotho National Party
BWP	Botswana pula
CCM	Chama cha Mapinduzi
CECAC	Conferences of East and Central African Countries
CNSFA	Committee on National Security and Foreign Affairs
COMESA	Common Market for Eastern and Southern Africa
CRC	Constitutional Review Commission
CSBM	confidence- and security-building measure
CUF	Civic United Front
DC	Defence Council
DFA	Department of Foreign Affairs
DoD	Department of Defence
DP	Democratic Party
DRC	Democratic Republic of the Congo
DRP	Democracy Research Project
DS	Defence Secretariat
EAC	East African Community
ECA	Economic Commission for Africa
ECCAS/CEMAC	Economic and Monetary Community of Central African States/Communauté Économique et Monétaire de l'Afrique Centrale
ECOMOG	ECOWAS Cease-Fire Monitoring Group
ECOWAS	Economic Community of West African States
ESAP	Economic Structural Adjustment Programme
EU	European Union
FADM	Forças Armadas de Defesa de Moçambique
FLS	Front Line States
FPTP	first past the post
FRELIMO	Frente de Libertação de Moçambique

GCC	Gulf Co-operation Council
GDP	gross domestic product
GPA	General Peace Agreement
HDI	Human Development Index
IEC	Independent Electoral Commission
IFI	international finance institution
IGAD	Inter-governmental Authority on Development
ILO	International Labour Organisation
IMF	International Monetary Fund
IOC	Indian Ocean Commission
IPA	Interim Political Authority
ISDSC	Inter-state Defence and Security Committee
ISPDC	Inter-state Politics and Diplomacy Committee
ISS	Institute for Security Studies
LCD	Lesotho Congress for Democracy
LDF	Lesotho Defence Force
LMPS	Lesotho Mounted Police Service
MDC	Movement for Democratic Change
MERCOSUR	Mercado Comun del Sur (Southern Cone Common Market)
MERP	Macro-economic Reform Programme
MLP	Mauritian Labour Party
MMD	Movement for Multi-party Democracy
MMM	Mauritian Militant Movement
MMP	mixed member proportional
MNR	Mozambique National Resistance (also RENAMO)
MoD	Ministry of Defence
MP	member of parliament
MUR	Mauritian rupee
NAFTA	North American Free Trade Agreement
NAD	Namibian dollar
NAMPOL	Namibian Police Force
NATO	North Atlantic Treaty Organisation
NDF	Namibia Defence Force
NDS	National Development Strategy
NEPAD	New Partnership for Africa's Development
NGO	non-governmental organisation
NNLC	Ngwane National Liberatory Congress
NOCZIM	National Oil Company of Zimbabwe
NSC	National Security Council
OAS	Organisation of American States
OAU	Organisation for African Unity
OECS	Organisation of East Caribbean States
OPDSC	Organ on Politics, Defence and Security Co-operation
OSCE	Organisation for Security and Co-operation in Europe

PAC	Public Accounts Committee
PAFMECA	Pan-African Movement for Eastern and Central Africa
PAFMECSA	Pan-African Movement for Eastern, Central, and Southern Africa
PLAN	People's Liberation Army of Namibia
PR	proportional representation
PTA	preferential trade area
PUDEMO	People's United Democratic Movement
RENAMO	Resistencia Nacional Moçambicana (also MNR)
SAARC	South Asian Association for Regional Security
SADC	Southern African Development Community
SADCC	Southern African Development Co-ordination Conference
SANDF	South African National Defence Force
SARPCCO	Southern African Regional Police Chiefs Co-operation Organisation
SCCCO	Swaziland Coalition of Concerned Civic Organisations
SFF	Special Field Forces
SFTU	Swaziland Federation of Trade Unions
SIPO	Strategic Indicative Plan of the Organ
SMB	Seychelles Marketing Board
SMF	Special Mobile Force
SNP	Seychelles National Party
SPDF	Seychelles People's Defence Force
SPPF	Seychelles People's Progressive Front
SPUP	Seychelles People's United Party
SSA	State Security Agency
SSO	SWAPO Security Organisation
SWAPO	South West Africa People's Organisation
TANU	Tanganyika/Tanzania African National Union
TRC	Tinkhundla Review Commission
TEMCO	Tanzanian Election Monitoring Committee
UDF	United Democratic Front
UDF	Umbutfo Swaziland Defence Force
UDI	unilateral declaration of independence
UN	United Nations
UNDP	UN Development Programme
UNIP	United National Independence Party
UNITA	Uniao Nacional para a Independencia Total de Angola
UNTAG	UN Transition Assistance Group
USD	United States dollar
ZANU	Zimbabwe African National Union
ZANU(PF)	Zimbabwe African National Union (Patriotic Front)
ZAPU	Zimbabwe African Peoples' Union
ZEC	Zanzibar Electoral Commission
ZIPRA	Zimbabwe African People's Revolutionary Army
ZNA	Zimbabwe National Army

Chapter 1:

Democratic Governance and Security: A Conceptual Exploration

Andre du Pisani

Democracy, like the state, is historically and socially constructed, and is a process rather than a single event or outcome. It is the outcome of historical struggles against arbitrary and authoritarian power, therefore different societies find themselves at different positions along a complex trajectory towards consolidating their democracies. Democracy mediates both political and civil society, for it has specific procedural implications for politics. By its very nature, it is contested. It tolerates peaceful dissent and disloyalty. For democracy to be legitimate, its institutions and practices need to be both apt and acceptable (Horowitz 1991: 32).

While democracy can be studied productively from both a normative and an empirical perspective, normative and empirical conceptions of democracy must remain connected to each other: what democracy *is* cannot be separated from what democracy *should be.*

Democracy is a political and social construct anchored on three key ideas. Following Nzongola-Ntalaja (1997: 8–24), these are: democracy as a *value,* a *process,* and a *practice.* These three ideas provide the very foundations of democracy as a *universal* concept and help to explain its appeal and institutional design in diverse historical and cultural contexts. These three domain ideas also provide the theoretical basis for exploring complex relationships among democracy, development, and human security.

Each of these ideas will now be briefly discussed.

Democracy as a value

For many authors and practitioners, democracy is above all a moral value or imperative. Perhaps it is true that in all human societies there is a need to improve the material conditions of life as well as to have a sense of freedom, whatever the real socio-economic and political conditions might be. Philosophically, it has been argued that this deep and innate human need provides the lubricant for demands for a new social or political project. While class consciousness may indeed be a necessary condition for social and political transformation, it is clearly not a sufficient condition for it. Innate human impulses for democratic values, practices, and human agency also play their part.

Democracy as a moral value or virtue is widely linked to four other core virtues. These are liberty (freedom), human dignity, justice, and tolerance. It has to be emphasised, however, that democracy does not necessarily resolve the problems of justice, equality, and tolerance, e.g. would it be just to give everyone the same things, when people have neither the same needs nor the same merits?

While it is widely recognised in the voluminous literature on democratic theory that majority rule is the best way, because it is visible, can be counted, and has strength to govern, it may also be the opinion of the least able – and sometimes of the least just. This raises questions of how the majority is qualified to pronounce on social and political choices. Questions of citizenship, a concept that is historically and legally tied to the apron strings of the state, also become important. In the West, as Falk (1995: 253) points out, 'positive participation has been associated with the shift from the status of "subject" (slave, vassal, serf) to "citizen".' The modern media-shaped political life, however,

> threatens individuals with a new type of postmodern serfdom, in which elections, political campaigns, and political parties provide rituals without substance, a politics of sound bytes and manipulative images, reducing the citizen to a mechanical object to be controlled, rather than being the legitimating source of legitimate authority.

Falk (1995: 253), responding to the devaluation of the notion of citizenship, proposes the concept of 'positive citizenship' as extending beyond state/society relations and involving all relationships of a participatory nature, i.e. institutions and practices that invoke authority. For Falk, 'positive citizenship' 'also draws on nonviolence and human rights as inspirational sources'. The greatest challenge is to 'reconcile the territorial dimensions of citizenship with the temporal dimensions: acting in the present for the sake of the future, establishing zones of humane governance as building blocks'.

Falk's notion of positive citizenship resonates in the work of Held (1992) on 'cosmopolitan democracy' and even, if one gives the imagination free reign, in the earlier Kantian notion of 'cosmopolitan justice'.

Rousseau's concept of the 'general will' is certainly useful in this instance, but is of dubious value. There is nothing to guarantee that the general will is always just, so its validity cannot depend on it being just (unless one defines justice as the general will, but in that case, the circularity of the definition would obviously make the guarantee worthless, if not simply meaningless). All democrats know this. The law is the law, whether just or not, but it is therefore not the same as justice. This brings us to justice not as a fact (legality), but as a value (equality, equity) or, finally, as a virtue.

The democratic values of human worth and solidarity that are evident in the writings of numerous philosophers and theologians are values around which the concept of democracy has taken root in African societies too. Nzongola-Ntalaja (1997: 11–12) comments succinctly:

> In African societies, the individual is conceptualised as a *vital force,* whose existence transcends the temporal body in which the person is objectified in his or her earthly life. This is the essential or more fundamental difference between humans and other living species, including animals. Hence the necessity of respecting the originality and the particularity of each person, respect of the latter's *individuality* or individual human worth. This is the foundation on which Africans, like peoples elsewhere, base the idea of the *inviolability* of the human person as well as his or her *inalienable* right to life and security. The security of people and their goods is one of the basic democratic principles recognised all over the world.

Owusu (1994: 132–33) makes a related point when he argues that African traditions provide a 'vibrant strand' for democracy to take root. In his analysis, 'leadership norms', often enshrined in oaths, songs and drum texts, maxims and proverbs, and prayers and ceremonies, as well as customary law that is based on the rights and duties of subjects and rulers, provide one foundation for constitutional democracy. The other foundations include the doctrine of the separation of powers and the democratic practices that render a constitutional democracy meaningful.

While the intrinsic worth of the individual is universally recognised, that individual is considered as fully human only through his or her dialectical relationship to society. Human existence has meaning to the extent that it is lived in society. The value of solidarity is expressed and reinforced through family and kinship ties, ethnic identity, language, patriotism, and nationalism. Needless to say, these very values can be – and have been – exploited to produce anti-democratic outcomes such as ethnic and racial particularism, neo-patrimonial rule and, in more corrosive cases, ethnic cleansing and genocide.

Experience in Senegal and Botswana underscores the importance of structured and mediated participation of different social formations and ethnic groups (in the case of the former) to make political contestation less violent and more amenable to compromise than in some African countries. In Senegal, the mediators are the *marabouts*: leaders of the important Muslim brotherhoods. In Botswana, the political class has been largely continuous with traditional leaders, and political participation has been mediated by the chiefdoms to which voters owe allegiance (Picard 1987: 190). Hence, it is worth emphasising that democracy needs tolerance of diversity. Universal tolerance, however, would be both morally reprehensible and practically impossible, since it would negate some of the very conditions that tolerance and democracy would need to flower.

This brings us to the second foundation of democracy: democracy as a social process.

Democracy as a social process

As a social construction, democracy is never complete or fully consolidated, but is a continuous social and political process of enlarging access to fundamental human rights and civil liberties for all. These fundamental human rights and liberties include, at least since the 1948 United Nations (UN) Universal Declaration of Human Rights, the following:

- the fundamental right of the human person to life, dignity, and security;
- freedom of religion, assembly, expression, the press, and conscience;
- economic, social, and cultural rights – the idea of democracy as a means of satisfying and responding to basic human needs (social democracy); and
- the right to political self-determination.

Central to this democratic process is the idea that a 'good' political order is one in which the state is capable of meeting the existential, material, and spiritual needs of its citizens. In fact, as Horowitz (1991: 116–17) points out, democracy

> is fostered by the development of more generally autonomous social forces, of voluntary associations and interests, of a civil society that stands apart from the state, of forces that can balance each other in utilizing the future state machinery for political ends.

The limited (and in some cases, declining) capacity of some African states to ensure human security and to promote human development is often the principal reason for instability and conflict. It is, paradoxically, the failure of development that has given rise to demands for more democracy. It is hard, however, to conceive of democracy (in whatever form) in the absence of state capacity. Enhancing and protecting democratic rights together form the starting point for responding to the problems many African countries face. In this sense democracy, like human security, is an actualising concept. (The nexus between democracy as a social process and human security will be explored in a subsequent section of this chapter.)

Democracy as political practice

Democracy constitutes political practice. It refers to specific institutional habits and practices for organising and exercising public power in accordance with universal norms and principles. Liberal democracy is arguably the most procedural of all types of democracy.

Understood as such, democracy can be examined at two levels: firstly, at the level of the principles themselves, and of the institutions, procedures, and practices that apply them; and secondly, at the level of whether the institutions, procedures, and practices are compatible with universal democratic principles.

The following, informed by the writings of Ake (1996), Pateman (1970), Dahl (1989; 1991), and Cheru (2002), provides a list of some of the key universal principles of democratic governance:

- the idea that legitimate power or authority emanates from the people, who exercise it either directly through popular assembly or indirectly through elected assemblies, elected executives, or other modes of representation;
- the concept of the rule of law, which means that power should not be arbitrary, and that its exercise must be circumscribed by agreed rules that define its scope (limits) and modes of operation;
- the principle that leaders are chosen by and accountable to the people. The element of choice logically implies that democracy is government by the consent of the governed;
- the right of citizens to participate in the management of public affairs through a variety of means, such as free, transparent, and democratic elections; decentralised governmental structures; non-governmental organisations (NGOs); and community-based organisations. This implies participation through civil society formations as distinct from the state; and
- the right of citizens to change a government that no longer serves their interests, or the right to revolution. This right is qualified in the sense that it can be exercised against non-democratic regimes.

Dahl (1991) adds to the above criteria five more. These include effective citizen participation, voting equality, enlightened understanding (on the part of citizens), popular control of the agenda, and the inclusion of adults.

While political institutions, cultures, and procedures vary greatly in Southern Africa, the test of their democratic worth remains the same: to establish whether they are consistent with these universal democratic principles. In this respect, Nzongola-Ntalaja (1997: 15), for example, argues:

> Neopatrimonialism, according to which the ruler is indistinguishable from the office he/she occupies, for example, pervades the entire system and erodes the formal institutions of government and any democratic content. Thus, even in states where democratic institutions and procedures are supposedly respected, the result is democratic *formalism*, or democracy in form rather than content.

The phenomenon of neo-patrimonialism has been widely researched by various scholars, among them Chazan *et al.* (1988), Clapham (1982), Jackson (1982), Joseph (1989), and Bratton and Van de Walle (1997).

One of the many reasons why neo-patrimonialism is so prevalent in much of sub-Saharan Africa goes back to a core distinction that is often forgotten in new democracies, that between *democratic politics* and *democratic institutions.* The former, democratic politics, is about how politics is conducted within the frame of democratic values and practices. The latter, democratic institutions, refers to the presence or absence of public institutions such as legislatures, judiciaries, political parties, and regular elections – the institutional architecture and more formal aspects of a democracy.

Democracy as political practice requires an effective state, and appropriate legal and political institutions to secure people's rights, safeguard their human security, and allow them to elect their own governments and make their own laws. The phenomenon of 'weak/soft' or 'failed' states, in Africa and elsewhere, substantively undermines the viability of democratic governance and by extension, the human security of these states' citizens. Since human security has as two of its dimensions the safeguarding of human rights and meeting the basic needs of people, these are difficult to envisage in the context of 'weak' or 'failed' states.

As political practice and social process, democracy is characterised by, among other features, a recognition of the rule of law, constitutional limits on government, the meaningful decentralisation of power, and procedures for arriving at collective decisions that seek to ensure the participation of important social formations and their representatives in public affairs. For Cheru (2002: 40), the decentralisation of power and responsibility should apply at both the political and economic levels.

At the political level, it concerns the form of representation and the practices for taking decisions at the local and regional levels. The political purpose of decentralisation is to provide meaningful ways for citizens to counter the monopoly of political decision making at the centre.

At the economic level, decentralisation not only concerns itself with the need for grassroots participation in development and budget deliberations, but should extend to addressing urban–rural divides and the skewed allocation of resources (both financial and human) between the centre and the regional and local state.

Competing understandings of democracy

Against these introductory remarks, several scholars, notably Ake (1994; 1996; 2000), have attempted to distinguish among competing understandings of democracy. In his latest work, published posthumously, Ake (2000) draws a distinction between 'liberal democracy' and 'social democracy'. The first he regards as 'minimalist': liberal democracy, for Ake, reflects the narrow interests of elites, privileges multi-party elections and democratic procedure, and has a belief in the supremacy of the constitution and the 'democracy of Western governments and the Bretton Woods institutions'. For Ake, the neo-liberal economic project undermines human security. This is so for various reasons, among them that the emphasis on procedure and rules detracts from the social imperatives of democracy, while liberal democracy is essentially based on elite pacts to the exclusion of vulnerable groups such as women and minority groups. Social democracy, on the other hand, has a different template. It demands material betterment, equality, social justice, the upliftment of citizens, and concrete rights. Ake argues for democracy of the second type if African civilisations are to survive and prosper.

In a somewhat differently constructed argument, Sandbrook (2000) offers a useful primer on a range of complex issues related to democratisation and market reforms in contemporary sub-Saharan Africa. He is especially concerned with the possible role of state agencies and institutions in promoting economic development, political stability, and social inclusion. For Sandbrook, 'getting the politics right' is a necessary precondition for enhanced prosperity, extension of civil and political liberties, and the achievement of human security. He conceives of 'democratic development' in terms of a 'virtuous and self-reinforcing circle of civil and political rights, growing prosperity, and state renovation'. In his view, democratisation is, 'at best', only 'one component of an effective preventive strategy' (Sandbrook 2000: 59). Democratic reforms are not sufficient on their own to trigger sustainable development. The challenge is more daunting: 'closing the circle' requires both the implementation of bureaucratic capacity building and effective conflict management institutions.

Diamond, writing in 1999, reminds us that it has become difficult to classify democracies in the current turbulent international system, as the conditions for making and consolidating democracy differ starkly from country to country and from region to region. He nonetheless distinguishes among three types of democracies. These are discussed briefly below.

Electoral democracy

This concept defines democracy as the regime in which governmental offices are filled as a consequence of contested elections, with the proviso that real contestation requires an opposition with some 'non-trivial chance' of winning office, and that the chief executive office and the legislative seats are filled by contested elections.

Depending on the political context and the nature of the electoral system used, the linkage between elections and electoral systems, on the one hand, and democratic governance, on the other, may be either positive or negative. Having said this, however, elections and electoral systems are key to democratic governance, although in themselves they are not a sufficient condition for democratic governance. The choice of electoral system is shaped by context and political history. Electoral system reform is an important requirement for deepening representation, legitimacy, and accountability. Contested, transparent elections as part of the architecture of democracy derive their meaning from democratic politics.

Proportional representation (PR) as an electoral system has several advantages. In the analysis of Reynolds and Reilly (2002), these include a fair translation of votes into seats, enhanced access to representation by minority parties, improved gender representation, and a more inclusive and socially diverse list of candidates. The principal disadvantages of PR include unstable coalition government, providing a platform for extremist parties, and leaving little room for independent candidates.

The first-past-the-post system, too, has several advantages. The following are the most evident: the system provides a clear-cut choice to the electorate, especially in a stable bi-party system; it favours broad-based parties; voters are given the opportunity to vote for candidates rather than for parties; and the system makes for strong constituency links between representatives and the electorate. The disadvantages include excluding minority parties, encouraging sectarian parties, and possibly excluding women.

Liberal democracy

Liberal democracy has the following principal institutional features:

- Control of the state and its key decisions and allocations lies in practice, as well as in constitutional theory, with elected officials.
- Executive power is constitutionally constrained by the relative autonomous power of other government institutions (such as an independent judiciary, parliament, and other mechanisms of horizontal accountability).
- Cultural, ethnic, religious, and other minority groups, as well as historically disadvantaged majorities are not prohibited (legally or in practice) from expressing their interests in the political process or from speaking their language or practising their culture.
- Beyond parties and elections, citizens have multiple channels for expression and representation of their interests and values, including diverse, independent associations and movements, which they have the freedom to join.
- Individuals have substantial freedom of belief, opinion, discussion, speech, publication, assembly, demonstration, and petition. The rule of law protects citizens from unjustified detention, exile, terror, torture, and undue interference in their personal lives, not only by the state, but also by organised non-state or anti-state forces.

The post-1989 period in particular has witnessed hybridised, sometimes inconsistent, constitutional engineering, with countries borrowing elements from different democratic constitutions. Moreover, many constitutional framers consulted foreign models and then proceeded to apply them to local conditions, sometimes with mixed success (Horowitz 2003: 16).

Dahl (1971; 1989) prefers the word 'polyarchy' to democracy. His notion of polyarchy, however, contains key elements of a liberal democracy. These include consent on the upholding of fundamental human rights and freedoms, and contest and competition for positions of public authority, principally through transparent elections.

Acknowledging that Diamond's classification of different types of democracies is based on *ideal* types, Ake (2000: 9) nonetheless believes that liberal democracy itself has atrophied in a 'long process of devaluation during which it lost much of its redeeming democratic elements'. In its classical, procedural understanding, liberal democracy can and does disempower marginal groups. It is inevitably socially less anchored than social or developmental democracy.

Pseudo democracies

Pseudo democracies are Diamond's (1999) third type. These 'democracies' tolerate alternative parties, which constitute at least some independent opposition to the governing party. This toleration is accompanied by more space for organisational pluralism and dissent in civil society than is the case in more repressive authoritarian regimes. Dominant party systems characterise such democracies.

Pseudo democracy is also known as 'facade' or 'virtual' democracy: democracy with the institutional architecture but none of the substance and social dimensions of a democracy.

Development democracies

Diamond (1999) argues that even liberal democracies fall short of democratic ideals. They have serious limitations in their guarantees of personal and associational freedom. Thus democracy should be understood as a 'developmental phenomenon'. Even when a country is above the threshold of an electoral (or even liberal) democracy, democratic institutions can be improved and deepened, or may need to be consolidated; political competition can be made fairer and more open; participation can become more inclusive; citizens' knowledge, resources, and competence can grow; elected and appointed officials can be made more responsive and accountable; civil liberties can be better protected; and the rule of law can become more efficient and entrenched.

More recently, with the tendency towards growing unilateralism on the part of the current United States administration, a new type of 'democracy' has emerged: 'imposed democracy', such as that being imposed on Iraq. The assumption, of course, is that the United States provides a model of democratic governance worthy of emulation by the rest of the world. (In parenthesis, the United States forgets its own history: democracy is always the outcome of concrete struggles against lack of freedom. It cannot be 'bought off the shelf', or imposed from above or from the outside.)

Democratic transition theory

Against the backdrop of the conceptual distinctions and argumentation introduced above, the inevitable question arises: When is a transition 'democratic' and when is it not? For Huntington (1991: 9), 'the critical point in the process of democratisation is the replacement of a government that was not chosen [freely and fairly] by one that is selected in a free, open, and fair election'. Bratton, who has been critical of democratic transition theory, since much of it has been based on the Latin American and Southern European experience (and more recently on Eastern and Central Europe), nevertheless believes that a country is held to have installed a democratic regime if, in a context of civil liberties, a competitive election is freely and fairly conducted and the election results are accepted by all contestants (Bratton and Van de Walle 1997).

Much of the literature has tended to define the subsequent consolidation phase of democratisation more comprehensively and in a more open-ended fashion. Linz and Stepan (1996: 15), for example, characterise the consolidation phase as

> a period when the overwhelming majority of the people [come to] believe that any further political change must emerge from within the parameters of democratic procedures ... when all the actors [are] habituated to ... [conflict resolution by] established norms ... and violations of these norms are likely to be both ineffective and costly.

They propose five key 'mutually interconnected and reinforcing conditions' that must be obtained for democratic consolidation to be achieved. These are: 'a free and lively civil society; a relatively autonomous political society; prevalent observance of the rule of law; a state bureaucracy "that is usable by the new democratic government"; and an institutionalized economic society' (Linz and Stepan 1996: 17).

Harbeson (1999: 42–43) argues that one of the limitations of much of the existing body of literature on democratisation is the 'election-centric' conception of the transition phases and the often unrealistic expectations that accompany this period. These expectations include

> the presumptions that (1) democratic elections will *ipso facto* produce regime change from an incumbent authoritarian to a new, democratically inclined regime; (2) initial multiparty elections and/or regime change will *ipso facto* generate the

> momentum necessary to produce subsequent, broader patterns of democratization; (3) this momentum will be sufficient to generate the means of fulfillment of tasks associated with the consolidation of democracy; (4) the initial multiparty elections taking place at the national level will lead to democratization processes at subnational levels; and (5) the polity will remain sufficiently stable to sustain transition and subsequent consolidation phases of democratization.

Time-series data for sub-Saharan Africa analysed by Bratton and Van de Walle (1997: 3–6) for the period 1988–94 shows that democratic transitions in Africa in this period were not linear. In their words, 'peaks in key transition events were followed by descents towards new valleys'. One of these 'valleys' has been a declining mean of civil liberties and a slide on the UN Development Programme (UNDP) Human Development Index (HDI) for some sub-Saharan African countries. Others, such as Namibia, South Africa, Malawi, Mozambique, and Eritrea (at least in the period 1991–98) could be cited as 'positive cases' of democratisation.

Acknowledging that the actual processes of transition to democracy differed in the various countries, Harbeson (1999: 43) boldly advances the proposition that

> African circumstances make it more likely that transitions will result in democratic progress to the extent that they commence with comprehensive multiparty agreements on the fundamental rules of the game, either through constitutional reform or by constitution-like pact making, than if they begin with initial multiparty elections in advance of such rule making.

While useful, Harbeson's proposition neither explains nor captures the specificity of particular transitions to democracy. Any theory of democratic transition needs to consider the specific circumstances and points of departure of individual countries. Luckham (2003: 9–10), for example, emphasises the importance of conceptualising new forms of conflict, produced by a 'series of interacting historical trajectories' that divert the 'Third Wave'[1] from its 'democratising course'. These 'trajectories' include, among others, 'transitional democracies', 'lapsed or stalled democracies', 'states under reconstruction', 'conflict-torn states', and 'failed or collapsed states'.

Such an approach would facilitate the incorporation of concrete African democratisation experiences into theories of democratic transition, which have hitherto been heavily influenced by the experiences of Southern and Eastern–Central Europe, and of Latin America. One illustration of this consideration is the fact that recent democratic transitions in Africa have not been linear, have taken a relatively short time to effect, have been differently sequenced, and have been fashioned by a largely hostile global environment that demanded political transition, regime change, and economic reform to occur simultaneously (Hyslop 1999).

Another consideration is that of the capacity of new and transitional democracies to come to terms with ethnicity. Ethnicity in itself is not necessarily a negative force in politics, but the way in which it is instrumentalised can cause conflict. For example, the preferential and exclusive treatment of different ethnic groups can release energy for ethnic mobilisation and destructive conflict, as happened in the cases of Rwanda and Burundi in the 1990s. If instrumentalised, ethnicity can culminate in a 'captured state' with one dominant ethnic group effectively controlling the state in its own interest.

Democratic transitions in Southern Africa

International and regional developments in the late 1980s resulted in Southern Africa experiencing a 'wave' of democratisation. This seemingly produced a broad acceptance, throughout much of the region, of the values and norms of multi-party democracy, regular transparent elections, constitutional rule, and adherence to human rights. Except for Swaziland, all Southern African Development Community (SADC) countries have held multi-party general elections since 1990, and most have held more than one (Matlosa 2000). This democratisation has been accompanied in most countries by the introduction of neo-liberal economic policies with their emphasis on market-led growth, privatisation, and commercialisation.

The expectation, held by many donors, international financial institutions (IFIs), and national policy-makers, was that liberal democracy would enhance human security. But has democracy brought stability and growth in its wake? If so, of what kind? For example, the region's dominant economy, South Africa, has been experiencing 'jobless growth' and ongoing social conflict in the context of liberal democratisation (Marais 1998). In important respects, such as its environmental security, neo-liberal South Africa may have become 'unsustainable' (Bond 2000). Countries such as Mozambique and Namibia also experience corrosive forms of unequal development and poverty. This had led many analysts to question the premise that with the introduction of liberal democracy countries 'stabilise' and 'develop' (Held 2000; Galtung 2000).

Ake (2000: 30) points to one of the fallacies that inform the widely held view that liberal democracy necessarily produces economic development and enhances human security. It is simply this: Africa is democratising in an international context in which there is apparently no allowance made for the fact that liberal democracy has been socially and historically constructed in the wake of the Industrial Revolution. Similarly, little or no attempt 'is made to separate the values and principles of liberal democracy from the particular historical practices which operationalise these values and principles in specific historical settings'. Contested understandings of what democratisation means, too, have resulted in a confusion of democratic processes and institutions with democratic outcomes.

In the heady 1990s, which breathed the air of a 'peace and democratic dividend', scholarly attention turned to the question of 'democratic consolidation' and its particular challenges. However, it is doubtful to what extent most states in Southern Africa may be considered to be consolidated or even consolidating democracies. In part, assessing the state of democratisation in the region depends on how democracy is defined and understood. Most countries have formal electoral democratic systems in place, but some lack entrenched and functioning mechanisms for protecting citizens' human rights and civil liberties, decentralising authority to lower levels, addressing gender inequality, and maintaining the rule of law. In other countries, democratic politics may be the preserve of an elite, even if formal democracy exists, and hence democracy may not resonate with citizens. Furthermore, deep economic inequalities, abject poverty, and marginalisation of vulnerable groups may threaten democracy.

Luckham, Goertz, and Kaldor (2000: 21) have introduced the concept of 'democratic deficits' in considering the quality of democracy in the 'new and transitional democracies'. Such deficits may be found in formal constitutional political arrangements (democratic institutions) or in the substance of political practices (democratic politics). Deficits may concern issues of citizenship (e.g. the exclusion of certain groups), issues of the vertical accountability of rulers to citizens or horizontal accountability within governance systems and practices, or issues of international accountability (e.g. policy strictures imposed by IFIs).

In one of the most insightful offerings on the feasibility of democracy in Africa, Ake (2000) raises more fundamental concerns. By all indications, the 'established democracies' are not able to offer the developing countries clear and meaningful standards of democratisation to relate to. This is because they themselves have

> no clear and meaningful standard of democracy, a condition arising from the growing alienation of the practice of democracy from the Western ideology of democracy and the concerted effort by powerful interests to deradicalize democracy by offering a profusion of definitions which trivialize it (Ake 2000).

The notion of 'democratic deficits' is arguably a more useful way of viewing Southern African countries than merely attempting to judge the extent to which they adhere to formal criteria, for it allows consideration not only of formal mechanisms, but also of the nature of political processes embedded in society and arising from political histories, as well as of the differential effects of globalisation on individual countries.

While recognising the introduction of electoral and liberal democracy in Southern Africa, one should not be blind to the democratic deficits and the stark socio-economic and gender inequalities that continue to exist throughout the region. Furthermore, it is unclear whether this has led to an improvement in either state security ('narrow' security) or human security (the wider security agenda), and whether this has been translated into regional common security. Human security can arguably be partially measured through the HDI, and the overall picture for Southern Africa since 1990 has been one of decline in this regard.

State security, common security, and human security

For several decades, the predominance of the realist paradigm meant that security was subsumed under the rubric of power and the state. Tickner (1995: 176) comments succinctly: 'conceptually, it was synonymous with the security of the state against external dangers, which was to be achieved by increasing military capabilities.' This state-centric understanding of security was based on the assumption of a firm distinction between domestic 'order' and international 'anarchy', the latter being a 'state of nature' where war is an ever-present possibility.

Given the absence of an effective international authority to keep aggressive ambitions at bay, states must rely on their own capabilities for achieving security. As classical realists acknowledge, this often results in what they describe as a 'security dilemma': what one state might justify as legitimate security-enhancing actions are likely to be perceived by others as threatening. For realists, what stability and security does exist in such a context can be attributed to the balance of power. The balance of power, in turn, is based on military security alliances.

These realist assumptions about the nature of the international system and the security-driven behaviour of states were partly vindicated by the behaviour of the former Soviet Union and the United States during the Cold War, and by state-sanctioned intervention in the affairs of other states. The escalation brought about as a consequence of the arms race between the United States and the former Soviet Union could indeed be viewed as a classic case of the security dilemma, yet the bipolarity produced a balance of power that assured a measure of global security and stability.

The notion of collective security, which continues to permeate thinking about security on the part of the UN (a notion that is still alive and well in SADC and the newly created African Union [AU]), sees only states as security objects. One could hardly enter into formalised guarantee systems, such as are involved in collective security, without having a functioning system of states. Similarly, the idea of common security, as advanced by the Palme Commission of 1982 and other proponents, remains essentially state-centric.

The concept of human security, on the other hand, refers to individual and societal security (Waever 1995; Buzan 1991; UN Commission on Human Security 2003). While this concept may be of recent origin, the ideas that inform it are far from new. For more than a century – at least since the founding of the International Committee of the Red Cross in the 1860s – a doctrine based on the security of individuals has been gathering force. Human security is the most recent formulation in a general broadening of the concept of security that has gained momentum over the past three decades.

The specific formulation is most commonly associated with the 1994 UNDP *Human Development Report*. The motivation behind the use of the phrase 'human security' was to capture the so-called 'peace dividend' and direct it towards a more developmental agenda. The definition advanced in the report was extremely broad, encompassing economic security, food security, health security, environmental security, personal security, community security, and political security. Though extensively used in preparatory work for the 1995 UN Social Summit in Copenhagen, the notion of human security was not reflected in the summit conclusions.

More recently, the excellent report of the UN Commission on Human Security (2003: 2) reminds the reader:

> Today's flows of goods, services, finance, people and images spotlight the many interlinkages in the security of all people .... The security of one person, one community, one

> nation rests on the decisions of many others – sometimes fortuitously, sometimes precariously.

Human security, as the UN Commission on Human Security (2003: 2, 4) puts it, 'complements state security, enhances human rights and strengthens human development. It seeks to protect people against a broad range of threats to individuals and communities and, further, to empower them to act on their own behalf'.

The commission (2003: 4) advances the following definition of human security: 'to protect the vital core of all human lives in ways that enhance human freedoms and human fulfilment'. Practically, this means

> protecting people from critical (severe) and pervasive (widespread) threats and situations. It means using processes that build on people's strengths and aspirations. It means creating political, social, environmental, economic, military and cultural systems that together give people the building blocks of survival, livelihood and dignity.

Human security: some key questions

The first question is: 'Security for whom?' The answer to this basic question is that human security is people-centred. Human security takes individuals and their communities, rather than territory, states, or governments, as its point of reference. It uses the effects on people as the criteria for assessing the success or failure of actions and policies. While not denying the importance of state security, human security complements the latter in specific respects, as will be shown later.

The second key question in respect of human security is: 'Security from what?' Human security addresses threats to the survival and safety of people from both military and non-military sources. The first category – military – includes, among others, intra-state war, small arms proliferation, communal-based violence, insurgency, rebel activity, and civil war. The second – non-military – can include serious human rights violations, famine, environmental degradation, violent crime, illicit drugs, economic collapse, infectious diseases, and natural disasters.

Human security highlights the complex interconnections among what were once deemed to be disparate issues (e.g. human rights violations, infectious diseases, mass displacement and migration, poverty, and sustainable development), and acknowledges, as the UN Commission on Human Security (2003) compellingly shows, that they cannot be treated in isolation. It recognises that many of the challenges to the survival and safety of people are global phenomena in their origins and their effects, and that they result in mutual vulnerability. The security of people is interdependent.

Human security needs to be situated in relation to state or national security. A fundamental point of departure is to see it neither as an alternative to, nor divorced from, national or state security. From a human security perspective, the security of the state is not an end in itself: it is a means of providing security for people. Thus, human security complements state security in four important respects:

- Its concern is the individual and the community rather than the state.
- Menaces to people's security include threats and conditions that have not always been classified as threats to state security.
- The range of actors is expanded beyond the state alone.
- Achieving human security includes not just protecting people, but also empowering people to fend for themselves (UN Commission on Human Security 2003: 4).

A further important question to ask is: 'Where do human security and state security overlap?' Inter-state war, generally recognised as the principal threat to state security, is also a prominent threat to human security. States with similarly strong, effective, and democratic characteristics enhance human security through their respect for human rights and their ability to meet basic human needs. The likelihood is greater that such states would foster international peace and security.

A further question that can help to situate human security in relation to state security is this: 'How does a human security perspective affect approaches to state security?' By assessing actions and policies on the basis of their effects at the level of the individual, a human security perspective challenges the legitimacy of some approaches to advancing state security, such as the use of land mines, destabilisation of contingent states, or broad-based economic sanctions.

In exploring the relationship between human and state security, one can ask: 'Is state security a sufficient condition for human security?' The answer to this important question is that where states are outwardly aggressive or inwardly repressive (e.g. Saddam Hussein's Iraq, apartheid South Africa, Israel), or where they are incapable of effective governance (Somalia, Sudan), they constitute a major source of human insecurity. The sad reality is that too often, state security has been used as a justification for actions and policies that have ultimately undermined rather than enhanced human security. The security of states is increasingly insufficient to safeguard human security.

At both the conceptual and practical level, additional questions can be posed. For example: Must human security concerns wait until state security has been assured? Is there a hierarchy of security concerns where the demands of the state inevitably take precedence over individuals? Could the advancement of human security actually threaten international peace and security by undermining the legal norm of non-intervention? While war inevitably results in human insecurity, human insecurity does not always result in war. Under what conditions does human insecurity cause violent conflict?

Human security and human development

Human security and human development together address freedom from fear and freedom from want. Human development is defined by UNDP as 'the process of widening the range of people's choices', while human security can be seen as the ability to pursue those choices in a safe environment.

But how do the two concepts interrelate? Since both take people as their principal point of reference, the two agendas are essentially complementary and mutually reinforcing. Human security is a necessary or enabling condition for human development, while promoting human development is a principal strategy for advancing human security. For example, eradicating malaria, currently responsible for 2 million deaths annually and affecting 300 to 500 million people, will require alleviating widespread poverty in sub-Saharan Africa.

Galtung's (1985) concept of 'structural violence' provides a possible conceptual link between human security and human development. Vulnerability and insecurity are experienced not only by people who live in extreme poverty, to paraphrase the recent report of the UN Commission on Human Security (2003). Human security is greatly diminished by food insecurity and lack of access to safe water and adequate sanitation. The HIV/AIDS pandemic is having a devastating impact on the most productive segments of the population, resulting in profound changes in household composition. Major investments in education and skills training are being lost, and the number of households headed by women and children is increasing. Much of the burden falls on the more vulnerable section of the population – women and children.

While the alleviation of poverty is clearly a key concern of both human security and human development, one may wish to ask: 'What does a human security perspective add to approaches to poverty alleviation already in existence?' A more challenging question then suggests itself: 'How can key developmental concepts such as gender, participation, and empowerment be comprehensively and meaningfully integrated into a conceptualisation of human security?'

One useful attempt to integrate gender into the wider equation of human security has been the 2002 UN *Study on Women, Peace and Security*. This important study explores the impact of war on women and girls. In particular, the study shows that women suffer economic dislocation and lose their access to land, food, and water, all of which deepen their poverty. Another factor that has a clear gender dimension to it is HIV/AIDS. Women and young girls are especially at risk, while peacekeepers (who are predominantly male) sometimes play an active part in the transmission of the virus.

Renewed interest in human security is not due to the emergence of 'new' conflicts and threats. Most of the challenges to the security and survival of people considered under the rubric of human security have been there for centuries. Due to globalisation, however, many threats to human security are increasingly transnational in their origins and their effects (particularly environmental concerns). Their intensity, too, is increasing. The post-Cold War agenda has created the opportunity to draw attention to these challenges and to place them on the global agenda. Advances in information and communication technology have greatly facilitated more international attention on these challenges. The contribution of civil society to advancing the human security agenda, too, continues to grow. While the engagement of non-governmental actors has a long history, new and innovative partnerships with governmental actors are becoming increasingly common. Broadening the definition of security, a process of the past three or more decades, is resulting in a more integrated conceptualisation that provides the theoretical foundation for a more comprehensive and integrated security agenda.

At the same time, however, one needs to sound a word of warning. A broadened security agenda, while desirable, particularly in a developing context, holds potential dangers. One of these is the risk that 'security services' appropriate responsibility for development matters once they designate these as 'security concerns'. This would inevitably collapse the development agenda into a security agenda.

Conceptually, it is important, as Waever (1995) and Buzan, Waever, and De Wilde (1998) have reminded us, that the concept of human security has as its primary referents the values and cultures of individuals, as well as how these relate to state security. Security is conceptually and practically different from development.

From theory to action

Enhancing the human security project requires co-operative, and often multilateral, responses, and approaches that are multi-sectoral emphasise preventive action and engage new partnerships. Human security is advanced through the protection of human rights, respect for the rule of law, democratic governance, sustainable human development, and the peaceful resolution of conflict. Many international treaties, agreements, and norms provide a foundation for human security: these include the Geneva Conventions, the 1948 Universal Declaration of Human Rights, and the Charter of the UN. Notwithstanding these conventions, the UN is premised on collective security, which is state-based.

Furthermore, approaches and targets to address many challenges to human security have been set out in the plans of action resulting from the series of UN World Conferences in recent years (Environment, Rio, 1992; Human Rights, Vienna, 1993; Population and Development, Cairo, 1994; Social Summit, Copenhagen, 1995; Women, Beijing, 1995; Habitat II, Istanbul, 1996; Sustainable Development, Johannesburg, 2002; Millennium Goals, 2000/1). In the European context, the development strategy of the Organisation for Security and Co-operation in Europe, 'Shaping the 21st Century', contains key elements for building human security.

The security architecture of SADC, too, provides a foundation for enhancing human security at the regional level, but the original SADC Organ on Politics, Defence, and Security, established in 1996, failed to move the sub-regional institution closer to a realisation of its core common security objectives. At the organisation's August 2001 summit in Blantyre, however, SADC adopted a Protocol on Politics, Defence, and Security Co-operation and reached important decisions on integrating the SADC organ more closely into the institution's other structures, and strengthening its accountability and operability.

The protocol also lists various policy objectives. Most of these concentrate on collective security; collective defence; governance, democracy, and human rights (linked to human security); development of common foreign policy approaches in international forums; and building joint capacities in areas such as peacekeeping, disaster management, and co-ordination of humanitarian assistance (also aspects of human security).

A number of related protocols, such as the Protocol against Corruption and the Protocol on the Control of Firearms, Ammunition, and Related Materials, embody similar principles, more particularly in the area of governance and collective security. A mechanism to deal with disputes arising between member states is also to be established following the signing of the Protocol on Tribunals and the Rules of Procedure Thereof. Still, substantial work remains to be done before these principles can be fully internalised as part of SADC's efforts to promote peace and human security actively (Baregu and Landsberg 2003).

Finally, at the continental level, mention has to be made of the New Partnership for Africa's Development and the AU. Both of these initiatives recognise a link, however complex, among democracy, human security, and development.

Conclusion

This exploratory chapter has examined the core ideas of democratic politics. These are democracy as a value, democracy as a social process, and democracy as political practice. Democracy is a process, and different states find themselves at various positions along a complex trajectory. There is also the ever-present risk of democratic reversal. Human security was defined as safety for people from violent and non-violent threats. This implies that human security is multidimensional and, like democracy and human development, actualising. However, democratisation does not in itself result in enhanced human security.

The chapter has also provided reasons for the renewed scholarly and political interest in the concept of human security and its relation to human development. In this respect, it has been argued that human security and human development together address freedom from fear and freedom from want. As both concepts take people as their principal point of reference, the two agendas are complementary and ultimately mutually reinforcing. It has also been argued that human security is neither an alternative to, nor divorced from, national or state security: it complements state security in important respects. From a human security perspective, however, the security of states is not an end in itself: it is a means of providing security for people.

Finally, giving operational import to human security will differ from context to context. In some cases it will involve affirming development targets and agendas already established; in others it will involve reinforcing or strengthening what has already been developed; and in others it will involve setting and developing new agendas or building state and governance capacity.

ENDNOTES

1 The term is taken from Huntington (1991).

Chapter 2:

Comparative Perspectives on Regional Security Co-operation among Developing Countries[1]

Gavin Cawthra

Regions (or sub-regions) can be defined in many different ways: through geographic propinquity or intensity of interactions, such as trade; through internal or external recognition and formal declaration as such; politically; historically; or culturally and in terms of 'civilisational areas'. Some regions are even defined in terms of river basins or shared seas or mountain ranges. In general, however, since this chapter is about formal security co-operation, regions are defined politically and in the context of the global collective security system personified by the UN.

Chapter VIII of the Charter of the UN is quite explicit about the security functions of regional organisations: 'The Security Council shall, where appropriate, utilize such regional arrangements or agencies for enforcement action under its authority' (art. 53.1), and: 'Members of the United Nations ... shall make every effort to achieve pacific settlement of local disputes through such regional arrangements or by such regional agencies before referring them to the Security Council' (art. 52.2). Regional organisations thus represent instances of first resort as far as the peaceful resolution of conflicts is concerned, but it is also underlined that different rules apply to the use of non-peaceful means: 'No enforcement action shall be taken under regional arrangements or by regional agencies without the authorization of the Security Council' (art. 53.1).

The division of the world into regions is not as clear as the UN charter might have envisaged, however, and is further complicated by the development of sub-regional organisations, especially in Africa, where the regional organisation, the AU, is shadowed by a number of sub-regional organisations.[2] There are also large parts of the world where there are no effective regional or sub-regional organisations, and often these are the areas where they would appear to be most needed: the Middle East (with the exception of the Gulf Co-operation Council [GCC]) and North-East Asia, for example.

Nevertheless, there has been a palpable rise in political collaboration, economic co-operation and integration, and security co-operation on a regional basis since the end of the Cold War. Hettne, Inotai, and Sunkel (2000) have argued that the recent expansion is different in quality as well as quantity from the efforts that preceded it. The characteristics of the so-called 'new regionalism' are summarised as follows:

- It is characterised by multidimensionalism or multifunctionalism, combining economic, political, social, cultural, and security aspects, and thus going beyond the 'traditional' forms of free-trade regimes or security alliances.
- It is driven by a combination of economic or security imperatives, as well as by ecological and other developmental objectives.
- It involves not merely states, but a wide variety of institutions, organisations, and movements, and to some extent is driven from the bottom up.
- It is outward looking, or 'open', in that it seeks to integrate organisations' member states into the global political economy rather than erecting tariff barriers.
- It varies widely in the extent of institutionalisation, with some organisations deliberately avoiding the construction of bureaucracies.
- It sometimes spans the divide between the developed and developing world, e.g. the North American Free Trade Agreement (NAFTA) (Fawcett and Hurrell 1995: 3–4; Hettne, Inotai, and Sunkel 2000: xix–xx).

An absolute distinction cannot be made between old and new regionalisms. Some long-established organisations have taken on many of the features of the more recent ones, but it is nevertheless evident that the globalisation process has necessitated the construction of new types of inter-state organisations.

Key issues

With this in mind, a number of old as well as new questions regarding the construction of regional organisations with security functions might be posed, which will inform this study.

Multilateralism, globalisation, and regionalism

Debates on regionalism of the old type often revolved around the issue of whether regional organisations were building blocks for the construction of the global collective security system (the UN and attendant organisations), or stumbling blocks to that process. On the one hand, military alliances such as the North Atlantic Treaty Organisation (NATO) and the Warsaw Pact appeared to inhibit the building of a global collective security system, while on the other, regional organisations such as the Organisation of African Unity (OAU) were given, and executed, an important peace maintenance role under chapter VIII of the UN Charter.

Similarly, some argue that the new regionalism in developing countries may allow states to protect themselves and their people from the pernicious and inequitable effects of globalisation, while others argue that it simply speeds up the process of globalisation and facilitates the penetration of exploitative capitalism, and still others (President Thabo Mbeki of South Africa, for instance) think it is the only way that developing countries can prosper in the current era. In relation to security, since the terrorist attacks in the United States of 11 September 2001, the UN collective security system has been placed under tremendous pressure by the rise of US militarism and the inclination of the Bush administration towards unilateralism. The role of regional organisations in this context will be highly contested.

Economic, security, and political co-operation

Is regional collaboration best led by economic, political, or security considerations? Is there a spillover effect, so that progress in one may lead to progress in another, as trust is built? Whatever the case, there is an undeniable tendency for regional organisations to move toward multifunctionality, and to link the various dimensions in what is hoped will be a relationship of synergy. The Organisation for Security and Co-operation in Europe (OSCE) is emblematic in this regard. Furthermore, is co-operation driven by mostly negative features (e.g. *threat* from a regional power, or the *hegemonic power* of a state) or mostly positive features (*affection* in the sense of shared values, or *gain* for mutual, mostly economic, benefits) (Baregu 2003: 21)?

Buzan's (1991: 190) idea of a 'security complex', i.e. 'a group of states whose primary security concerns link together sufficiently closely that their national securities cannot realistically be considered apart from one another', is a useful point of departure for any discussion of security co-operation. Of course, a security complex does not a region make, let alone a regional institution, but security interactions of this nature are bound to have a profound effect on regional organisation. Furthermore, as regions move toward higher degrees of institutionalisation and develop common values, a much closer correlation between security linkages and political co-operation emerges, for obvious reasons. This may eventually lead to the construction of a 'security community' (Deutsch 1957; Adler and Barnett 1998), where armed conflict between states has become inconceivable, e.g. in Scandinavia.

Regional hegemonism

Is the presence of a regional hegemon, both able and willing to exercise its military and economic muscle, a desirable or even a necessary condition for the evolution of regional organisations? Neo-realists would tend to argue that it is; others regard this as a negative feature. The answer to this may be context-specific. It might also be the case that at different stages, or under certain conditions, hegemony may either accelerate or retard organisational development. Whatever the case, it is a critical issue in many regional organisations.

What type of security collaboration?

Security collaboration can take several different forms, each of which may require a different process of construction. These include:

- military alliances such as NATO, in which states seek to combine their defence capabilities against a common external enemy;
- mutual assistance or mutual defence treaties, where states pledge to come to the assistance of any other member state in the event of it being attacked (and sometimes in the event of internal threats as well);
- non-aggression pacts, which are quite often linked to mutual assistance agreements; and
- common, collaborative, co-operative, or comprehensive security arrangements, where member states agree to a set of ground rules governing relations among them (and sometimes also to internal practices), institute confidence- and security-building measures (CSBMs), and develop co-operative approaches to security.

Which of these are the most useful and successful? Can they be combined?

Issues related to institutionalisation

Should developing countries follow the European Union (EU) model of building an extensive array of institutions supported by a bureaucracy, or should a more flexible, less institutionalised approach be followed? Put another way, should regional organisations evolve as inter-state structures or as supra-national institutions? A related issue is that of multiple institutionalism: is it possible (or even desirable) to have more than one regional organisation with overlapping memberships (as in Europe)? This debate is closely related to that of how best to deal with hegemonic powers.

As institutionalisation progresses, particularly in the security area, the issue of managing the periphery becomes more pressing. Certain forms of security co-operation can act as 'force multipliers', potentially threatening neighbouring states and leading to counter-bloc formation. And successfully institutionalised organisations will inevitably create demands for new members, as with the EU.

Sovereignty and 'non-interference in internal affairs'

While there have not yet been any examples in modern history where regional organisations have ended the sovereignty of member states, there is no doubt that they inevitably – as with any international regime – require that states agree to work within certain limits, which may become progressively restrictive as institutionalisation progresses. This is particularly the case in multifunctional organisations. Furthermore, states are naturally very concerned not to lose their ability to act independently in security matters. Under what conditions will states be willing to 'trade' some of their sovereign decision-making capacity for the benefits of inter-state co-operation?

While the principle of 'non-interference in internal affairs', entrenched in the UN Charter (although also potentially contradicted by the assertion of universal human rights), may have utility in terms of confidence building, in the long run it could be argued that it feeds instability, as it may result in tolerance of human rights violations, authoritarianism, and the like. Even more importantly, it demands the following question.

Regime security or human security?

Most of the organisations in this study are essentially state-driven projects, and in many cases the motivations for security co-operation appear to be driven by the mutual insecurities of state elites. They may have contributed to stability – essentially, maintenance of the status quo – and to the security of the regimes involved, but have they contributed to socio-economic development and to the security of their citizens – in other words, to human security?

Democratic values

It can be asked whether regional security co-operation has merely shored up undemocratic regimes, or contributed to, and been built on the basis of, democratic values. This inevitably leads to a consideration of the arguments centred on the 'democratic peace' theory: if all countries in a region are democracies, can this lead to peaceful interactions and assist in building a security community? And is security organisation possible in contexts where democracies are not the norm?

This chapter will seek to answer all these questions by examining, in a selected way, the experience in the developing world of building regional organisations with security functions.

Latin America

The emergence of regional security co-operation organisations in the Western Hemisphere has been overshadowed by the hegemony of the United States. Nevertheless, like Europe and Africa, the Americas have evolved a continental security structure and a number of sub-regional ones, as well as a major trading organisation, NAFTA, which also has a limited political and security role. Of the sub-regional organisations, the most successful is the Mercado Comun del Sur (Southern Cone Common Market – MERCOSUR), but others, notably the Organisation of East Caribbean States, have also played a security role.

MERCOSUR

Like Africa, Latin America is littered with the corpses of failed sub-regional co-operation and integration organisations. But there is at least one recent success: MERCOSUR, launched in 1991 by Argentina, Brazil, Paraguay, and Uruguay. The primary focus of MERCOSUR is on trade, and it has succeeded in substantially increasing inter-regional exports, but it has also increasingly taken on political and security functions. One of its first actions was to implement a nuclear weapons-free zone (a process that started with the Treaty of Tlatelolco of 1967); it has facilitated joint military exercises and joint meetings of chiefs of staff; and in 1999 it declared itself a 'Zone of Peace', and member states agreed to enhance co-operation and promote CSBMs. This process has been facilitated by the demilitarisation of the region, with all countries moving – albeit in different ways and at different speeds – to reduce military power and influence in domestic and foreign policy, and to cut defence spending substantially.

MERCOSUR's success comes despite its relatively low level of institutionalisation. It has not sought to develop large supra-national institutions, and it has no standing security co-operation mechanism. This has created some problems. In the words of one commentator: 'The absence of any community entity with any advisory or decision-making power gives rise to conflicting responses that must always be resolved *a posteriori* through political decisions, which are not always transparent' (Pereira 1999: 20).

On the other hand, this lack of institutionalism has necessitated continuous and informal high-level contact, which has helped to build trust and has allowed for flexibility. Heads of state and senior officials remain in regular contact with each other to discuss issues as they arise.

MERCOSUR's relative success has been attributed to a number of factors, including:

- the fact that the members are all relatively strong, well-established states with relatively efficient bureaucracies and policy management capacities (by developing-world standards, anyway);
- the small size of the organisation;
- shared values, chiefly a commitment to democracy following periods of military dictatorship;
- common economic interests and a commitment to opening up economies; and
- regular contacts and good personal relations between heads of state and senior officials (Cleary 2001: 92).

MERCOSUR emerged at a time when all the member states were undergoing processes of transition from authoritarianism to democracy, and there was a conviction – which is common in many new regional organisations – that democracy would provide a firm foundation for inter-state peace. This may not really be true, as the chapter's conclusion argues, but an argument can certainly be made that MERCOSUR has assisted in stabilising and consolidating the democratic transitions in its member states. That the organisation is mostly concerned with trade, rather than politics or security, has not necessarily blunted its effectiveness in stabilising relations among states.

Organisation of American States (OAS)

One of the oldest regional organisations in the world, and one of the few to bring together developed (United States, Canada) and developing countries (Latin America), the OAS has as its main feature the complete dominance of the United States.

Multi-functional in nature and highly institutionalised, the OAS also has a mutual assistance function, through the 1947 Inter-American Treaty of Reciprocal Assistance, better known as the Rio Pact, in terms of which members are required to assist another member under attack until the OAS or the UN Security Council can recommend a course of collective action. But this principle was steadily eroded by US military actions, and when Britain launched its fleet against Argentina in 1982 in order to reclaim the Falklands Islands/Islas Malvinas, and Argentina tried to invoke the treaty, the United States instead supported Britain.

Although the OAS is constituted as a regional security organisation under chapter VIII of the UN Charter, and it states its intention to work as part of the UN system, it can be argued that in practice it has allowed the United States to operate outside of the UN system in the Western Hemisphere, by using the OAS to legitimise its actions. And when the OAS has not suited its purposes, e.g. in its invasion of Grenada in 1983, the United States has simply acted unilaterally, without consulting the regional organisation at all.

Despite the failures, efforts have been made since the early 1990s to revitalise the concept of mutual assistance, and a Permanent Hemispheric Security Commission was incorporated into the OAS's institutions, ensuring that security – along with a commitment to democracy – was mainstreamed in the organisation. It has also developed mechanisms for preventing military coups, by establishing procedures for co-ordinated responses (Mills, Shelton, and White 2003: 10; Hurrell 1995: 265).

Asia

The security challenges facing Asian countries are as diverse and often as complex as the countries themselves, and have been compounded by the strategic 'overlay' of the Cold War and interventions by external powers. These factors, as well as the interpenetration of conflicts, have made it difficult for regional security co-operation to emerge. In North-East Asia, competition among the four major powers influencing the region (the United States, the Soviet Union, China, and Japan), as well as the conflicts over Taiwan and Korea, have in the past prevented the emergence of regional co-operation (Alagappa 1998: 109). In Central Asia, the overlay of the Cold War was the major security feature, and the new states that have emerged since then have not yet found their way towards substantive security co-operation, although there is some progress through the Commonwealth of Independent States. The most successful effort at regional co-operation has been in South-East Asia, and an effort has also been made in Indian-dominated South Asia.

Association of South-East Asian Nations (ASEAN)

There would seem to be little that would draw the countries of ASEAN together. Even the original members (Indonesia, Malaysia, the Philippines, Singapore, and Thailand) were extremely diverse in size, culture, ethnic composition, colonial history, religion, and political system (military rule, authoritarian rule, and democracy), and the organisation's diversity has increased as it has expanded to include countries such as Brunei, Cambodia, Laos, Myanmar, and Vietnam. But ASEAN is a classic case of states drawing together because of shared threat perceptions and common convictions about how to counter the threat. All the founding states were faced with communist insurgencies and believed that their regimes were threatened. They also all believed that they could 'buy' their way out of domestic crisis through growth and economic development. ASEAN was essentially about regime survival at a time when Western-leaning states in the region were made profoundly insecure by domestic insurgencies, the Cultural Revolution in China, and the Vietnam War.

Because of political sensitivities, the original members concerned themselves initially more with economic than political and security co-operation, even though security was one of the main motivations for collaboration (the predecessors of the EU and SADC took a similar course) (Than and Singh 2001: 173).

As time has gone on, however, ASEAN has become quite institutionalised and now involves itself in a wide range of issues, including security. That the original communist threat has largely evaporated has not led to the organisation's demise; instead, the benefits of regional co-operation have become so evident that it is highly unlikely that there will be any turning back. But ASEAN's weaknesses have all been exposed through its failure adequately to address the major challenges that have faced it in the past several years (Henderson 1999: 36–47).

ASEAN's weakness in dealing with these challenges stems from the same root that is often seen as the key to its relative success: the so-called 'ASEAN way'. Essentially – and this stems in large part from the organisation's diversity and the fact that it has always had non-democratic or semi-democratic member states – this practice may be summarised as follows:

- strict non-intervention in member states' internal affairs (although informal, private discussions may take place);
- informal decision-making by consensus after (mostly) closed-door discussions;
- reliance on national institutions rather than building a strong centralised bureaucracy; and
- 'compartmentalising', postponing, or simply ignoring difficult or divisive issues (Than and Singh 2001: 176–77; Bessho 1999: 48).

There can be little doubt that in the first 20 years or so of its existence, these principles allowed ASEAN to emerge on the basis of a rather unlikely partnership of states and to create some stability in an otherwise turbulent region. However, since the end of the Cold War, and with the complex economic and political challenges facing ASEAN states, the organisation has been less successful. The principle of non-interference in particular has come under pressure. Critics have argued that it has resulted in ASEAN in effect collaborating with massive human rights abuses, such as those perpetrated by the Indonesian regime in East Timor or the abuses of the Myanmar military rulers.

Whatever the case, it is clear that the principle of non-interference is difficult to uphold and has proved inadequate for dealing with the more recent crises. ASEAN effectively began 'interfering' as long ago as 1997, when it delayed Cambodia's admission for two years – under strong Western pressure – after the Hun Sen coup. If ASEAN is to prosper in the new century, it will need to find a way of balancing its traditional respect for sovereignty with effective intervention strategies for upholding human rights and promoting democratic practices: not easy when member regimes include paranoid military juntas such as that in Myanmar, or nominally communist regimes such as that in Vietnam, which cling tenaciously to the principle of 'non-interference'.

In line with its informal, non-institutionalised approach, ASEAN has not developed comprehensive multilateral institutions to deal with security issues. Co-operation tends to take place bilaterally, and typically involves intelligence exchanges, exchanges between military staff colleges, joint military or policing exercises, and co-operation in fighting transnational crime such as narcotics. A complex web of security interactions has thus been established, contributing significantly to building confidence, especially among the longer-standing members (Than and Singh 2001: 178). A non-aggression regime has also been put in place through a number of treaties.

One of the most innovative security and political initiatives was the establishment in 1993 of the Asian Regional Forum (ARF), with the aim of enhancing ASEAN's ability to deal as a bloc with strong external powers, and to build confidence in the region (and, unspoken, to rein in China, which was then aggressively pursuing territorial claims in the South China Sea). The ARF is very loosely modelled on the OSCE, and involves ASEAN member states and their major trading partners and regional actors – Australia, the EU, Japan, New Zealand, South Korea, the United States, Canada, China, Russia, India, and Mongolia.

South Asian Association for Regional Security (SAARC)

In part inspired by the success of ASEAN, SAARC was established in 1983 with the aim of enhancing security in the South Asian region (India, Pakistan, Bangladesh, Bhutan, Sri Lanka, and the Maldives are members). However, it adopted the same approach as ASEAN – and many other regional organisations – in that it concentrated on economic, social, and technical issues, even if its aim was to enhance security, and tried to avoid dealing with contentious and bilateral issues. This has not been easy, however, given the regional fears of Indian hegemony, and the long and apparently intractable conflict between India and Pakistan.

Nevertheless, it has chalked up some successes, including a bilateral agreement between India and Pakistan not to attack each other's nuclear facilities, a preferential trade agreement, and settlement of some complicated bilateral disputes (Alagappa 1998: 109). In general, however, SAARC has largely failed to break the mould of a zero-sum or relative-gain approach to security by South Asian states, and it has also been largely unsuccessful in promoting intra-regional trade. This is in large part because its activities have been overshadowed by the Indian–Pakistani conflict, in which it has been unable to play any major role, given the weakness of the other member states. The asymmetric nature of SAARC, coupled to a dyadic conflict, appears to have inhibited its development.

Middle East

The conflict-ridden Middle East (which straddles two continents and in its widest definition extends east–west from Morocco to Iran, and north–south from Turkey to the Sudanese–Egyptian border, and takes in the Arabian peninsula) is the homeland of some of the world's great religions and civilisations. One of these, the Arab civilisation, has given rise to the League of Arab States (Arab League), while two sub-regional organisations with security functions have emerged: the GCC and the Arab Maghreb Union (AMU), which is dealt with in the Africa section. For the rest, conflict formations and the penetration of great-power interests have prevented the emergence of substantive regional organisations.

Gulf Co-operation Council

None of the GCC member states is a democracy – all are ruled by feudalistic royal families who govern with varying degrees of authoritarianism (Saudi Arabia, United Arab Emirates, Kuwait, Bahrain, Qatar, and Oman). As with so many regional organisations, it was a specific security threat that triggered co-operation: in this case the 1979 Iranian Revolution and its domestic overspills, and the subsequent Iran–Iraq War (Tow 1990: 45–48).

The GCC is thus yet another example of states coming together on the basis of shared threat perceptions and regime insecurities. Again, however, the initial emphasis was on 'economic security', with military and other forms of security co-operation being dealt with more quietly – in part to avoid the impression of military-bloc formation.

Nevertheless, the GCC states have entered into a mutual defence pact, established a small multinational regional defence unit, carried out joint military exercises, and worked towards setting up a common air defence mechanism (Tripp 1995: 291–95). As such, the GCC is one of the most advanced examples of military co-operation among regional organisations in the developing world. But – typically of such pacts – when it has come to the crunch, with Iraqi and Iranian threats, the member states have been largely unable or unwilling to act. Instead, the GCC states have largely relied on external security guarantees, chiefly from the United States (Tripp 1995: 302–3).

The GCC is also an example of a regional organisation dominated by one power, Saudi Arabia, the gross domestic product of which exceeds that of the others combined. Lawson (1999: 10) argues that this has provided stability – not so much because of Saudi dominance, but because the relative balance of power among the member countries has remained consistent over time.

League of Arab States (Arab League)

Like the OAU, the Arab League is driven by an ideology of a shared identity and a common past and future; unlike the OAU, however, it is based not on a geographical framework, but on a 'civilisational' or ethnic commonality, although some of its 22 members – Sudan, for example – include sizeable populations that are not Arab.

One of the oldest regional organisations, it was formed in 1945 and its members entered into a collective defence agreement in 1950, through the Treaty for Joint Defence and Economic Co-operation, which typically states that an act of aggression against one member should be regarded as an attack on all (Al-Bab n.d.).

Much of the Arab League's security focus has been on Israel (Palestine is a member state), and it has been fairly successful in keeping this issue alive, even if it has not always projected a common position (and felt obliged to expel Egypt after it signed the Camp David Accords). It has been far less successful in mediating disputes between member states, nor has it succeeded in presenting a common front against external interventions – it was unable, for example, to play a significant role in preventing the US-led attack on Iraq in March 2003.

Most of the 'Arab world' remains highly militarised and tensions among states are high. Just as in the OAU, political divisions centred on the national interests of states have proved more important in security terms than an assumed inclusive commonality: Arab states – like African ones – are very heterogeneous, and the differences among them are replicated by differences within them, thus inviting interventions and fomenting tensions (Farer 1993: 173). The Arab League remains a weak organisation because 'mutual distrust is high, both between regimes and their citizens and between regimes themselves' (Aarts 1999: 207).

Africa

Africa appears at first glance to be far more developed than Asia or the Americas in terms of security co-operation, and far more logically organised, with an overarching regional organisation and – at least at present – a fairly neat division of sub-regional organisations with security functions more or less organised according to Africa's five geographical divisions (North, Southern, East, West and Central). As in the Arab world, there is a strong inclination towards an inclusive African identity – despite the vast cultural, ethnic, and other diversities of the continent.

But on closer inspection, it becomes clear that Africa's ruling regimes are just as wedded to the concept of national sovereignty as regimes anywhere else in the world, that many regional organisations are weak or even empty shells, and that more than 30 attempts have been made at constructing regional organisations, often through grandiose plans, most of which have failed. Many of these have been overlapping, and development has been haphazard. Furthermore, a pattern of intervention by individual states or ad hoc coalitions has been established (Furley and May 2001). Most of the 'civil wars' that have plagued African states since independence have in fact involved other states. Seldom has a formal commitment – to 'non-interference in internal affairs' – been more honoured in the breach than in the observance, and yet this fiction has been one of the longest-standing principles of African unity, and has only recently been revised.

Nevertheless, commitment to regionalism remains probably stronger in Africa than anywhere else, except Europe, and it is the intention of Africa's leaders that the new AU should rest on five or possibly more strong sub-regional organisations, each with a security management system that to some extent mirrors that of the AU itself, and which in turn is based on and integrated with the UN system. The most obvious candidates for these 'building blocks' of continental security are the AMU, the Economic Community of West African States (ECOWAS), the Economic and Monetary

Community of Central African States/*Communauté Économique et Monétaire de l'Afrique Centrale* (ECCAS/CEMAC), the Inter-governmental Authority on Development (IGAD), the Common Market for Eastern and Southern Africa (COMESA), the East African Community (EAC), and SADC. It is to these seven organisations (with the exception of SADC) that the chapter now turns its attention: other overlapping organisations will continue to exist, but as time goes by they are likely to become less important in security management terms. It should be noted that other sub-regional organisations, notably the Manu River Union, have taken on security functions and developed institutions for security management.

AMU

The AMU, the weakest of all the putative sub-regional building blocks of the AU's security system, is moribund, and its presidential council has not met since 1994. Established in 1989 by all five Maghreb states – Algeria, Libya, Mauritania, Morocco, and Tunisia – the AMU is a multifunctional organisation that deals with issues as diverse as sanitary standards and taxation, but the 'trigger' for its formation, and one of its chief preoccupations, was the need to engage with the EU. It was also seen as a building block for Arab unity, a cause then being espoused (no longer) by President Gadaffi of Libya.

The AMU has no functional security structures although, as in many regional organisations, member states have entered into a mutual defence pact. Political and security co-operation has been hampered by the dyadic conflict between Algeria and Morocco over Western Sahara. Some analysts argue that the problem with the AMU is that it is too small (whereas the Arab League is too big): when two member states disagree, the three others are too weak to intervene collectively.

Whatever the case, it is clear that considerably more will need to be done if the AMU is to become one of the building blocks of the AU's Peace and Security Council. But this will depend on the resolution of political divisions and on the mercurial will of Gadaffi.

ECOWAS

In contrast, ECOWAS has the most sophisticated security management system in Africa, and the most experience in terms of peacekeeping and peace making. From the outset, ECOWAS, and what has come to be its security arm, the ECOWAS Cease-Fire Monitoring Group (ECOMOG), has been driven by the dominant sub-regional power, Nigeria. In some ways, like the OAS, ECOWAS/ECOMOG has been a fig leaf for what would otherwise be unilateral Nigerian intervention in neighbouring conflicts, but in other ways it has emerged as a genuinely regional initiative.

As in many other regional organisations, ECOWAS member states have signed both a non-aggression treaty and a mutual military assistance treaty whereby an attack on one is deemed to be an attack on all, but the principal objective is described as regional economic integration. Since 1998 ECOMOG has been recognised as the peacekeeping arm of ECOWAS, and an elaborate security architecture has been erected to support it. Through a somewhat ad hoc succession of military interventions, coupled with *ex ante* formalisation and institutionalisation – always led by Nigeria – ECOWAS has evolved a sophisticated but functional system for security management. However, its strength – that it has been activated by a regional hegemon – is also its weakness: if Nigeria is unable or unwilling to act, then ECOWAS is fatally weakened, and this is compounded by anglophone–francophone divisions. Furthermore, it is deeply ironic that ECOWAS has intervened to 'restore democracy' in war-torn states when the leading power, Nigeria, itself was not a democracy. ECOWAS's limitations have been made clear in its inability to act over the civil war in Côte d'Ivoire, when Nigeria felt unable to help out. This may increasingly be the case, given the growing political tensions within Nigeria (Berman 2002: 38).

ECCAS/CEMAC

Primarily an economic grouping, the 11-member ECCAS has recently taken on security functions and is envisaged as part of the AU's security architecture.

In 1999, the ECCAS summit decided to set up a Council for Peace and Security in Central Africa/*Conseil de Paix et de Securité en Afrique Centrale,* which includes a conflict monitoring unit as well as a putative Central African Multinational Force – a standby peacekeeping arrangement consisting of earmarked military and civilian contingents. The apparently mandatory mutual military assistance pact has also been signed. With assistance from external powers, some joint military exercises aimed at developing the regional peacekeeping capacity have been carried out.

However, ECCAS is a weak organisation, and formal structures seldom have any significant content (Berman and Sams 2000: 205–6). Member states do not agree on the relationship between the security and economic functions of the organisation, and a number of countries retain membership of other regional organisations as well (IPA 2002: 36). Considerable work will have to be done if ECCAS is be a substantive building block for continental security, and this will require political will.

IGAD

Originally a functional co-operation agreement focusing on drought and development issues, IGAD began to take on conflict resolution activities in the mid-1990s (notably the Sudan peace process) and is now developing more elaborate security arrangements. Bringing together Sudan, Somalia, Uganda, Eritrea, Ethiopia, Djibouti, and Kenya, IGAD not only involves countries facing internal conflict, but also states that have been at war with each other. IGAD intends to establish a conflict early warning and response mechanism, but its capacities remain very limited. It has been unable to intervene significantly in the Eritrean–Ethiopian conflict or the Sudan conflict, for example, and commentators have remarked that 'IGAD member states seem more willing to devote significant scarce resources to actively undermine their neighbours than to help bring about a sustainable peace' (Berman and Sams 2000: 210).

EAC and COMESA

The potential status of these two organisations as sub-regional building blocks within the AU's emerging security architecture is somewhat unclear, as most of their member states are also members of other sub-regional organisations (mostly IGAD and SADC), and there is thus a high degree of overlap.

The EAC is a resurrection of the earlier community of the same name, and involves the same three countries: Kenya, Tanzania, and Uganda. It has economic as well as security functions, and a memorandum of agreement has been signed among the defence forces of the three countries, which, among other things, provides for joint training, joint operations, and the sharing of intelligence; the organisation also aims to conclude a defence pact (Berman and Sams 2000: 200).

COMESA, the largest sub-regional organisation, with 20 member states, was originally formed to promote economic co-operation through trade, and grew out of the Preferential Trade Area. But like so many such organisations, it has also taken on security functions in the belief that peace and security are essential for investment, trade, and development. COMESA member states have made a series of commitments to non-aggression, respect for human rights, the rule of law and democracy, the peaceful settlement of disputes, and so on. It has managed to establish a number of semi-autonomous and ad hoc arrangements to deal with regional conflicts (IPA 2002: 38). However, its main achievements have been in reducing trade barriers, and tensions have arisen among member states over trade imbalances and other issues, as well as the overlap with SADC, with some members leaving in order to concentrate scarce resources on SADC instead. Its future as a sub-regional building block for African security thus remains uncertain.

Conclusion

Far more research will have to be done if the complex questions posed at the beginning of this chapter are to be answered satisfactorily. In many cases, no clear patterns have emerged, and it appears that answers may have to be context-specific. Nevertheless, a few general points may be made on the basis of this brief and selective survey, and we thus return to the key issues posed at the beginning of this chapter.

Multilateralism, globalisation, and regionalism

In virtually all cases, sub-regional organisations in the developing world appear to have acted more as building blocks for regional and global collective security than as stumbling blocks. This is seen perhaps most clearly in Africa, where a conscious effort has been made to construct a regional security mechanism on sub-regional organisations. However, it can also be seen – e.g. in relation to the OAS, with the United States, and possibly also in relation to Nigeria in the OAU/AU – that sub-regional or regional organisations may act as 'fig leaves' for unilateral interventions by hegemonic powers, to some extent thus undermining global collective security objectives.

It is clear also that regional organisations are increasing in scope and extent as a direct response to globalisation. But the 'new' type of regionalism emerging is far more about opening up regions than closing them off. As such, these organisations can be seen both as a response to and providing further impetus for globalisation. Whether they serve to mitigate the exclusionary effects of uneven global development, however, is unclear. It could equally be argued that they serve to accelerate inequalities by servicing neo-liberal economics through their outward orientations.

Economic, security, and political co-operation

The vast majority of organisations surveyed started out with the stated aim of economic co-operation, but took on political and security co-operation tasks. In probably a majority of cases, however, the actual motivation for initiating the regional organisation was a shared regime threat perception, often triggered by a particular event or by a shared fear of a hegemonic or revisionist power, or by a common perception of domestic security threats. In quite a number of cases, economic co-operation was promoted in order to address the actual issue of regime threat perception, and this seems to be by far the most important driver in the initial stages of institution building.

But it need not remain so: some regional organisations have continued to thrive on the palpable benefits of multifunctional co-operation, even when the initial threat disappears. Such 'spillover' is a product of increased levels of inter-state communication. Moreover, as Waever has argued, as regional organisations progress towards security communities, interactions may become increasingly 'desecuritised'; i.e. there may be 'a progressive marginalisation of mutual security concerns in favour of other issues' (Adler and Barnett 1998: 414–15, 432).

Regional hegemonism

This brief survey has shown that regional hegemons can play a critical role in promoting regional co-operation, either by utilising their military and other power to secure a type of peace (Nigeria in ECOWAS) or more subtly (Indonesia in ASEAN). At the same time, hegemonic powers weakened by internal divisions (Nigeria and Indonesia both) can slow the growth of regional organisations, and may also so distort relations within them that the organisations become hollow, as member states seek bilateral arrangements with the regional power. In other words, the benefits or drawbacks of regional hegemonism appear to be context-specific, and quite likely time-specific as well. In the early period of regional formation, powerful states that can provide leadership and 'a sense of purpose' seem to play an important role (Adler and Barnett 1998).

In most of the organisations studied, hegemonic powers were present and, despite their sometimes negative roles, it seems that they can play an important part in the establishment of functional regional security organisations, although it is unlikely that they are a necessary or sufficient condition. A key driver in this seems to be the need to 'embed' hegemonism by constructing agreements that serve to rein in the regional power; of course, they may also serve to consolidate that power.

Types of security co-operation

This study has reaffirmed a general truth about mutual assistance pacts: they don't work. Political realities tend to take precedence over treaties when push comes to shove, and if a regional power is involved, its calculation of national interests is likely to override any pledges it might have made. There are few examples of successful defence alliances that have been put into operation in the developing world.

Nevertheless, mutual assistance pacts seem to be vital to the process of institution building, as virtually all the organisations examined have developed them, always in conjunction with non-aggression treaties. As confidence-building measures, they are probably a necessary stage. However, the most effective form of co-operation seems to be collaborative security, moving on through time to common security.

Issues related to institutionalisation

Some organisations have been successfully built on the basis of informal interactions ('loose' organisations), while others have failed because they have not developed a high enough level of institutionalisation. Again, this probably varies over time. Informality may work for some years, but in due course some type of institutionalisation will be needed to take co-operation to a higher level. Institutionalisation – in the form of agreements or organisations – may also be required in situations where a hegemon is involved, in order to establish checks and balances and to rein in the dominant power, as argued above.

Size matters, but it is not clear how. Arguments have been put forward that small organisations, with, say, four or five members, cannot deal with conflicts between two members because the others are collectively too weak (AMU); alternatively, it is argued that small organisations can build confidence and common values (MERCOSUR), and that very large ones encompass too many political divergences to succeed (the Arab League or COMESA). What can probably be concluded with some certainty is that small organisations will not be able to withstand dyadic conflicts (SAARC and AMU).

It would be expected that the type of security organisation would affect the challenge of the periphery, with military alliances posing a threat to non-member neighbours and collaborative security regimes being much less threatening. This has not been empirically proven in this study, possibly because there are in practice few effective military alliances in the developing world, and mutual assistance pacts are usually ineffectual and seen to be so (see below).

Many of the organisations studied here work on consensus, or at least pretend to do so. While this may slow down institutional progress, it also makes it much more difficult for countries to back out of agreements once they have been made. Furthermore, institutions seem to evolve on the basis of 'sunk costs' – as the effort put into regional organisations increases and the costs of extraction grow, stability seems to set in.

Sovereignty and 'non-interference in internal affairs'

The principle of non-interference has been a stabilising and confidence-building factor within some regional organisations at some (usually early) time. Often, however, especially in Africa, principle and practice have borne little relation to each other, and states that have signed up to such principles have blatantly violated them.

There seems to come a time when progress toward regional co-operation or integration is hampered by an over-insistence on national sovereignty. Further development will come to depend on states being willing to cede some sovereignty in order to reap the greater benefits of co-operation. It is also evident that many issues remain unaddressed if the principle of non-intervention is made into a shibboleth, and it can be a fig leaf for the tolerance of dictatorship and human rights abuses.

However, if the principle of 'non-interference in internal affairs' is to be ditched in regional organisations, it is obviously desirable that some other principles are put in place to govern relations between states, especially in situations where there is a regional power. Such principles could typically be based on democratic and human rights norms, and opposition to non-constitutional changes of government and military interference in governance (as in MERCOSUR).

Regime security or human security?

This cursory survey has strongly suggested that the principal driver of regional security co-operation is shared regime threat perception (both internal and external) and a common interest among regimes – be they democratic or not – in supporting each other against sources of threat to internal and external security. As such, regional security co-operation in developing countries is clearly aimed at stability and regime security.

However, as Adler and Barnett (1998: 37–48) argue, the mere presence of the increased communication and transactions among states and peoples required in building a regional organisation can become 'the wellsprings of both mutual trust and collective identity', even if these processes are initially elite-driven.

It is difficult to determine in a survey of this nature whether the regional organisations under consideration have contributed to human security and community and social development, and far more in-depth research will need to be carried out. Indeed, it is not clear what the measurements of human security are (do they approximate to the UNDP HDI?) or whether it is possible to determine a contingent relationship between stability and human security. Again, this may vary over time.

Democratic values

Our brief survey has shown that some organisations, albeit very weak ones (such as the Arab League), have been built on the basis of common 'civilisational' values, while in others (such as MERCOSUR), a common commitment to democratic political values appears to have played an important role. However, other organisations (ASEAN, for example; possibly also ECOWAS) have survived, even thrived, despite very different political values and systems in member states. Common political values, as noted earlier, can be – probably have to be – constructed. Their development is a necessary process as part of the forward movement of security complexes to becoming security communities. As noted earlier, there is also evidence that a failure to move beyond 'regime collaboration' and to develop common democratic values probably puts a cap on the growth and utility of regional organisations.

Regime collaboration and beyond

There seems to be strong evidence that incremental, functional co-operation on a widening range of issues can eventually lead to co-operation on grander issues such as security – this is probably, on the basis of empirical evidence, the more successful model. This is closely related to the debate about whether functional (usually economic) co-operation should precede security and political co-operation, or vice versa. As this chapter has concluded above, security is the most important motivator, but it may be expedient to concentrate on economic co-operation at first.

In virtually all the organisations studied, states have been the primary actors. It may be argued that this is entirely inappropriate (see, for example, Vale 2003), but it is nevertheless the way it has happened. Time has not provided for an analysis on other forms of regional co-operation, e.g. among NGOs or social movements, nor whether there is a symbiotic or adversarial relationship between such collaboration and that of states. This is a necessary issue for further research.

Although security-motivated 'regime collaboration' – with or without a hegemon, and whether the threat lies within or without – appears to have a stabilising effect on regional security complexes, and although such interactions have a cumulative and 'spillover' effect, it is not clear that such collaboration contributes to 'social gains' in the sense of promoting democracy, human rights, and human security, even if it usually leads on to other functional forms of co-operation. It is likely, furthermore, that in the current era of globalisation and the universalising claims (although sometimes also exclusionary effects) of political liberalism, the utility of 'regime collaboration' will be reduced in the quest for the construction of security communities. The relationship between outward-oriented 'new regionalism' and the evolution of human rights and democracy needs to be further explored.

ENDNOTES

1 This chapter examines some of the conceptual issues related to the rise of regional inter-state co-operation, in particular, in security and defence co-operation. It does not deal with organisations in the developed world, save to use them as examples, and it does not aim to be comprehensive with regard to the developing world.

2 In this chapter, the term 'region' is taken to include 'sub-region' unless otherwise specified.

Chapter 3

Southern African Security in Historical Perspective

Abillah H. Omari and Paulino Macaringue

Southern Africa is a region defined and structured by a history of conflicts. Colonialism, anti-colonial resistance, apartheid, wars of liberation, Cold War rivalries, and destabilisation campaigns entered the historical lexicography for this region, testifying to the structural conflict that afflicted it until the 1990s. Within this historical legacy, the region witnessed the formation of alliances and counter-alliances and was forced to consider a co-operation formula to resolve the endemic conflicts. SADC's co-operation on politics, defence, and security is a child of this historical process and continues to bear the marks of the legacies of these conflicts (Macaringue 2004).

This chapter highlights the salient features of the Southern African historical transformation from the 1970s to the present. It argues that the regional conflict paved the way for co-operation, but also that the many years of conflict have strengthened the national sovereignty of the region's states, which may slow down forms of regional co-operation. The region was, for a long time, engaged in what has been called a 'war of visions' (Deng 1995; see also Khadigala 1994). This history has resulted in certain preferred modes of co-operation that have necessitated a slow and painful process towards institutionalised regional integration. Nevertheless, Southern Africa is now slowly moving towards a regional security regime that can ensure democratic governance and common security.

Conflict

What is unique about Southern Africa is not the existence of conflict and co-operation at one and the same time, but essentially co-operation for conflict resolution. As this chapter will argue, this is unique, and has tended to influence other regional developments.

The traditional aspect of the conflict has been the colonial one, Africa being the last continent to be decolonised. Southern Africa has a special place in history: the character of colonialism is different from most colonial situations, as it was a combination of classic and settler colonialism. There were also some differences within one type of colonialism, which complicated the process of decolonisation of the 1960s and beyond.

Within the classic set-up there was Portuguese, German, Belgian, and British colonialism. Angola and Mozambique were administered by Portugal, always an imperial anomaly in that Portugal was both the first European nation to colonise Africa and virtually the last to leave. While the British were decolonising Africa in the 1960s, Portugal maintained that its African colonies, like those of France, were part of the mother country (Gibson 1972: 4; Isaacman 1988: 16). Portugal tried to isolate its colonies from the changes occurring elsewhere in Africa; under those circumstances, attempts to use persuasion and dialogue failed, and that made it clear to many that the Portuguese colonies would not have a negotiated or a peaceful transition to independence. Armed struggle therefore became the only way to liberate Portugal's African colonies. The British had colonies in Lesotho, Swaziland, and Botswana. These countries were administered as typical colonies. Tanzania was a British mandated territory, as Namibia was to South Africa. Malawi, Zambia, and Rhodesia/Zimbabwe were also classic British colonies, which were forced into the Central African Federation in 1956, an arrangement that was heavily contested in Zambia and Malawi. Dissolution of the federation in 1964 paved the way for constitutional negotiations, which brought independence to Malawi and Zambia, but not to Rhodesia/Zimbabwe. Constitutional developments in Tanzania, Malawi, and Zambia, and later in Botswana, Lesotho, and Swaziland, enabled the British to grant independence peacefully.

However, due to settler colonialism, which developed over time, Rhodesia/Zimbabwe shifted away from the classic colonial trend. The white settlers in Rhodesia/Zimbabwe moved to disassociate themselves from the British colonial authorities, culminating in their unilateral declaration of independence (UDI) in 1965, which unleashed the armed liberation war in that country.

South Africa effectively made Namibia its colony, therefore defying the authority of the UN over the country. The problem in South Africa was racism, institutionalised as apartheid in 1948.

Therefore, the colonial conflict in Southern Africa was partly resolved by the classic British colonies getting independence constitutionally, while in the settler and Portuguese colonies, liberation war became the only way to gain independence. The democratisation of apartheid South Africa was also achieved in part in that way. Portugal, Rhodesia, and South Africa were in concert to perpetuate colonialism, white settlerism, and minority rule in Southern Africa. The three regimes were in direct conflict with the majority of people in their respective territories and also with the countries that had received independence earlier on. The magnitude of this conflict varied, as did the range of its active actors. The colonial and settler regimes were determined to fight the wars of liberation to the end. In all these cases, the colonial powers accepted negotiation as a basis for settlement only when pressure on them mounted or when there had been substantial changes that directly affected them, such as the coup in Portugal in 1974, itself a product of the colonial African wars.

The colonial conflict was not the only one in Southern Africa: from the 1970s to mid-1990s the region experienced both old and new forms of conflict. Wars of liberation, which were the remnants of the 1960s and 1970s, were intensified. The victories gained in Mozambique, Angola, and Zimbabwe were superseded by internal conflicts. Destabilisation policies emanating from South Africa affected most majority-ruled states in Southern Africa at a time when they were experiencing declining economic performance, which necessitated structural adjustment programmes. The Namibian problem dragged on to 1990, and South Africa was not democratised until 1994.

By the mid-1980s the major conflict pattern in Southern Africa was between the majority-ruled states and the Republic of South Africa, manifested in apartheid in South Africa itself and the destabilisation by South Africa of those states opposed to its internal policies. The independent states treated apartheid and colonialism similarly. They condemned apartheid and sought the international isolation of the apartheid regime, and recognised and supported the liberation movements' fight against apartheid. South Africa perceived the alliance between the liberation movements and the majority-ruled states as an onslaught against it, supported by international communism, and reacted in the form of a militaristic 'Total Strategy' supplemented by destabilisation.

There were also conflicts within each group of primary actors in the regional conflict, which shaped the behaviour of various actors towards conflict and co-operation. Examples exist in varying degrees, some catalysed by destabilisation, including the differences among the South African liberation movements, and also among the various movements in the then majority-ruled countries – Angola, Mozambique, Zimbabwe, and even Zambia.[1] An additional aspect of the regional conflict was the differences among the majority-ruled states regarding the nature of their co-operation, the way they treated the liberation movements, and their perception of the common enemy, apartheid South Africa. This has left a political legacy and influenced the conception of good governance and common security in the region.

Co-operation

When attempting to understand the intertwining of conflict and co-operation in Southern Africa, it should be emphasised that in some cases conflict catalysed co-operation, and sometimes co-operation caused certain types of conflict. Three major types of co-operation can be identified, namely bilateral, multilateral, and transnational co-operation, and these complemented each other over time. These categories are outlined here as a prelude to the history of the major actor in the area of co-operation and conflict in Southern Africa: the Front Line States (FLS) (Omari 1991b).

The general conflict patterns in Southern Africa made sustained bilateral relations possible, mostly in the political and diplomatic spheres. Personal relationships between the then presidents of Zambia and Tanzania, Kenneth Kaunda and Julius Nyerere, respectively, helped to forge political links between their countries in an effort to hasten the regional liberation process. The ad hoc summit system they practised in the 1960s developed into a number of regional groupings. They initiated a series of conferences of East and Central African countries, which became an informal organisation (CECAC) (*Africa Research Bulletin* 1966: A484). The two countries related to the various liberation movements in particular ways, which had some consequences for the regional patterns of the 1980s and beyond.[2] One cannot ignore some bilateral ideological relations: the ongoing relations between Angola and Mozambique, Namibia and Angola, and Mozambique and Zimbabwe exemplify this.[3]

Bilateral economic relations have also been a feature: this co-operation provided an impetus for the current forms of regional integration. Crucial in this process during the 1960s through to the 1980s were Zambia and Tanzania. The hub for some joint economic ventures between these countries was the landlocked position of Zambia.[4] Relations between Zimbabwe and Mozambique have also shown this feature, with Zimbabwe reliant on the Beira corridor for access to the sea.

As an adjunct to the FLS, there was also some bilateral co-operation in defence and security matters well before the multilateral efforts of the present-day SADC. Several bilateral defence agreements were in place in the period under discussion (Omari 1991b). The nature of this co-operation has influenced the character of multilateral co-operation, as well as the resultant institutions. Most of such institutions in the region are loose, which reflects conflicting interests. These institutions were formed in the 1970s through to the 1990s: the FLS, the Southern African Development Co-ordination Conference (SADCC), the Preferential Trade Area, and COMESA. The current existing security co-operation frameworks, including the Organ on Politics, Defence, and Security Co-operation and the Mutual Defence Pact in SADC are a culmination of this long process.

Ironically, there was also some co-operation between the major adversaries in the regional conflict. Some of the majority-ruled states were forced by circumstances to co-operate with apartheid South Africa, as the economic realities of the regional political economy, centring on transportation infrastructure, overtook political and diplomatic considerations. Among such efforts was the Constellation of Southern African States, which never got off the ground, and the Rand Monetary Area and Southern African Customs Union, both of which still exist.

At the height of destabilisation, some majority-ruled states were forced into non-aggression treaties with apartheid South Africa in the mid-1980s, mostly notably the Nkomati Treaty between South Africa and Mozambique of March 1984. Similar non-aggression accords between South Africa and other majority-ruled states are known to have been signed and kept secret. Obviously, the signing of such treaties symbolised the end of an era – from the politics of confrontation to the new age of co-operation and accommodation, pre-dating the end of apartheid.

One may also cite some transnational relations that have endured over time, which have now been consolidated. Such relations have increasingly defined inter-state relations, becoming more regional than their inter-state counterparts. Apart from capital, technology, labour, and cultural exchanges, there have been the flow of people, informal (including illegal) trade and trafficking, and the activities of NGOs. Transnational relations of the past have now been consolidated, especially in the area of capital investment. What such relations did during the apartheid era was to undermine the isolation of the apartheid regime.

Co-operation for conflict resolution

It was alluded to above that the basic tenets of the regional political history in the 1960s and beyond were the co-existence of conflict and co-operation, and regional co-operation for conflict resolution. That the FLS triumphed as the most important actor in co-operation for conflict resolution does not mean that it was the only one: it was the culmination of various attempts towards regional co-operation for conflict resolution. Unlike formally constituted alliances, the formation of the FLS was not a product of a negotiated inter-governmental agreement. It evolved over time, arising out of specific needs of the 1970s, which reflected regional political, social, and economic needs.

There were thus some regional groupings before the formation of the FLS. Such groupings differed in size, focus, structure, and leadership, reflecting the general overview of African international relations at the time. Despite their differences, the groups preceding the FLS had similar objectives to this institution, namely, regional political and economic freedom. Thus the FLS had a long gestation period.

Pan-African Freedom Movement for East and Central Africa/Pan African Freedom Movement for East, Central, and Southern Africa (PAFMECA/ PAFMECSA)

Established in 1958, PAFMECA brought together the leaders of the nationalist movements in East and Central Africa (Cox 1964: 10). The founding conference approved the PAFMECA constitution and signed the Freedom Charter of the Peoples of East and Central Africa. The right to self-determination of the colonial peoples was upheld and a call to fight against apartheid was emphasised. The PAFMECA snowballed into a huge organisation in terms of membership (Cox 1964: 10–11). It changed its name to PAFMECSA to reflect its geographical growth and changed its constitution to accommodate independent countries. It was dissolved following the founding of the OAU in 1963. The founders of the FLS pointed out that PAFMECSA was suited to deal with classic colonialism, while in Southern Africa that problem was complicated by settlerism and apartheid (Cox 1964: 2–3).

CECAC

CECAC was initiated by Tanzania and Zambia to fill the vacuum left by the dissolution of PAFMECSA, which could not cater for the special needs of the region (Cox 1964: 3). Like the preceding PAFMECSA, CECAC grew in size and finally became ineffective. Despite its wide membership and friction with the OAU, CECAC is remembered for its Lusaka Manifesto (1969), which appeased the West and displeased the active liberation movements, as it attempted to balance negotiation and armed struggle as mechanisms for decolonisation. The OAU and the UN adopted the manifesto. However, that controversy was corrected by CECAC itself through the Mogadishu Declaration (1971), which upheld the virtues of armed struggle.

The Mulungushi Club

This was the most short-lived of all the groups pre-dating the FLS. Established in 1970, while CECAC was still in existence, it was dissolved in 1974, paving the way for the FLS. Formed among the leaders of Zambia, Uganda, Tanzania, and Zaire, the 'club' was more for the respective heads of state than an inter-state institution, and focused on the liberation of Southern Africa. It was formed in order to streamline the contradictory manifestos of CECAC, and also to follow up on resolutions.

The origins of the FLS can be found in the Mulungushi Club. Tanzania's Nyerere and Zambia's Kaunda formed the nucleus. Other founding presidents were Sir Seretse Khama of Botswana, Olusegun Obasanjo of Nigeria, Samora Machel, whose was then heading the transitional government in Mozambique, and Agostinho Neto, whose Movement for the Liberation of Angola was struggling to seize control in that country. Due to his ambiguous behaviour within the Mulungushi Club, President Mobutu of Zaire was excluded, signalling some realignment after the dissolution of the club.[5]

Some key characteristics of regional security co-operation emerge from this history. Firstly, all the organisations preceding the FLS had loose structures, with neither headquarters nor secretariats. They were informal and operated mainly at head-of-state level. Secondly, the institutions for conflict resolution enjoyed some coexistence, i.e. with a new organisation being formed before the existing one was disbanded. And thirdly, there was a proliferation of such institutions in the region, all having similar objectives. Such characteristics were imbedded in the FLS, and were to become major features of the regional integration process.

The FLS

The dominant view is that the FLS was founded on the basis of the anti-colonial conflict in Rhodesia/Zimbabwe (Omari 1991b).[6] The ineffectiveness of the Mulungushi Club, especially with Mobutu in it, and also the politics of détente initiated by South Africa to find a settlement to the Rhodesian/Zimbabwean problem, were the main catalysts. The coup d'etat in Portugal in April 1974 was also a contributory factor, as the new regime in Lisbon was forced to promise positive changes in Angola and Mozambique. Détente was conceived by South Africa in order to save itself, Rhodesia/Zimbabwe, and South West Africa/Namibia from the effects of armed struggle, so South Africa extended a hand of goodwill and attempted to normalise relations with its hostile neighbours, thinking that it was in the interest of African leaders to co-operate with it in resolving the conflict in Rhodesia/Zimbabwe peacefully. South Africa was assuming the role of peacemaker, thus defending apartheid through its involvement in Southern Africa.

To respond to this offer, concerted efforts were needed among independent states so as to have co-ordinated responses and policies. Other leaders who were relevant and willing were therefore courted to join Kaunda and

Nyerere, which is how Khama and Machel came to join forces with them. In addition, within Rhodesia/Zimbabwe a possibility presented itself of an internal settlement, to exclude the externally based liberation movements, the Zimbabwe African Peoples' Union (ZAPU) and the Zimbabwe African National Union (ZANU). Meanwhile, Britain had agreed to sponsor constitutional talks. Fundamental to what might have precipitated the establishment of the FLS is, arguably, the necessity to co-ordinate the efforts to convince ZAPU and ZANU to form a united front. The actual origin of the FLS can be traced to attempts to achieve this: the ambivalent Patriotic Front between ZAPU and ZANU was thus formed in Dar es Salaam in September 1976.

Arising out of the colonial conflict in Rhodesia/Zimbabwe, the FLS became one of the most important institutions in Southern Africa. However, it continued to operate in the same way as its predecessor organisations. It worked through a summit system, with no secretariat or headquarters, thus following the traditional tendency of avoiding written and signed charters and constitutions, as well as the formality enshrined in modern institutions (Omari 1991b). However, it was differentiated from its predecessors by its *modus operandi.* The FLS's importance in the regional liberation process and in that of Zimbabwe in particular was that it was a credible institution. The OAU mandated the FLS to work for the liberation of Southern Africa on its behalf. The UN provided a similar mandate. In addition, the big powers with interests in the region, especially Britain and the United States, found it useful to work with the FLS. In short, the FLS carried more weight internationally in matters pertaining to the liberation of Southern Africa than any other institution of the same nature before and even after.

The other difference is that, in addition to the summit system, the FLS had a functional arm of the summit, the Defence Staff Committee, which later became the Inter-state Defence and Security Committee (ISDSC), which has endured to date. Focusing on liberation meant that the FLS had to play a major security role, and the ISDSC was its security mechanism, generating practical advice and recommendations for the summits. The ISDSC planned and discharged various operations in collaboration with the active liberation movements, including training, logistics, and transits and infiltration of freedom fighters. It also had a liaison role with the summit to which it was accountable, and with other organisations such as the Liberation Committee of the OAU.

It can be contended that the main factor behind the establishment of the FLS, i.e. the colonial conflict in Rhodesia/Zimbabwe, was also a factor leading to its decline. With the independence of Zimbabwe in 1980, the FLS began to wane, but remained crucial in co-ordinating support to the Namibian and South African liberation efforts and assistance to the governments of Mozambique and Angola.

In 1980 the SADCC was formed as a precursor to the present-day SADC. The treaty establishing SADC in 1992 attempted to commit member states to peace and security, as well as economic development and integration. The unfortunate ambiguity that followed with the empowering of the ministers of economic planning and finance to form the Council of Ministers rather than the ministers of foreign affairs inherently caused the failure of the marriage of politics, defence, and security with economic development.

Anticipation of a new regional security regime

The onset of the 1990s brought mixed feelings to Southern Africa. The release from prison of the region's political legend, Nelson Mandela; Namibia's independence; and the provision of political space to opposition groups inside South Africa all showed the irreversibility of change in the region. Apartheid was coming to an end, and the regime's last president vividly captured this by providing his vision of a new Southern Africa that would plan and work together (De Klerk 1991: 24). The vision provided some optimism that a new regional regime was in the making. But there were a number of unanswered questions:

- Would the end of colonial conflict signify the end of all conflict?
- Would the end of apartheid mean the beginning of a new regional security regime?
- Would the rest of the region be able to tame post-apartheid South Africa?
- What would the peace dividend be?
- In reality, what type of security did SADC want to establish?

These and other questions dominated the Southern Africa of the early 1990s. They were genuine questions that had no easy answers. The end of the colonial conflict did not mean an end to all conflict. The legacies of the wars of liberation were raging on in Angola and Mozambique, and a new regional security regime was impossible to build when there were crises throughout the region. Pertinent among these was the crisis of governance in many countries, especially in Lesotho, which divided Southern Africa's leaders. There were even uncertainties as to how the new South Africa would behave towards the rest of Southern Africa. Influenced by global changes under way at the time, these developments sent waves of pessimism over the region. It was a period of transition, which had to be adequately managed.

After Nelson Mandela was sworn in as president, it became clear that the new South Africa had decided to be an African country in Southern Africa.

It did not assume its alleged role of a regional superpower, thus quelling the fears among its neighbours of their inability to tame the leviathan. Symbolically, the new South Africa downgraded itself to become a regional member, just like the others. It thus joined apartheid's long-time opponents, namely, SADC and the FLS. At the same time, South Africa had to manage its own difficult process of transition.

There were, however, some problems in the regional transition. One of these was the debate over the accommodation of FLS activities within SADC. The options consisted of the proposed transformation of the FLS to an independent Association of Southern African States (ASAS), or alternatively the establishment of a specialised body within SADC to deal with security. The latter argument won the day, and the Organ on Politics, Defence, and Security Co-operation (OPDSC) was established.

While such a transformation was meant to build a new regional security regime, which was to support the momentum being built up on the economic front through SADC, there were some problems that watered down these achievements. The Angolan crisis was raging, a crisis of governance emerged in Lesotho, and there was a serious civil war in one of SADC's new members – the Democratic Republic of the Congo (DRC). As will be shown below, the debate on whether to intervene or not in Lesotho and the DRC may have slowed down the process of concretising a new regional security regime. The signing of the OPDSC protocol was delayed, probably due to this – and thus for a long time the region was without an appropriate mechanism through which to exercise democratic governance and common security.

The new regional security regime

It was observed above that one of the features characterising organisations pre-dating the FLS was personal relations among the leaders. This was symbolised by the Nyerere–Kaunda–Khama axis in the FLS. Organisations founded along these lines presuppose a low turnover in leadership, a feature notable during the one-party state era. However, a change of leadership in any one member country may cause ripples through the entire organisation. Although this has not happened in Southern Africa,[7] the new leaders may not have the same priorities as the outgoing leaders. Personal relations among leaders went along with the preference for summitry, informality, and hesitancy with regard to strong secretariats.

This tendency points towards the reluctance of the summiteers to surrender part of their national sovereignties for the regional good. 'High politics' has been strong on the agenda. Organisations that avoid strong structures tend to plan regionally and implement nationally, creating a gap between policy and implementation. This tradition was carried forward from the Mulungushi Club through the FLS, and its remnants are today found inside SADC. It would seem logical, however, that to have a regional security regime, states must share quite a number of common policies – relating to economic, defence, and security issues – that entail the erosion of a certain amount of national sovereignty.

Flexibility embedded in loosely structured organisations, as shown by the Southern African inter-state institutions, has had an impact on the nature of regional politics. In most cases, the independent states conferred an 'authentic movement' status on liberation movements of their choice. In Southern Africa there were several liberation movements in each of the countries to be liberated. Depending on which movement finally assumed power, the inter-state relations that consequently followed were not so harmonious – again, depending on who supported whom.[8] The levels of previous support for and solidarity with the liberation movements tended to determine the depth of regional integration. Under such circumstances it has been difficult to develop sound common regional policies to which every member may subscribe.

Of late, there has been a shift from one-party to multi-party systems. This has manifested itself as a crisis of governance in most states. Along with the remnants of the wars of liberation and a few military dictatorships (Omari with Swatuk 1995), internal strife has also been a feature, hampering the establishment of a sound footing for a regional security regime.

History, therefore, has dictated the present circumstances in Southern Africa as a region where there has been co-operation for conflict resolution. That type of co-operation necessitated the establishment of loose organisations in which member states came together for specific objectives, but without affecting their national core values and interests. When former enemies become friends, old fears and sensitivities are hard to overcome, hence the tendency towards 'planning regionally, implementing nationally'. This may be different from experiences elsewhere in the world, where countries usually begin by functional co-operation in less sensitive issues that create confidence, and then move on to the sensitive areas of defence and security.

The OPDSC

The SADC Treaty was signed in 1992, two years before apartheid came to an end. The establishment of SADC occurred in a changed security environment. The goal then was to establish a regional organisation for collective security that best addressed the common threats in the region. The concept of security had changed dramatically and was perceived differently throughout the region.

Political instability in the region is now associated with the difficulties of establishing and consolidating democratic systems and promoting stability, peace, and sustainable development. One challenge facing SADC has been the establishment of an appropriate and effective institutional framework for executing its new mandate. This has required the organisation to rethink security and adjust its mechanisms to deal with the new challenges, especially a new security agenda that favours the peaceful resolution of conflicts and prefers prevention rather than resolution.

The debate from 1992 to 1996 was that some member states felt that bringing the old issues of the FLS and ISDSC within the SADC framework would divert the organisation's attention from its main objective of economic development. Others felt that the new concept of security tended to view development as part and parcel of building common security in the region. They argued that much regional insecurity arose from the way resources and political space were distributed and shared. Accordingly, the issue of security was so important and sensitive that it could not be subordinated to the debate on economic development and handled by a bureaucracy that would be dependent on a secretariat often insensitive to such issues.

This line of argument led some SADC members to advance a proposal to create an association of states, ASAS, which would function independently of the SADC Secretariat and would report directly to the summit. However, other members argued that that would increase expenditure, as the proposal implied the creation of a new secretariat to deal with security affairs in a situation where SADC's main sources of funding were extra-regional.

These arguments, among others, led the heads of state and government to reject the ASAS proposal in August 1995 and direct that further consultations should take place between ministries of defence and security on new structures, terms of reference, and operational procedures. Consequently, the ministers proposed the establishment of the OPDSC in January 1996. The summit formally accepted the proposal in June of the same year, which provided a response to many issues regarding the rejected ASAS. The OPDSC would function at the summit level, operating independently of SADC structures. The chair would rotate annually among the troika (see below), and the OPDSC was allowed to create new structures, including technical committees, as it deemed necessary, while the ISDSC could continue to act as its secretariat.

However, there was no real consensus on the way the OPDSC should function. A troika system was introduced by the 1996 summit and was to comprise one chair and two vice chairpersons: the outgoing and incoming chairpersons. Some member states expressed their dissatisfaction that the OPDSC functioned outside the SADC framework. Efforts were made to overcome these differences, including a review and rationalisation of the SADC Programme of Action of 1997. The August 1997 summit in Malawi agreed to suspend the OPDSC and appoint a committee composed of Malawi, Mozambique, and Namibia to identify a suitable solution.

Some members proposed that the OPDSC should be transformed into committees and work on an ad hoc basis; others suggested that it should be integrated into the SADC framework and be chaired by one of the vice chairpersons in the troika. And some believed that the OPDSC should operate on the basis of a specific protocol. Not even the Luanda summit of August 1998 came up with a solution. It was the Maputo summit of August 1999 that directed the Council of Ministers to review the operation of all SADC institutions, including the OPDSC, and report back within six months. At a subsequent meeting of the ISDSC and ministers of foreign affairs in Swaziland in October 1999, it was recommended that the OPDSC should be part of SADC and should report to the SADC summit.

At its meeting in February 2000 in Mbabane, Swaziland, the Council of Ministers agreed on the terms of reference for a review of SADC operations. It also established the Review Committee comprising the troika plus one, i.e. Mozambique (chair), Namibia (deputy chair), South Africa (outgoing chair), and Zimbabwe (as chair of the OPDSC). The extraordinary summit in Windhoek, Namibia in March 2001 finally approved the report on the restructuring exercise.

The disagreements over the OPDSC were based on the core issue of how security should be viewed in the present era. It was a debate between the old thinking, of viewing security in strictly military terms, and the new one, of understanding security as an all-embracing concept. Some participants still continued to conceptualise security in terms of threat perception, which is consequently reactive rather than proactive.

The dialogue between defence and security officials and their civilian think-tank counterparts was yet to produce a consensus. The August 2001 summit in Blantyre, Malawi was important in that the Protocol on the OPDSC was finally signed, and it was ratified by the end of 2003. The consequences of this lengthy debate are obvious. Although the ISDSC has functioned since the establishment of the FLS, formal co-operation in the defence and security area is still far behind the level achieved in the other sectors within SADC.

It will take some time and additional effort before the region has in place a mechanism ready to respond to the pace, pressures, and fluctuations of regional demands. The region needs a multidisciplinary approach to the issue of defence and security, a common vision, and common policy and planning mechanisms. Organisational and operational problems have continued to afflict the OPDSC. One could argue that the troubles started back in 1992 at the signing of the SADC Treaty. Instead of empowering a committee of foreign ministers to manage the affairs of SADC, the treaty identified the ministers of economic planning and finance to form the Council of Ministers, thus inherently marginalising issues of politics, defence, and security.

Since the 2001 Malawi summit, where the OPDSC was signed and the decision made to rotate the OPDSC chair annually, interesting developments have been taking place. The region has come to terms with reality by going beyond regional co-operation to focus on sectors that will enhance regional integration. A lot of work has been done on the SADC restructuring programme. The Inter-state Politics and Diplomacy Committee (ISPDC) is now functioning. This has completed the two legs of the OPDSC, namely the ISDSC and the ISPDC. But the efficiency of the two committees' functioning is questionable, and the region surely has to rethink how all these processes are integrated across the SADC Secretariat.

The Dar es Salaam summit of 2003 finally approved the Mutual Defence Pact that should operationalise the Protocol on the OPDSC. The Strategic Indicative Plan for the Organ (SIPO) was also approved at that meeting. It is expected that SIPO, a strategic vision for the OPDSC, in conjunction with the Regional Indicative Strategic Development Plan, would provide a road map through which SADC can achieve peace, stability, prosperity, and development.

Challenges

The SADC Protocol on the OPDSC, the Mutual Defence Pact, and SIPO come at a time when SADC is facing the challenges of placing itself within the transformed AU peace and security agenda. This is informed by the establishment of the AU Protocol on the Peace and Security Council, which provides for the establishment of the African Common Defence and Security Policy, African Standby Force (ASF), and Military Staff Committee. The materialisation of these brings added responsibility for SADC.

The AU peace agenda foresees the regions as the building blocks for the creation of the ASF, by establishing regional brigades. By early 2005, the ISDSC had established a framework for a regional brigade under the ASF initiative, which is likely to become an important tool in the hands of the OPDSC.

The core challenges in the exercise of building viable regional security architecture remain the following:

- issues arising from the governance and management of security in a democratic society;
- the changing role of the defence and security establishments;
- the disarmament, demobilisation, and reintegration of ex-combatants;
- the repatriation and resettlement of refugees and displaced people;
- the collection and control of illegal weapons;
- the reconstitution of state institutions;
- the promotion of national reconstruction; and
- the establishment of a favourable environment for the return of emigrated human capital.

The key argument is that security issues in SADC are no longer military in a conventional way: they are more political–military in their nature, causes, and consequences. The shift is that security in Southern Africa is no longer conceived against, but rather with other members.

Conclusions

Despite the sensitivity of defence and security issues, which need confidence to make them operational, the post-independence Southern African states opted to organise loosely to avoid enduring structures, most probably to maintain and safeguard their national sovereignties. Thus the four decades of regional co-operation have not provided the region with adequate lessons, techniques, and even mechanisms to co-operate on the less sensitive issue of economic development. It would seem that regional circumstances necessitated the reversal of the natural process of moving from economic to security co-operation.

Instead of being a confidence-building mechanism, the many years of co-operation for conflict resolution have been a drawback to meaningful regional co-operation. Co-operation for conflict resolution has not been a catalyst or a motivation for deepened regional integration, as it was basically conducted amid secrecy, enmity, and suspicions. It is only now that the region is discovering itself. And the models of co-operation adopted seem to be carefully chosen so as to ensure that they themselves constitute confidence-building measures. So the loose forms and structures are meant to be piecemeal measures to enhance future deepened co-operation.

Southern Africa can hardly be termed a viable integrated regional political economy, nor a regional security regime. There is a notable absence of regional (common) policies – harmonised or otherwise. Governance is upheld, in most cases, not through fear of a regional reprimand, but through the political maturity of the citizens in individual countries.

The region is thus caught between the traditional and modern, which is a serious transition trap. Democratic governance (see Du Pisani, this volume) and common security are the prerogatives of modernity, and if the regional states shy away from these features, then they will be rejected by the rest of the regional 'commons' – the regional citizens. Traditional garb has to be shed in order to achieve democratic governance and common security. This cannot be done in a short period of time. King (1986) has rightly observed that the age-long 'African winter' – consisting of poverty, drought, and war, all of which have to be first dealt with – continues to bite. It may take a long time for Southern Africa to match democratic governance with common security, the subject of this book.

ENDNOTES

1 A group called the Mushala gang ravaged Zambia for almost a decade.

2 Zambia supported Joshua Nkomo's ZAPU, while Tanzania supported Robert Mugabe's ZANU. This consequently affected Zambian–Zimbabwean relations in the early 1980s.

3 Angola and Mozambique related to each other from their similar colonial perspective and Marxist–Leninist socialist ideology. Angola was the rear base for Namibia's liberation movement, SWAPO. After independence, Namibia intervened in the DRC, probably in support of Angola.

4 This became important after UDI in Rhodesia (1965). A joint petroleum pipeline, highway, and railroad were built between Tanzania and Zambia, enabling the latter to utilise Dar es Salaam harbour.

5 Mobutu allied himself with Holden Roberto's *Frente Nacional de Libertação de Angola*, thus disqualifying himself from membership of the FLS.

6 This was ascertained through the authors' research in the region.

7 East Africa experienced this when Milton Obote of Uganda was overthrown in 1971, causing the collapse of the EAC less than a decade thereafter.

8 After independence, Zimbabwe was closer to Mozambique than it was to Zambia, reflecting Zambia's support for ZAPU and Mozambique's close relations with ZANU.

Chapter 4

Botswana

Mpho G. Molomo, Zibani Maundeni, Bertha Osei-Hwedie, Ian Taylor, and Shelly Whitman

Since independence in 1966, Botswana has been a functioning liberal democracy, albeit dominated by one political party: the Botswana Democratic Party (BDP). This party has pursued policies that have fostered a relatively high degree of social and economic development.

The character of democracy in Botswana

Analysis of Botswana's democratic credentials has largely been favourable, with an 'African Miracle' school (a term originally coined by Thumberg-Hartland) being mainly positive if largely economistic in its approach.[1] This group of scholars frequently invokes the question of whether Botswana is indeed 'a model for success'? (Picard 1987). Indeed, the intriguing way Botswana has managed to uphold a broadly liberal democratic tradition since 1966 while incorporating aspects of its pre-colonial governance is quite unique in the region. Ever since independence, the post-colonial government has acknowledged the crucial part that pre-colonial structures such as the chiefs and the *kgotla* (local traditional assembly) could play in modern Botswana's politics. Indeed, the *kgotla* has been deployed by the state as a forum where government policies are clarified for the people, and also where the people can voice their problems and concerns. This, combined with the more 'modern' aspects of an electoral representative democracy, has crafted a sustainable democratic culture in the country. Moreover, the installation of a woman *kgosi kgolo* (paramount chief) – Kgosi Mosadi Seboko of Balete – who also became chairperson of Ntlo ya Dikgosi (the House of Chiefs), is clear testimony of the softening of patriarchal tendencies, manifesting the reformation of *bogosi* (chieftainship) to become more inclusive and democratic.

However, while Botswana's democratic development is routinely hailed as a 'model' for Africa, this developmental path has not been unproblematic and, in fact, has engendered inequalities, while the character of democratic practice in the country – although qualitatively better than many of its neighbours' – is at times somewhat problematic.

Having said all this, the limitations of Botswana's celebrated liberal democracy are noteworthy. Although it is true that the state has provided social services in the form of schools and clinics to the populace, and has exhibited features of the 'developmental state', major contradictions within the country's political economy and the qualitative nature of its democracy mean that the country exhibits authoritarian liberalism. Like the East Asian developmental states of Malaysia, Singapore, South Korea, etc., Botswana has combined high growth rates and visible 'development' with a structured autocracy.

Political parties

The limitations on Botswana's celebrated liberal democracy are noteworthy. Opposition parties are generally weak due to interminable intra-party faction fighting and internal splits. The fragmentation of opposition parties has meant that the ruling BDP has enjoyed dominant – if not wholly unchallenged – status since independence (Mokopakgosi and Molomo 2000; Molomo 2000a; Osei-Hwedie 2001). In addition, the country has feeble organisational structures and poor capacity to promote alternative policies. The failure of opposition parties to unite and the propensity of opposition leaders to pursue their personal agendas have denied the opposition the possibility of unseating the BDP from power. As a result, this has meant that Botswana is, and has been since 1966, a *de facto* predominant-party system. The incumbent BDP has won each and every election by a clear margin (Selolwane 2001). It is only really at the local level that the opposition has made some meaningful inroads into the BDP's power base. In the past, the absence of a strong and vibrant opposition meant that BDP backbenchers effectively performed the role of the opposition in parliament – a serious indictment, indeed, of the opposition.

The BDP thus towers over the political scene in Botswana. The opposition suffers not only from poor leadership, but also from a lack of funds. In contrast, the BDP is wealthy and also enjoys the benefits of incumbency. Political party funding is not provided by the state, and as the incumbent party, the BDP is able to attract generous donations from various sources. Because of its predominance and the seemingly hopeless chance opposition parties have of unseating the BDP, alternative parties attract limited funding. As a result, during elections the BDP is comparatively advantaged with a financial strength and visibility unmatched by any of the other parties. It is the BDP that deploys advertisements, erects election billboards, and drives around in new vehicles – all contributing to a high and active level of visibility, which the opposition manifestly does not achieve. In addition, the party is able to use its predominance in government to appoint additional members of parliament (MPs), the so-called 'specially elected members'.

In a country where the ruling party has been dominant for so long, the distinction between party and government interests is clearly blurred. The adoption of the National Vision 2016 by the BDP as the thrust of its election manifesto during the 2004 general elections is a case in point: BDP policy has become national policy. Botswana's developmental state is strengthened by the party's capacity to influence business opportunities, award contracts, and, importantly, operate in a largely non-transparent fashion through the control of access to vital data and information. The control of vital information on state-owned and controlled companies is bolstered by the relatively weak state of the media and civil society.

The media

The fairness of the democratic system in a country is affirmed not only by what happens at the polling station on the day of elections, but by the broader milieu within which the political process plays itself out. In particular, access to information, freedom to campaign, and equal and fair access to the media are but a few crucial features in this regard. In Botswana, with the exception of small, localised private radio stations, such as Gabz FM, the electronic media is government controlled. The national radio station, Radio Botswana, is a government mouthpiece, and so is the only daily newspaper, the *Daily News*. Although opposition activities are covered, the overall perception of the contents of such media products is that the BDP government is given greater weight. Certainly, the government is perceived by the people to have an inordinate amount of influence over the press – in contrast to the opposition parties (see Leepile 1996). There are allegations to the effect that government blocks programmes that put it under the spotlight with a view to making it account to the public for its actions and policies. The most cited incident is its decision to stop the broadcasting of a call-in Radio Botswana programme known as 'Masa a Sele'.[2]

There are, however, a number of private weekly papers that maintain considerable independence from the ruling party. It is these papers that have in the past exposed government corruption. Having said that,

> from independence up until the twilight of the 20th Century, the Botswana government has done little to promote or strengthen media freedom, diversity and expansion. It instead continues to thrive on restrictive media legislation,

bureaucratic red tape and unclear policies (Media Institute of Southern Africa n.d.).

Civil society

In the past it has been argued that the autonomy of the state machinery has been largely facilitated in Botswana by the fact that civil society has been poorly developed and disorganised, and democratic input weak (Holm and Molutsi 1989). Threats to media independence and media surveillance of the government and elites are profoundly amplified in the context of a polity such as Botswana, where civil society is very weak (Holm, Molutsi, and Somolekae 1996). However, it is now believed that civil society input to society has been contributed through dialogue with government (Maundeni 2004).

Comparatively speaking, civil society groups in Botswana are not as developed as in other African countries. This reality may be partly attributable to the political and economic stability that has prevailed since independence. Furthermore, the lack of any violent 'struggle' for independence and an essentially top-down traditional culture of acquiescence before one's superiors may explain the relative weakness and disorganised nature of civil society. One argument has been that civil society in Botswana is readily co-opted into state structures, lacks a strong grassroots base, and is prepared to work within the parameters deemed permissible by the state – and not beyond. However, that some leaders are co-opted into government may provide evidence that civil society is not weak but valuable.

The state apparatus in Botswana has been commonly deployed to promote political and economic goals that reflect the BDP leadership's understanding of the limitations and opportunities presented by the national, regional, and international economies. At the same time, this has reified existing structures of power and privilege within the country. Having said that, a note of caution regarding criticism of Botswana's democracy should be sounded. Though ruling for nearly 40 years, the BDP has *not* subverted the constitution; it has *not* outlawed opposition parties or declared the country a one-party state. There are no political prisoners. Despite the handicaps the media face, the press in the country is flourishing and critical. The material benefits accrued through diamond sales have been dispersed (albeit unevenly), and evidence exists that poverty levels are falling. The constitution *does* guarantee citizens free political activity and freedom of speech and association. However, there are clearly things in Botswana that could be done much better if it truly wishes to retain the label of a democratic 'African miracle'.

Drivers of democratisation

The primary drivers of democratisation are numerous and include political parties and civil society, including churches, the media, and academics. With regard to academics, the Democracy Research Project (DRP) has been an important player in the democratisation process in Botswana. Surveys have been carried out and their findings publicised in ways that have clarified issues involved in the democratisation process. The project is a non-partisan, multidisciplinary research group that derives its membership from the Faculties of Social Sciences and Humanities at the University of Botswana. The DRP has conducted surveys, opinion polls, and symposiums; in fact, opinion polls have been conducted during every election year since 1994.

Intra-party democracy

Obviously political parties are also important players in the democratisation process. As primary agents of political mobilisation and voter education, they occupy an important space in the democratisation debate. Perhaps what is most pertinent is that they should not only be seen as facilitators of democracy at the national level, but should also ensure that there is intra-party democracy. Intra-party democracy is, without doubt, one of the hallmarks of liberal democratic practice.[3] It manifests itself in the general workings of political parties: how various structures of the party relate, how office bearers of party committees are elected, the reporting lines within the party, and the conduct of primary elections, with this last factor being perhaps an important litmus test of the existence of intra-party democracy. These elections are mechanisms through which political parties choose candidates to contest elections on their ticket. The process was initiated by the ruling BDP in 1984, followed by the Botswana National Forum (BNF) in 1989.

Primary elections within the BDP were initially limited to an electoral college that comprised designated office bearers within the party structures, and the rest of the party members were excluded from the process. Moreover, the party central committee could veto the appointment of candidates voted in by the electoral college. As political office became a more and more contested terrain, outcomes of primary elections became sources of serious disputes, which often led to resignations, defections, and expulsions.

Upon realising that the limited primary elections were not only undemocratic, but also divisive, the BDP adopted a new system, known as *bulela ditswe* (free for all), which was first tested in a by-election in 2002 and was fully implemented in the primary elections for the 2004 general election. In this new dispensation, aspirants for political office first apply to the party central committee, which is empowered to vet the candidates, and only those that pass the screening process are allowed to contest the primary elections. Candidates who win the primary elections after the party vetting process become the party's candidates for the constituency. *Bulela ditswe* has not only opened the floodgates for political competition, but has ensured that the party becomes vibrant and responsive to the aspirations of its membership. Yet its challenges have still to unfold.

Democratisation also manifests itself in disputes on political succession. This has been a factor within the ruling BDP and opposition parties. The jostling for political power among candidates for positions in the parties and candidates for the national echelons of the parties has opened the greater debate on political succession within parties, as well as the presidency of the country. What is most problematic is that although intra-party democracy is wanting, the country's constitution does not provide for direct presidential elections. The presidential candidate of the majority party in parliament stands duly elected as president of the country.

The country's constitution has also been amended to ensure automatic succession of the vice president to the presidency should that office fall vacant. In the past, if the president vacated office – as happened with the death of Seretse Khama – parliament elected a president from among the MPs to complete the remaining term of office, and the party would then choose its presidential candidate for the next election. During that time, aspirations to hold political office were not high, and Khama's trusted deputy, Ketumile (Quett) Masire assumed office. Given the factional fights within the BDP, the constitution was amended to ensure that Festus Mogae, the current president of Botswana, would succeed Masire when he stepped down in 1998.

As is becoming increasingly clear, the tussle for control of the chairmanship of the BDP was actually a contest for succession to the presidency of the party, and ultimately of the country. President Mogae correctly read the lines of political battle and aligned himself with Ian Khama. Such political posturing was meant to ward off the impending challenge from P. H. K. Kedikilwe for the party presidency in 2004. In the same way that Masire handpicked Mogae to succeed him, Mogae has also handpicked Ian Khama to succeed him.

Based on the above, developments across the political divide cause serious doubts about intra-party democracy. The lack of it is likely to lead to the erosion of democracy at the national level. The likelihood of Ian Khama assuming the presidency does not inspire confidence that democracy will be nurtured and strengthened, and there are fears that the country will slide into authoritarianism. Khama's governance style; his reluctance to shed his military mantle; his insistence on flying an army helicopter despite the ombudsman's report that he should not do so; his unsavoury remarks to fellow parliamentarians, calling them 'vultures' and 'barking dogs'; and his inclination to flaunt established democratic structures all point to his authoritarian tendencies (Molomo 2000b: 100–6).

Democratising election administration

Democratising the administration of elections has also been a significant development. In 1984 the BNF took the government to court, claiming that there had been rigging in the Gaborone South constituency, where its president lost to the BDP vice president.

As a result of opposition pressure, the Office of the Supervisor of Elections ceased to be a department in the Office of the President and was established as an independent office. But the supervisor was still appointed by the president, and that did not satisfy the opposition alliance. The opposition questioned the impartiality of the supervisor of elections and called for the establishment of an Independent Electoral Commission (IEC). In 1998, the Office of the Supervisor of Elections was abolished and the IEC established to run elections. Other electoral concessions included the lowering of the voting age from 21 to 18 years and recognition of an absentee ballot. Yet questions regarding the independence and operational autonomy of the IEC continue to be raised.

The media in democratisation

The private media constitute a pillar of the democratisation process in Botswana. Ethical questions are the central domain through which the media have participated in the process. The *Botswana Gazette* and *Mmegi wa Dikgang* have been central in publishing stories about scandals, most notably during the 1994 elections. One such scandal was the failure of prominent individuals in government to pay their debts to the National Development Bank, thereby creating a threat of retrenchments and possible closure. While corruption had not been a serious political issue before the 1994 elections, the media's publication of corruption scandals was significant, and the press has also exposed mismanagement and other miscarriages of justice. In the case of allegations of corruption and mismanagement, such media reports struck at the heart of the ruling BDP and government, involving President Masire and a number of his senior government ministers. These incidents involved allegations of impropriety in parastatal organisations such as the Botswana Housing Corporation and the National Development Bank.

The state media have also introduced programmes that have opened up debate and deepened the democratisation process. Radio Botswana's 'Live Line', 'Round Table', and 'Maokaneng' programmes and Btv's 'The Eye' and 'Mmualebe' have contributed enormously by providing forums for discussing national, regional, and international issues. These programmes have brought government ministers and officials in contact with academics and other enlightened citizens in debates that allow a three-way flow of information. This has enhanced participatory democracy, a key aspect of the democratisation process.

Various players contribute to the democratisation process in Botswana. Some, such as the DRP, have concentrated on carrying out surveys on aspects of the political system and on holding workshops for local and national politicians and for civic organisations to disseminate their findings. Such findings have played the crucial role of sparking the democratisation process. Other players have concentrated on court cases in order to induce constitutional and political reforms on the part of the government. They have used legal means, and involved the High Court and the Court of Appeal to achieve reforms. Other democratising efforts, such as media publications on ethical issues, wrongdoing, and corruption among politicians and civil servants have targeted those who wield political power and have generated the emergence of important institutions such as the ombudsman and the Directorate on Corruption and Economic Crime.

Botswana's security concerns

Botswana's security architecture is premised on the Tswana tradition of *ntwakgolo ke ya molomo* (the best way to resolve differences is through dialogue). By and large, Batswana are known to be a peace-loving people. However, the ethnic debate that was intended to make sections 77, 78, and 79 of the Botswana constitution ethnically neutral, healthy as it was, indicated that Botswana is not as ethnically homogeneous as it is perceived to be, and is also premised on a false sense of stability. Botswana's security threats are primarily national: the sustenance of peace for the people and the security of the state.

Botswana's security concerns that determine its involvement in security co-operation include both actual and potential threats, such as cross-border crime, illegal immigrants, refugees, small arms, and HIV/AIDS, all of which threaten national security. According to interviews with both the deputy commissioner of police and representatives of the Department of Foreign Affairs, these problems are partly caused by the influx of political and economic refugees attracted by Botswana's economic affluence.

The end of the Cold War and, perhaps more profoundly, the demise of apartheid and its destabilisation campaign have led to the reconceptualisation of security in the Southern African region. With the decline of regional destabilisation, the redefinition of security became an important academic concern, especially for Botswana, which shares borders with four countries in the region. Inevitably, its defence policy has to take cognisance of this geopolitical reality. The Botswana Defence Force (BDF) was constituted by an act of parliament in 1977 and mandated to defend the country and carry out any duties as may be assigned to it by the president.

Botswana's defence policy was first conceived in 1977 out of a fragile sense of security emanating from attacks from Rhodesia. Following the institution of South Africa's 'Total Strategy' (in response to a purported 'Total Onslaught') during the 1980s, which was geared towards the destabilisation of the region, the security of the people and state became the primary preoccupation. From the mid-1990s, Botswana enjoyed relative peace compared to other countries in the region. As a result of this peace dividend, many have wondered why Botswana continues to allocate about 14 per cent of its budget to defence. For instance, in 1996 the BDF was allocated BWP 209 million (USD 61.4 million) or 11.4 per cent of the overall development budget. This budget allocation constituted 68.1 per cent of the total budget allocation of the Ministry of Presidential Affairs and Public Administration. However, while the commander of the BDF, Lieutenant-General Matshwenyego Fisher, recognises that Botswana enjoys relative peace and stability, he is of the view that the BDF should maintain a certain level of military readiness to meet challenges ranging from low-intensity to high-intensity conflict. He supports his argument with a quotation from Sullivan and Twomey (1994: 12):

> We cannot know with precision the character of our future enemy, the weapons he will possess, or actions he will employ; but that does not relieve us of the responsibility to prepare carefully for the future. That preparation cannot be for a single, predetermined threat.

Military roles

Given the nature of some internal security challenges that are beyond the capacity of the police, the military is often asked to render assistance. Perhaps what limits the police is that the relevant act mandates them to protect internal law and order, and not, as it were, the survival of the state. The disintegration of the state, as was the case in Somalia, constitutes the greatest threat to any country. As a result, a strong military is believed to be necessary to deal with such a threat, if and when it occurs.

As commander-in-chief of the armed forces, the president has the prerogative, as mandated by the constitution, of deploying the BDF in other duties, as national security may determine. Under the umbrella of aid to civil authority, the BDF co-operates with the police on an operation called *Kalola Matlho*, which involves surveillance on matters of armed robbery, hijacking, and other related robberies. In this operation, more than 100 soldiers are attached to the serious crime squad of the police service Criminal Investigation Department. In addition, it is engaged in low-intensity operations, such as anti-poaching patrols. It is also deployed along the borders between Botswana and Zimbabwe to reinforce police operations to curb the movement of illegal immigrants.

However, Fisher was quick to concede that some of these operations do compromise the professional integrity of career soldiers. First of all, the ethos of the police is different from that of the military. The police are trained to use minimum force, while soldiers are trained to use maximum force. Even though soldiers of the BDF are thoroughly briefed when they go into such operations, it is conceivable that their military training might lead them to take actions that are not consistent with the operation. Secondly, military personnel who do police-type jobs have to learn new skills, such as securing evidence and assisting with prosecution. But what is more daunting is how to appraise such personnel, i.e. should they be appraised by police or military standards? Moreover, upon completion of their task, how are they to be reintegrated into the BDF?

Defence policy

Botswana does not have a ministry of defence, and its security policy is developed in the Ministry of Presidential Affairs and Public Administration (MPAPA). It is perhaps with the development of the defence policy that one realises that political power is highly centralised in the Office of the President, and that policy is the prerogative of the president, cabinet, and senior officials in the MPAPA. In matters of BDF administration, the president relies on the Defence Council to superintend conditions of service, welfare, and career progression.

The reality of Botswana's defence policy is that there is no formalised structure by which it is formulated. Its formulation is ad hoc, centralised in the Office of the President, and largely a response to issues as they arise. Perhaps this is a reflection of the non-existence of a ministry of defence. In contrast to other countries in the region, in the 25 years' existence of the BDF there has never been a defence review. Borrowing a leaf from other experiences, it appears that periodic defence reviews are important because they would develop a strategic vision for the BDF in terms of its development as a professional entity that is 'effective, affordable and accountable to the people' (Mbabazi 2002: 2).

If Botswana were to embark on a defence review, such an exercise would address some of the vexing questions in the political system. Time and again the admission of women into the BDF is raised, but it is never adequately addressed. An excuse has always been given that there is not enough accommodation in the country's barracks. Such a response sidesteps important issues of gender equality and the empowerment of women. However, the minister of presidential affairs and public administration recently announced that women would be admitted into the BDF during his term in office. Another pertinent question, given the size of Botswana's population, the size of the BDF, and the need to create an effective defence system, is whether a reserve force is needed. More fundamental, however, is the perception that the BDF appropriates a disproportionate share of the national budget. As in many other years, when presenting the 2003 defence budget, the minister of finance and development planning had to defend the BDF budget, which is generally regarded as too high. Out of a total allocation of BWP 802 million for the Ministry of the State President, the BDF was allocated BWP 415 million – more than half of the allocation to that ministry, and about 14 per cent of the total budget allocation (Balise 2003: 15).

A defence review would help Botswana in a number of ways. It would provide the government with a better appreciation of the nature and origins of 'security threats', if any, and enable it to respond to them more effectively. A defence review would also streamline the operations of political instruments and other civil structures, which may compromise military professionalism and integrity. In addition, such a review would entail greater consultation, which would give a wider understanding of how security problems affect various groups in society. Such an exercise would also address broad public sector reforms and the location of the defence sector in the overall national context. It would address issues of the size of the defence force, the training and equipment it needs, and its welfare concerns. It would facilitate greater dialogue, legitimacy, and eventual ownership of the defence policy by the society at large. The results of such a review would be subject to discussion by cabinet, parliament, and the general public, and arising from such a debate, a white paper would be developed that would constitute a defence policy (Uganda Ministry of Defence 2002).

Botswana's perception of SADC's security concerns

As Botswana's foreign minister has noted,

> regional security is a complex phenomenon, which is a derivative of interplay of various societal factors. It is an internationally accepted fact that respect for human rights, fundamental freedoms, and adherence to principles of democracy and good governance enhance and bolster security (Merafhe 2000).

Botswana's security policy is in part determined by its geopolitical situation. As a landlocked country, its sense of security is predicated on the security interests and goodwill of its neighbours (Molomo 2001: 5). This perception has clearly dictated many of the foreign, defence, and economic policies pursued by the Government of Botswana since independence. The key security issues faced by Botswana may be summarised into the following categories: cross-border crime, refugees, illegal immigrants, HIV/AIDS, poverty, and small-arms trafficking.

With regard to cross-border crime, the head of the sub-regional bureau of Interpol in Harare, Commissioner Frank Msutu has stated:

> There are very clear relationships and interlinking factors between crime syndicates operating in Southern Africa. It is not a secret to law enforcement agencies in the region that the criminals in the region have better co-operation links than the police officers. They seem to know whom to contact at all times and budgetary constraints, foreign currency shortages, visa problems or governmental authority to travel do not control their movements (Gastow 2002: 1).

It is, therefore, not surprising that Botswana is concerned about the increasing cross-border crime occurring in the region. According to the Ministry of Foreign Affairs, cultural and linguistic similarities make it very easy for Batswana to co-operate in cross-border crime operations with South Africans. The Institute for Security Studies, located in Pretoria, has recently conducted a study in which police agencies in Southern Africa were asked to identify the three transnational organised criminal groups that constituted the most serious threat to their countries. The Botswana Police Service identified Zimbabweans as the top threat, South Africans as the second-biggest threat, and Zambians as the third-biggest threat (Gastow 2002: 1).

Refugees are always a potential threat to the security of any country. Often the country from which the refugees fled has suspicions about the activities of the refugees within their host country. Botswana has tried to diffuse this problem by handing the problem of refugees to the UN High Commissioner for Refugees. As a signatory of international conventions on people who flee their countries for political reasons, Botswana welcomes genuine refugees. However, asylum seekers constitute a security threat if they use the host country to attack or destabilise their home country. A case in point was Meshake Muyongo of the Caprivi Liberation Army crossing into Botswana with his armed men masquerading as refugees. However, Botswana has always maintained an open-door policy regarding refugees and always ensures that they are treated according to the international legal instruments that apply. For example, the Government of Botswana allowed the Namibian minister of foreign affairs to come and view the Namibian refugee camp on its border. Following bilateral discussions between the two countries, some of these refugees were given amnesty and repatriated to Namibia.

Refugees and illegal immigrants are a very serious threat to security within Botswana. Illegal immigrants are very difficult to keep track of because they cross the border at unauthorised points and also do not report their presence to the police. Often they are not only originators of crime, but also its victims. Many of the prisons in Botswana are filled with large populations of illegal immigrants. Illegal immigrants and refugees are also potential contributors to the problems of both poverty and HIV/AIDS: 'the related phenomenon of illegal immigrants is a serious security threat to some of our countries, including Botswana ... poor people will trek anywhere where they hope to find some food and shelter' (Merafhe 2000).

HIV/AIDS has been perceived as a security threat to Botswana. Many have blamed the extensive spread of the disease in the country on the many people in transit through it. 'AIDS is by far the most serious security threat to our region' (Merafhe 2000). With an infection rate in the country of 25.3 per cent, which is among the highest in the world, government has a daunting challenge to combat it. Nevertheless, Batswana need to change their sexual behaviour of having multiple partners as a way of curbing the spread of the disease.

Poverty is also perceived to be a security risk in Botswana. According to Merafhe (2000), '[a]s a SADC government, our general view is that poverty is the greatest threat to our national and regional security. Prospects for external aggression on any of our member states at the moment appear to be remote.' This view has been corroborated by Fisher, who pointed out that most of the conflicts in the world are internal (in the order of civil wars, religious wars, ethnic wars) and not externally driven.[4]

Again, if the region is facing drought, economic sanctions, or economic problems, then that also affects Botswana's economy. Currently, it is estimated that 36 per cent of Botswana's population is living below the poverty datum line. It is understandable that poverty exacerbates social divisions and therefore may be a source of conflict: 'Forty per cent of Southern Africans live in absolute poverty … a hungry man is an angry man' (Merafhe 2000).

The small arms problem in Botswana is considered to be negligible compared to other countries in the region, according to the deputy police commissioner, Edwin Bantsu. There are 31,000 registered small arms in Botswana. Registration is restricted due to strict rules for issuing permits. In any given year, only 400 new licenses are issued. However, Botswana has taken the issue of a small arms threat seriously, as witnessed by its creation of the Committee on Small Arms. The main aims of this committee are to look at potential problems and to focus on the transit of small arms through Botswana. This decision came after the creation of the SADC Working Group on Small Arms and a subsequent declaration in 1999, and following the first major conference in New York in 2000 of the UN Working Group on Small Arms and Light Weapons.

The relocation of Basarwa ('bushmen') from the Central Kalahari Game Reserve is also a security threat for Botswana. Following a campaign mounted by a British NGO, Survival International, Botswana's diamonds have been dubbed blood or conflict diamonds. Botswana's political stability and economic success derive from diamonds, and if they were to be boycotted by the international community, the country's economic sparkle would fade. Botswana therefore needs to tread with great sensitivity and caution when addressing this matter.

As previously discussed, questions have been raised about Botswana's defence budget:

> Why is Botswana embarking on a massive military build-up when the region appears to be moving towards peace? Lt. General Merafhe argues that it is not a contradiction that Botswana is engaging in military build-up when the region is moving towards peace. After all ... armies are built during peacetime (Molomo 2001: 6).

There are strong indications that Botswana finds it imperative to spend a large proportion of its budget on the country's defence. However, in light of the security threats outlined above, it appears to be inconsistent with addressing the issues that threaten the country the most. For example, HIV/

AIDS, poverty, and refugees are unlikely to be addressed through a strong military presence:

> While I am a strong proponent of the concept of state sovereignty in security matters, and will not blink an eye in protecting the interests of Botswana against external aggression, I am aware that that is only one side of the equation. There are other equally important security challenges such as abject poverty, inequitable socio-economic development, environmental degradation and ethnic/political intolerance (Merafhe 2000).

Botswana's involvement in the region's security co-operation practices

Botswana's security concerns are best understood within the context of a redefined conception of security and the regional configuration, especially in Southern Africa. Post-independence security problems not only require regional security co-operation, but also a redefinition of security that focuses 'on internal rather than external threats' (Shaw 1994: 392). They also include the defence of the incumbent government against threats, and the pursuit of democracy, sustainable economic development, social justice, and environmental protection (Shaw 1994; Swatuk and Omari 1997).

The regional context is crucial because Botswana's foreign policy is largely a response to its geopolitical situation, and partly determined by commitments to a regional organisation. Since independence, Botswana has pursued a pragmatic foreign policy orientation towards neighbours. As a landlocked country, it places high priority on security in a bid to safeguard its territorial integrity, sovereignty, order, and peace, as well as good relations with neighbours to prevent spillage of problems. As a member of SADC, Botswana has to adhere to collective objectives. Southern Africa is striving to promote both good governance and economic development, but political and economic development is only possible when political order and stability prevail. Therefore, the aim of SADC members is to promote peace and security, because they realise that peace, security, and development are intertwined. The latter can only be achieved through collective action, preferably through a security regime such as the Organ on Politics, Defence, and Security, and adherence to democratic principles (Osei-Hwedie 2002).

Botswana's involvement in regional security co-operation has evolved from the use of peaceful means, diplomacy, and negotiations to the use of force or military participation. But, in reality, a mixture of both has been the common practice, depending on the nature of the security problem. Similarly, the nature of Botswana's involvement in security co-operation has changed in accordance with the leadership's preferences. The country's first president, Seretse Khama, was preoccupied with the development of Botswana, and therefore emphasised economics in foreign relations, especially with neighbours such as South Africa, the country that was its biggest trading partner, the source of private investment in Botswana's diamond mines, and the recipient of migrant labour. Thus, he avoided military confrontation. President Masire also emphasised development, but it was during his time that Botswana became involved in direct military intervention in regional affairs and peacekeeping activities. President Mogae is preoccupied with minimising the costs of participating in neighbouring countries' conflicts, but sent the BDF to intervene in Lesotho. However, in spite of the reservations of its leaders, the government appreciates the need to participate in regional security co-operation due to its geopolitical situation and to promote the common principles of stability and prosperity that are the basis of security.

From 1970 to 1994, Botswana, as a member of the FLS, contributed to regional policy and co-ordinated collaborative efforts in the area of politics, peace, and security. Following the Lusaka Manifesto of 1969, the FLS simultaneously used negotiations and armed struggle to assist liberation movements, with neighbouring states providing bases from which to launch attacks, training to combatants, and refuge to refugees. However, Botswana, mindful of its small size and lack of resources and capabilities at that time, refrained from giving material support to liberation movements. Instead, it preferred to provide verbal and diplomatic support, as well as asylum for refugees (Osei-Hwedie 1998; 2002). The successful liberation of all Southern Africa testifies to the success of the FLS.

Botswana has, on several occasions, depended upon negotiations and diplomacy to promote security through good relations with neighbours. For example, the Botswanan–Namibian dispute over ownership of the shifting sands of the Sedudu island in the Chobe river was handled peacefully through discussions and, ultimately, through both countries' acceptance of the decision of the International Court of Justice. Similarly, there have been threatening incidents with South Africa, which have been resolved amicably through talks between government officials, thereby preventing armed confrontation. Former President Masire is currently involved in mediating peace talks between contending parties in a bid to promote peace in the DRC. Botswana and other SADC members have refrained from public criticism and isolation of Zimbabwe in spite of pressure from Western powers. Instead, in spite of their disagreement with President Robert Mugabe's land distribution programme and pressure from donors, they have opted for quiet diplomacy to exert influence, which has dismally failed to register any positive results. Only President Mogae has criticised Mugabe recently. In addition, officials of Botswana and Zimbabwe have held consultations over allegations of mistreatment of their respective nationals, in spite of Zimbabwe's recall of its high commissioner from Gaborone (Baraedi 2002; Letsididi 2002; *Mmegi* 2002).

With the establishment of its army in 1977 and its acquisition of better equipment, Botswana became involved in military operations, both in the form of direct intervention and peacekeeping operations, to ensure its own security and that of its neighbours. In 1994, under the auspices of the then SADC troika, Botswana, South Africa, and Zimbabwe intervened to quell political instability in Lesotho. The presidential troika forced King Letsie III to reinstate the democratically elected government of Prime Minister Mokhele. In 1998, Botswana and South Africa, as the allied forces of the SADC OPDSC and at the invitation of the Lesotho government, intervened again in Lesotho. In accordance with the SADC Protocol on Peace, Security, and Conflict Resolution, member states unanimously agreed to military intervention as the most appropriate response to the deteriorating political situation in Lesotho. The restoration of peace and security in Lesotho indicates the OPDSC's success (Osei-Hwedie 2002).

Military capabilities have enabled Botswana to participate in peacekeeping activities. The BDF is renowned for its peacekeeping services, which it has handled with professionalism. Under the auspices of the UN, in 1993 Botswana participated as a peacekeeping force and acted as a buffer to separate two Mozambique warring parties, FRELIMO and RENAMO, during the cease-fire to secure peace and order. Botswana has also participated in peacekeeping operations beyond the region in Somalia and Sierra Leone.

Botswana has taken part in Southern African regional military training exercises. Moreover, it is also a member of the Joint Commission on Defence, Security, and Police with South Africa, Zimbabwe, Zambia, and Namibia. The hotlines connecting the commanders of the armies allow for co-ordination and monitoring of the situation across borders. To date, the commission has been functioning very well; it also reviews the crime situation across borders.

To contain the problem of small arms in the region, the SADC Protocol on Firearms, Armaments and Related Materials recommended that the Southern African Regional Police Chiefs Co-operation Organisation (SARPCCO) implement law and order matters. The SARPCCO, established in 1995, is responsible for controlling cross-border crime. It has three sub-committees dealing with training and legal matters, and the Permanent Co-ordinating

Committee of Heads of Criminal Investigation Departments. This committee has conducted joint operations very successfully, resulting in recovery of vehicles – mostly from Zambia, a few from Zimbabwe and one or two from Malawi. However, at first there was no trust among the members of the SARPCCO, until joint training on border control, intelligence gathering, and harmonisation of legal provisions regarding motor vehicle penalties was carried out, and this led to improved relations. In September 2002, ministers responsible for the police agreed on a plan on regional security, which will be implemented by the SARPCCO.

Conclusion

Botswana has a functioning liberal democracy that has been remarkably stable since independence. The country has enjoyed a high degree of social and economic development and is generally regarded as a safe site for investment. However, it does have its problems, particularly regarding inequality, as well as the quality, at times, of its democratic practices. The failure of the opposition has meant that Botswana is, and has been since 1966, a *de facto* predominant-party system. Furthermore, the lack of internal party democracy, as well as the absence of direct presidential elections, present serious challenges for Botswana as a beacon of democracy. With regard to Botswana's security concerns, the main issues centre on cross-border crime, illegal immigration, refugees (primarily from Zimbabwe), small arms, and HIV/AIDS.

As a member of SADC, Botswana adheres to collective objectives, primarily good governance and economic development, which of course can only prevail if political order and stability also prevail. The nature of Botswana's involvement in security co-operation has changed in accordance with emerging challenges. The democratic nature of the state means that Botswana is one of the few countries in the region where the issue of national security is frequently discussed, and although one should not exaggerate the effect such debates have on security policy, it is a fact that security policy in Botswana is a concern for a growing number of its citizens.

INTERVIEWS

Deputy Commissioner Batshu, police headquarters, Gaborone, 11–12 December 2002.

Lieutenant-General M. Fisher, commander of the BDF, 21 February 2003.

M. Merafhe, minister of foreign affairs and former commander of the BDF, 11 December 2000 and 27 January 2003.

Oscar Motswagae, deputy permanent secretary, Ministry of Foreign Affairs, Gaborone, 10 December 2002.

David Rendoh, deputy permanent secretary, Ministry of Foreign Affairs, Gaborone, 7 April 2004.

S. Segokgo, MP, 29 January 2003.

ENDNOTES

1 See Thumberg-Hartland (1978); Picard (1985; 1987); Harvey and Lewis (1990); Danevad (1993); Stedman (1993); Dale (1995); Samatar (1999).

2 In an interview with *The Monitor*, the former minister of communications, science and technology, Boyce Sebetela, tried to clear his name on a number of accounts. Firstly, he denied that he personally stopped the broadcasting of the Radio Botswana programme 'Masa a Sele', arguing that as minister he was only implementing a government decision. He was also at a loss to explain why he was perceived as an 'enemy of the press' when he had opposed the 'draconian mass media bill', which he thought was not in consonance with the constitution of Botswana and Vision 2016. He felt that the proposed bill would 'erode press freedom'. On the liberalisation of the press, he maintained that the establishment of the National Broadcasting Board meant that the state-owned Radio Botswana would no longer be controlled by the minister of communications, science and technology.

3 The articulation of intra-party democracy also manifests itself in the election of office bearers for various party committees. The election of candidates to positions in the central committee, women's wing, and youth wing in various parties has in recent years been highly contested. For the BDP, the contest for central committee elections held in Ghanzi in July 2003 was perhaps the mother of all battles within the party. For the opposition BNF, splits resulted in the formation of the Botswana Congress Party in 1998, which split up again following the central committee elections in Kanye in 2001, leading to the formation of the New Democratic Front. Perhaps what was most dramatic about the latest split was that Dr Kenneth Koma, the founder of the BNF and its mentor, left it to form the new party. The BDP, which over the years has been plagued by factional fights, went to the Ghanzi congress in July 2003 more polarised than ever – there was a noticeable rupture in the cohesion of the elite. Much as Vice President Ian Khama wanted to project himself as being above factionalism, and preached a message of party unity, he went to the Ghanzi congress as a leader of a faction that opposed the Kedikilwe faction. Needless to say, the Kedikilwe faction was defeated at that congress, but it remains to be seen whether Khama's victory has led to an end to factions. What is clear is that the party is now under a new guard, which rode to power on the crest of the Seretse Khama legacy.

4 Interview with Lieutenant-General M. Fisher, 21 February 2003.

Chapter 5

Lesotho

Khabele Matlosa

Lesotho presents an interesting case study for an investigation of the interface between democracy and security, primarily because it is the only country in the Southern African region that has experienced military rule. Although a constitutional monarchy, the Kingdom of Lesotho experienced *de facto* one-party authoritarian rule during the period 1970–86; military rule between 1986 and 1993; and democratic rule from 1993 to date. The implications of all these trajectories of governance have been quite profound for security, as will be shown below.

External context of democratisation

The external context for our understanding of the democracy–security nexus in Lesotho is extremely important. The Lesotho democracy and security landscape has been shaped and influenced to a great extent by both global and regional developments over which the small nation state has little (if any) control or leverage, much as it has been conditioned by endogenous development within the country itself (see Matlosa 1998a; 2001; Matlosa and Pule 2001). The major external developments are surely the end of the Cold War on a global scale in 1990, which coincided with negotiations to end white minority rule in South Africa. These epoch-making developments reshaped Lesotho's democratic and security architecture in a number of ways.

Firstly, Lesotho's military dictatorship of the time could no longer feed on the Cold War ideological bipolarity and the threat of apartheid South Africa for its survival and razor-thin international credibility, but instead had to bow to democratic pressures which, in turn, led to a democratic election in 1993. This election was a watershed political development, for it marked the return to a democratic path, even if it brought about a fragile democracy bedeviled by both violent and non-violent conflicts, and political instability. Secondly, given Lesotho's overwhelming dependence on foreign aid, political conditionality weighed heavily on the military junta, adding more pressure for the regime to chart a democratisation path and allow the military elite to retire gracefully to the barracks, and in this regard, pressure was exerted by the country's major donors at the time, namely Germany, Sweden, Britain, and the United States (see Matlosa 2000). Thirdly, the West could no longer find strategic value in Lesotho after the end of the Cold War and the ending of apartheid in South Africa.

The incoming government of national unity in South Africa was also eager to contribute to the normalisation or democratisation and demilitarisation of Lesotho politics, primarily for its own national security interests, and exhorted the military to relinquish power in favour of an elected civilian government. The 1993 election in Lesotho decisively reversed the culture of militarism, although pockets of violent conflict still remained as a painful reminder of the politics of militarisation. Developments in Namibia, Mozambique, and South Africa pointed to a region-wide transition away from authoritarian governance of both civilian and military varieties to a multi-party system of democratic governance to which the military junta could not turn a blind eye. It was obvious that this regional political sea change would leave no single country untouched, beginning with Zambia's landmark election of 1991 in which the ruling party, in power since independence, was turned out of office. All one-party and authoritarian regimes in Southern Africa, including the military junta in Lesotho, were in retreat from the wave of democratisation surging through the region.

Internal context of democratisation

Lesotho is small, landlocked, and impoverished, with a population of about 2.1 million people. It gained its political independence from Britain in 1966 following about 100 years of colonial rule. The governance regime in Lesotho is basically a parliamentary constitutional monarchy in which the king, currently Letsie III, is the head of state, and the prime minister, currently Pakalitha Mosisili, is the head of government.

However, this governance system does not have domestic roots in Lesotho, as it is essentially a replica of the British Westminster system. The Lesotho state is both in theory and practice a borrowed concept and entity framed according to the Westphalian notion of a state. Thus it remains a state in the making, structurally weak, dependent, fragile, and extremely vulnerable to external pressures.

There has clearly been a pattern of authoritarian and *de facto* one-party rule in Lesotho. During some five years following political independence, the then ruling party – the Basotho National Party (BNP) – fearing electoral defeat, embarked on a period of authoritarian rule, relying solely upon repressive governance and the most horrendous abuse of the security establishment to quell oppositional politics. It was interesting, though, that while it was assumed that a fairly strong bureaucratic–military authoritarianism had developed, that ostensibly had cemented firm links and a community of interests between the BNP political elite and the military elite, the two forces parted ways abruptly in the 1980s, culminating in a bloodless military coup in 1986 that dislodged the BNP and saw the military assuming state power for about eight years. Thus civilian authoritarianism turned into an even more repressive military regime, which effectively banned political party activity.

Following the eight-year period of military rule, prospects for the mountain kingdom to revert back to democratic rule and exercise civilian authority over the security establishment, while at the same time depoliticising and professionalising the security forces, were heralded by the return to civilian rule and the 1993 election, which was won overwhelmingly by the Basutoland Congress Party (BCP) over the by then discredited and disgruntled BNP. This was an election whose outcome was aptly described by many observers as the 'righting of the wrongs' for the BCP, since the BNP had snatched electoral victory from it by violent means in 1970.

A fairly feeble and fledgling democratic experiment began, which was marked by conflicts between the state on one hand and the monarchy, the opposition BNP, and the security forces on the other (Matlosa 1998b; Matlosa and Pule 2001), culminating in violence in 1998 that nearly precipitated a civil war. The crisis itself was precipitated by the May 1998 national election. Prior to the vote, the BCP had split into two factions, leading to the formation of a new party, the Lesotho Congress for Democracy (LCD), which unexpectedly won 60 per cent of the national vote, but because of the first-past-the-post (FPTP) electoral system functioning at the time, gained all but one of the parliamentary seats. Defeated parties charged fraud, and the BNP used its connections in the security forces to foment a rebellion, culminating in an army mutiny led by junior officers on 11 September. On 22 and 23 September, at the invitation of the prime minister, and acting under the aegis of SADC, which had long been involved in trying to resolve the issue, South Africa and Botswana sent in military forces to restore order. In the process, 113 Basotho and 11 South Africans were killed, and parts of the capital, Maseru, were destroyed in riots and looting.

This ushered in a new phase in the governance–security nexus. Deliberate efforts have been made since 1998 to nurture and consolidate Lesotho's conflict-ridden democracy and bring the security forces firmly under civil authority. This has taken the form of reforms, primarily revolving around the electoral system, which was changed in 2002, and security sector reforms, which are still ongoing.

Democratic consolidation

Whereas Lesotho's fledging democracy experienced turbulence and violent conflicts during the period 1993–98 following long years of authoritarian rule, commendable progress is now being made to nurture democracy, with the ultimate objective of democratic consolidation (Matlosa 2002a; Matlosa and Pule 2001). First and foremost, a violent major conflict in 1998, which nearly escalated into a civil war, was resolved through both military intervention by SADC states and political settlement involving belligerent forces in a dialogue mediated by South Africa (Matlosa 1999; Elklit 2002). The most innovative and constructive strategy aimed at political settlement through dialogue was the establishment of the Interim Political Authority (IPA). The IPA comprised two representatives for each of the 14 political parties that contested the 1998 election, including the ruling LCD.

The overall mandate of the IPA was as follows:

- the creation and promotion of conditions conducive to the holding of free and fair elections;
- the levelling of the playing field for all political parties and candidates that seek to participate in the elections;
- the elimination of any impediments to legitimate political activity;
- the elimination of victimisation of people on account of divergent political beliefs;
- the creation of conducive conditions for all political parties and candidates to canvass political support from voters freely, to organise and hold meetings, and to have access to all voters;
- the elimination of political patronage of any kind; and
- the creation of conditions for equal treatment of all political parties and candidates by all governmental institutions, and in particular by all government-owned media, prior to and during the elections (Kingdom of Lesotho 1998: 29).

Although the IPA encountered numerous difficulties in the execution of its mandate, due mainly to a multiplicity of conflicts between the structure and government, which in turn delayed the holding of general elections, it achieved its objectives in more ways than one. The most important achievements of the IPA were that:

- the structure created a viable forum for continued dialogue among belligerent parties;
- the political dialogue certainly facilitated the process of national healing, political reconciliation, and peace;
- the dialogue also facilitated the process of the demilitarisation of Lesotho politics;

- the structure proposed various policy measures that added value to the nurturing of democracy; and
- the structure played a pioneering role in the process of Lesotho's electoral reform, which culminated in the replacement of the FPTP electoral system with the mixed member proportional (MMP) electoral system, which was used in the elections of 2002 (Elklit 2002; Matlosa 2003a; 2003b).

As Elklit (2002: 1) rightly observes:

> on 25 May 2002 Lesotho became the first African country to test the MMP electoral model in a parliamentary election. The elections went well and the results produced by the new MMP system represent a significant political and democratic achievement. There can be no doubt that the experiences from this first national level application of this electoral system to African soil will be studied carefully in many quarters, including outside the mountain kingdom.

Some countries that have this system in place thus far are Germany, New Zealand, Wales (for regional assemblies only), and Scotland (for regional assemblies). Unlike the earlier FPTP system, the new MMP system in Lesotho adopted a dual ballot system in which a voter casts two ballots: a constituency vote and a party vote. According to the IEC report,

> the constituency vote determines who will represent the constituency in the National Assembly. The party vote is used to elect candidates from party lists and compensates parties who have won fewer constituency seats than they would be entitled to under pure proportional representation, or who have won no constituency seats even though entitled to under proportionality (IEC 2002: 3).

This system has many advantages, primarily because it attempts to combine the positive elements of both the FPTP and the proportional representation systems. In the 2002 elections, while the LCD won the large majority of constituency seats, the BNP, which did not win even a single constituency seat, received 21 compensatory seats in parliament. While almost all the previous elections had produced a parliament dominated by one party (especially the 1993 and 1998 elections), 2002 produced a clearly multi-party parliament. Thus, to a large extent, the introduction of the MMP system has addressed a major democratic deficit in Lesotho's political landscape.

However, the electoral reform process in Lesotho still faces critical challenges if political stability is to be assured. In any case, the electoral system, in and of itself, does not really provide a total panacea for Lesotho's multifaceted political crisis. Major and far-reaching constitutional reforms are still required on various governance issues. Such reforms, of necessity, need to dovetail neatly into the security arena as well, and it is to this particular issue that the next section turns.

Democratisation and security sector reform

Hampered by ostensibly intractable conflicts for close to three decades, Lesotho today seems poised for some relative political stability, which surely augurs well for its democratisation project. Nowhere is this positive development so vividly demonstrated as in the current security sector reform process covering, among other things, the Lesotho Defence Force (LDF) and the Lesotho Mounted Police Service (LMPS). These organs of the security establishment had been thoroughly politicised by previous regimes, especially during the period 1970–93, with the sole purpose of turning them into mere political instruments of the ruling elite of the time.

LDF

A plethora of policy initiatives have been taken since 1994 to reform the LDF with a view to entrenching civil authority over the armed forces (Mothibe 1998; 1999). The first major initiative was the establishment of the Ministry of Defence (MoD) in August 1994, a vivid political expression of civil control of the military through both the executive and legislative arms of government. The ministry is headed by the prime minister, Pakalitha Mosisili, as minister of defence, and is managed generally by civilian staff, although army officers also form part of the staff complement.

Through the efforts of the Defence Council, the MoD has developed a defence policy that aims to transform the LDF into an apolitical, accountable, capable, and affordable defence force. The establishment of the MoD itself represents another attempt by the executive authority to strengthen civil–military relations. The MoD has the primary responsibility of administering, organising, and accounting for the activities and operations of the LDF. The overall operations of the MoD are governed by four main principles:

- separation of military and civilian powers in order to restrain involvement of the army in partisan politics;
- legality of all operations of the armed forces to ensure that their functions are in accord with the rule of law as defined by the constitution and the Defence Act;

- accountability of the LDF to the elected civilian authority through the MoD and parliament; and
- transparency of the activities and functions of the LDF through the provision of critical information on security and defence to the general public.

The MoD's mandate is confined mainly to administrative and executive functions, while all operational responsibilities of the armed forces still remain the sole responsibility of the LDF through the leadership of its commander. It does seem that there are expansive institutional mechanisms (including a policy framework) in place for ensuring stable civil–military relations and ensuring successful implementation of security sector reform in Lesotho. However, the major missing link in this institutional arrangement is effective parliamentary oversight of the armed forces and defence policy. The challenge lies in the reform of the parliamentary system in a way that provides room for the establishment of portfolio committees, among which must be a parliamentary portfolio committee on defence and security.

The second most important element of the security reform process in the LDF has to do with the adoption of a defence policy since 1995. The defence policy aims at developing a vision for the LDF and corroborates the mission of the MoD in terms of nurturing and consolidating the ongoing process of security sector reform. Within this overarching policy, the mission statement of the LDF is to contribute to the

> maintenance of the constitution and territorial integrity of the state. [The LDF] is committed to contributing to the stability, security, peace and progress of the country and its entire people. It shall always aim to enjoy the full support of the population and international respect as a result of its professionalism and high standards (Kingdom of Lesotho. Ministry of Defence 1998: 16).

The defence policy will be augmented considerably by a strategic plan for the LDF. The strategic vision is that the LDF shall be a prepared, flexible, and affordable force, which renders a military service to the state and not individuals. The primary role is the successful protection of the territorial integrity of Lesotho.

Yet another area for security sector reform in Lesotho has to do with the resource endowment of the country and how scarce resources are allocated. The state of economic growth and development plays an important role in influencing civil–military relations. This is because the economy determines the amount of resources that the executive authority is able to assign to the security forces. This is crucial for the defence budget, which often competes with other demands for the country's scarce resources. Thus far, the defence budget has always ranked among the traditional top three in terms of size – namely, education, health, and defence. For the first time, the 2002 national budget relegated defence spending to fifth position in terms of prioritisation of resource allocation.

Although Lesotho's transition to civilian rule in 1993 was perceived by many as a positive development for the county's democracy, tense relations between the executive arm of the state and the armed forces still linger. This tension bred the seeds of political instability that became more manifest during the 1994 and 1998 political turmoil. Undoubtedly, these tense relations further undermined the impact of major efforts towards establishing stable civil–military relations elaborated above. Following the 1993 election, the armed forces were unsure whether to work closely and collaborate with the new government, or to undermine the government in order to support the return of BNP rule. Perceptions within the forces were sharply divided on this thorny issue. As a result, the BNP took advantage of this to try to lure the army to its side in order to undermine the BCP government. The faction fighting in the armed forces in 1994, which invited external intervention by the Commonwealth, OAU, and SADC countries, was precisely about disagreement within the forces as to whether to accept or undermine the authority of the BCP.

At this time, the executive arm of government had not fully established civil supremacy over the armed forces. This became abundantly clear during post-election violent conflict that engulfed the country. Although the primary protagonists in 1998 were the ruling party and opposition parties, the secondary players with a vested interest in the conflict were the monarchy and the security forces. Clearly, therefore, the armed forces were directly and indirectly involved in the 1998 conflict. Subsequently, a commission of inquiry was established in order to find out the causes of the conflict and identify the key players who propelled the civil strife. The three-person commission, known as the Leon Commission, comprised judges from South Africa and was headed by Justice Nigel Leon. It established beyond any shadow of a doubt that:

> With regard to the role of the Lesotho Defence Force in the preservation and maintenance of law and order, the Commission found that a large number of soldiers not only failed lamentably to preserve law and order but contributed to the state of anarchy which prevailed at the relevant time (Leon Commission 2001: 5).

Further evidence abounds that suggests that the armed forces were again sharply divided into those supporting the opposition protest against the election outcome and thus sympathetic to opposition calls for the dissolution of the LCD government, and those supporting the outcome of the election and the authority of the LCD as a legally constituted government. It will be recalled that it was during this major conflict that Botswana and South Africa undertook a military intervention in Lesotho at the request of the Lesotho government. Part of the mission of this external military intervention was to neutralise the military's involvement in this conflict and to seek a political solution. Following the political settlement of the violent conflict, a major restructuring of the armed forces is ongoing and this includes, among other things, downsizing of the forces and training of the officer corps in order to ensure both efficiency and professionalism. Technical assistance for security reforms in the armed forces has come from South Africa and, more recently, India.

LMPS

Pretty much like the military, the police force in Lesotho evolved in the 1960s as a highly politicised force primarily used as an instrument of coercion by the then ruling BNP to control or eliminate its political opponents. Given that during most of its tenure of office the BNP was anchored more upon the bullet than the ballot, the police force was used (or abused) mainly to reproduce *de facto* one-party rule and undermine any form of opposition to the government of the day. So it was that to all intents and purposes, the police, like the military, suffered a severe legitimacy crisis in the eyes of the general public, as the force was closely identified more with the BNP as a party than with a neutral government institution.

The deliberate politicisation of the police by the BNP considerably diminished its professionalism and impartiality in discharging its law and order functions. Many of the brutalities and repressive measures of the BNP regime during the 1970s and 1980s were perpetrated through both the police and military forces. It should be emphasised, though, that this politicised role of the police and the military cannot be blamed squarely on the forces alone. Rather, the largest culprit in the politicisation of the forces and their lack of professionalism for that period was the government of the day.

The BCP, after its landslide 1993 election victory, inherited a highly politicised police force, and a critical challenge was how to reform the police force and subject it to civil authority, especially within the context of a new administration. This process was not easy, as the new government locked horns in a bitter conflict with the defence and police forces in the early days of its administration. In 1994 the police demanded a salary increase from government and went on strike to pressurise the government to meet their demand. Under duress, the government acquiesced and granted a 50 per cent salary increase. The political pressure by the police dovetailed neatly with a similar demand by the military, which resulted in violent conflict between the military establishment and the government, as well as among factions inside the military itself. The 1994 political conflict in the police force resulted in the killing of about three police officers. The same violent conflict witnessed the most unfortunate intervention by King Letsie III, in a fairly partisan fashion, when he dissolved the BCP government and established a transitional council to run the affairs of the country. This move triggered internal dissent and protest, which in turn invited external actors, especially Botswana, South Africa, and Zimbabwe (the SADC troika), to intervene and reverse the king's unilateral and partisan political move.

Consequently, the BCP regime was reinstated a month later, in September 1994, in a political settlement that resulted in the troika countries acting as guarantors of Lesotho's fragile democracy. A year later, the LMPS once again suffered internal factionalism and faction fighting, due mainly to political differences on how best to deal with a national teachers' strike organised by the Lesotho Teachers' Trade Union. It was fairly clear by this time that internal wrangling within the force was a manifestation of the contradictions between the past culture of a politicised force under an authoritarian regime and the new culture of a professional service under a democratic order. The climax of the major problems that the BCP faced in its attempt to professionalise the police came in 1997, when a faction attempted a mutiny that was ultimately quelled through the intervention of the military. During the violent political conflict of 1998, political cracks within the police were clearly visible, and it was also clear that there was a wide gap between the police and the military; the two forces even exchanged fire as a result of differences on how best to bring about law and order.

Three major initiatives towards the reform of the LMPS have been introduced: the 1997 white paper on police reform (Kingdom of Lesotho 1997), the 1998 Police Service Act, and the five-year development plan for the LMPS for the period 1998–2003 (LMPS 1998). Whereas the 1998 act provides the legal framework for the reform programme, the development plan provides a programme of action for the implementation of reforms over a period of five years.

The essence of the white paper is to build a professional police service able to discharge its law and order functions without political bias and in partnership with communities. It also aims to ensure that the service operates under the principle of the supremacy of civil authority. In this regard, the mission of the LMPS is as follows:

> To provide a high quality Police Service in Lesotho and in conjunction and consultation with the community, other organisations and agencies seek to promote the safety and security of the individual, reduce crime, disorder and fear and enhance confidence in the rule of law (Kingdom of Lesotho 1997: 2).

At the heart of the white paper is the commitment to maintain an effective, efficient, and accountable police service, as well as to enhance internal discipline, and build confidence and trust between the police and the public. It emphasises democratic partnership between the police and the public in order to achieve three basic strategic goals: reduction of crime, improvement of service to the public, and efficient management of police resources (Kingdom of Lesotho 1997: 7).

The new approach to policing emphasises strategic planning wherein, among other things, the annual policing plan will set out key national priorities and objectives for policing each year. This plan is accessible to the public and will incorporate some views and opinions from the public. The plan is submitted to the minister of home affairs by the commissioner of police after public consultations. The annual policing plan will be accompanied by regional and local plans, which elaborate the strategies for realising the key objectives of the overall plan. As in the case of the annual plan, regional and local action plans will be drawn up in close consultation and collaboration with the communities. On the basis of the implementation of the annual plan, the commissioner of police is expected to produce an annual report and submit it to the minister of home affairs at the end of each financial year. This approach strengthens the accountability of the police to both the civil authority and the public at large. On a longer-term basis, the LMPS developed a five-year development plan which, among other things, set out the nature and scope of the necessary reforms in the police force over the specified period. The white paper emphasises the operational autonomy and independence of the LMPS as follows:

> the government intends to take the opportunity to clarify in law the independence of the police from political interference .... The Commissioner alone must have the direction and control of the Lesotho Mounted Police Service. No politician should be allowed to give the Commissioner or his officers instructions about particular police operations

> .... Such instructions are incompatible with policing in a free democratic society (Kingdom of Lesotho 1997: 12–13).

The white paper then introduces a new participatory approach to the following critical areas of the policing service: police–community partnership, resource mobilisation and utilisation, new police management, and a new directorate of police.

The police–community partnership has already been discussed at length above. The white paper gives the commissioner of police greater latitude to determine, plan, and utilise resources required for policing through approval of the minister of home affairs – with minimal 'external interference and bureaucratic delays' (Kingdom of Lesotho 1997: 21). In respect of the new management approach, the police force is no longer considered strictly as a department of the Ministry of Home Affairs and subject to the bureaucratic red tape of the civil service. Rather, it is regarded as a special unit within the ministry, and this includes the establishment of a Police Negotiating Council through which staff interests are mediated and represented. In order to ensure implementation of the reforms suggested in the white paper, a new Directorate of Police has been established within the Ministry of Home Affairs. The directorate is basically the administrative arm of the ministry to ensure that the reforms do lead to an effective, efficient, and accountable service. Headed by the principal secretary and independent of the LMPS, it is thus another instrument for ensuring accountability.

The white paper also prescribes that the LMPS should evolve the five-year development plan, which provides a framework for annual regional and national plans. To this end, the LMPS (1998) produced *Beyond 2000: A Development Plan for the Lesotho Mounted Police Service, 1998–2003*. The main thrust of the plan was to set out a clear framework for the professionalisation of the police force, focusing specifically on six key areas.

Firstly, the plan provides a strategic guideline for crime management. It sets out a crime management strategy that targets crime prevention. This will further facilitate smooth and efficient processing of crime cases.

Secondly, the plan singles out the critical importance of police collaboration and partnership with communities. This partnership will help assist the LMPS to respond directly to changing needs of communities and provide a sense of community responsibility in crime prevention. This partnership is also crucial for the LMPS to develop clear strategies for community policing in the medium to long term.

Thirdly, another principle that undergirds the five-year plan is people management, by which is meant human resource management in the LMPS, as well as a cost-effective deployment strategy for policing. This will also involve capacity building so that the LMPS is better able to discharge its core mandate, as well as manpower planning to establish appropriate force levels through right-sizing and cost containment, taking due cognisance of the country's future policing needs. One of the most important components of this principle will be the civilianisation policy, which basically aims at gearing policing towards a firmer integration of civilian and police staff.

Fourthly, improvement of the quality of police services is one of the most important cardinal pillars of the five-year development plan. This will aim at improving police–community relations; quality of service delivery in terms of crime prevention; effectiveness, efficiency, and professionalism; processing of crime cases by the responsible law enforcement and adjudication agencies; accountability to the executive and legislative arms of government; and giving the public high-quality deliverables from the LMPS.

Fifthly, the plan aims at developing service-wide integrated information management. This will help enhance effective and efficient decision making and implementation of decisions and policies, as well as monitoring and evaluation of the progress made in undertaking reforms in the LMPS. This will entail, among other things, development of high-technology information systems for the LMPS, including computerisation of the services.

Finally, the plan aims to help the LMPS manage its meagre resources effectively and efficiently. This will entail providing modern radio and telecommunication systems, effective transport infrastructure, and appropriate offices and equipment, and improving utilisation of funds and accountability for all expenditure incurred.

Considerable progress has been registered in terms of security sector reform in both the military and police forces in Lesotho, although more still remains to be done. The most critical challenge that still confronts the Lesotho government is how parliament monitors and oversees the roles and functions of the security establishment and, indeed, plays a key role in this process of security sector reform.

Gender dimensions of democracy and security

Gender dimensions of democracy and security in Southern Africa in general, and Lesotho in particular, present one of the most daunting challenges for democratic consolidation today. These relate to power relations between men and women insofar as policymaking and the construction of the legal and institutional framework for democratic governance and security are concerned. Existing literature points to a lot of work already done in terms of the participation of women in the public policymaking spheres of the governance machinery. We are, however, still ignorant about the degree of influence, authority, and power that women who get involved in key state organs have in order to drive the policymaking machine in a direction that further consolidates gender balance in governance. In other words, whereas we are more aware today of advances or obstacles in respect of women's participation – in quantitative terms – in the political world, much more still remains to be done to unveil the exact influence, authority, and power that women in these state organs wield in order to drive a gender-sensitive agenda as part of the nurturing and consolidation of democratic governance.

Broadly speaking, the debate on gender and democracy turns mainly on the level of participation of women in key organs of the state, in particular, the legislature, cabinet, judiciary, and security establishment. This section of the chapter focuses discussion mainly on women in parliament.

The Southern African experience in respect of women empowerment in both quantitative and qualitative terms is a mixed bag. The SADC member states took a positive step in 1997 when they signed the Gender and Development Declaration in Blantyre, Malawi. The member states committed themselves individually and collectively to the following policy measures, among others:

- the achievement of equal gender representation in all key organs of the state, and a target of at least 30 per cent women in key political and decision-making structures by 2005;
- promoting women's full access to and control over productive resources to reduce the level of poverty among women;
- repealing and reforming all laws, amending constitutions, and changing social practices which still subject women to discrimination; and
- taking urgent measures to prevent and deal with the increasing levels of violence against women and children (Molokomme 2002: 42).

The declaration was further reinforced by an addendum entitled 'The prevention and eradication of violence against women and children', adopted by SADC in 1998.

The signing of protocols and declarations by the political elite in the SADC region is one thing, and translating those political commitments into reality through deliberate policy reform measures is quite another. Progress towards reaching the 30 per cent minimum target of women in key organs of the state, especially parliament, is not only mixed, but points to a quiet resistance by male-dominated political institutions. Only a few SADC states – most prominently Mozambique and South Africa – have achieved this threshold. Namibia and Tanzania have come near to reaching the target, but progress in general has been disappointing.

Following the 2002 Lesotho election, in which the MMP electoral system was used for the first time, 12 women formed part of the 120-person strong National Assembly. Despite the increase of parliamentary seats from 80 to 120, after the 1998 political debacle, the number of women in the National Assembly remains low. However, the speaker of the National Assembly, Nthloi Motsamai, is a woman, and evidently her leadership role has injected some enthusiasm and commitment into parliament for the political empowerment of women.

The number of women has tended to be higher in the Senate relative to the National Assembly. Of the total of 33 members, there are 11 women (five of them appointed and six who are chiefs). Over the years, women have increased their participation in the institution of chieftainship. This participation, however, has been more by default than design, since women can only act as chiefs in circumstances where a male is unable to perform due to absence, youth, or incapacity, or where there is no male in direct line of descent (Letuka, Matashane, and Morolong 1997: 23).

The relatively low levels of participation of women in government, politics, and the legislature can be explained in various ways. The most plausible explanations rotate around the political and legal content of the state system. African political systems are often marked by instability and violence. Given this and the zero-sum nature of the political game in Africa, plus the marginalisation of the gender question in political discourse, women have not been involved. The political sphere and the state system are perceived as male domains, while women are expected to participate in the economic sphere and the domestic realm of life. The legal systems in Africa also inhibit women's participation in politics and national legislatures both by design and by default. The patriarchal nature of the state system, perforce, excludes women, and according to Williams, 'African states cannot behave in a manner different from the general characteristics of their society steeped in patriarchy and in a patrilineal stance despite the noises they make about democratising their societies' (quoted in Motebang 1997: 57).

Lesotho and common security in Southern Africa

The size and geopolitical location of Lesotho to a considerable degree shapes and influences the country's role and position in regional common security efforts. Put much more explicitly, and rather provocatively, Lesotho's small size, impoverishment, and landlocked situation have inhibited the country's influence in the current efforts towards regional common security in SADC. It is worth noting, though, that Lesotho is an active member of SADC, participates meaningfully in all SADC activities, and was in fact the chair of the ISDSC in 2001, and the chair of the OPDSC in 2003–04. In a sense, therefore, Lesotho's foreign policy in the region, though somewhat weak and reactive, does embrace the conviction of the political elite that national security today, under conditions of globalism and regionalism, is inextricably interwoven into regional security. In this regard, Lesotho definitely embraces the significance of a regional security institution such as the OPDSC.

Despite near-paralysis of the OPDSC between 1996 and 2001, and the lack of a clear role for SADC on the security front (see Omari and Macaringue in this volume), South Africa, Botswana, and Zimbabwe have been extensively and directly involved in containing Lesotho's protracted, and often violent, conflicts, and today the three countries, together with Mozambique, remain the guarantors of Lesotho's democratic governance. This development has naturally triggered an interesting debate in terms of its implications for Lesotho's national security and sovereignty.

One school of thought perceives the South African-led SADC interventions in Lesotho as premised on altruism aimed at ensuring Lesotho's political stability and peace for the good of the SADC region as a whole. The second school posits that South African interventions in Lesotho are primarily predicated upon the former's national security and strategic interests, rather than the quest for democratic governance in Lesotho as such. Whichever school of thought one follows, a key challenge facing Lesotho today in relation to regional security imperatives is precisely how best the leadership of the country can reposition this small and landlocked nation in the context of post-apartheid South and Southern Africa. Lesotho needs much stronger bilateral co-operation arrangements with South Africa, without necessarily sacrificing its commitment to multilateral regional efforts towards regional common security. Although it has taken a painstakingly long time for the leadership of both countries to appreciate this stark reality, it is encouraging, and indeed commendable, that they established the Joint Bilateral Commission of Co-operation in April 2001, the key objectives of which are to:

- guide the strategic partnership between the parties;
- promote mutually beneficial economic integration between the two countries, with the aim of closing the existing economic disparities;
- promote co-operation in the field of science and technology, with the aim of bridging the technological divide;
- cultivate and promote good governance, and beneficial social, cultural,

humanitarian, and political co-operation, and facilitate contact between the public and private sectors;
- maintain peace and security between the two countries and general stability in the Southern African region through collective action based on respect for democratic institutions, human rights, and the rule of law;
- co-operate with each other and harmonise the position of the two countries in addressing multilateral issues of common interest; and
- facilitate movement of people, goods, and services, taking into consideration the unique geographic position of Lesotho.

In order to operationalise the commission and facilitate the realisation of the above objectives, working groups or clusters have been established, namely the economic, good governance, security and stability, and social clusters.

It is only fair to observe that slowly but surely positive steps are under way in the redefinition of Lesotho–South African relations, and only time will tell whether or not the two countries will reap mutually beneficial developments arising from the bilateral commission, especially in respect of democratic governance and security.

Conclusion

This chapter has attempted to tease out possible linkages between democracy and security in Lesotho. The first of the main findings and conclusions of this study are that insecurity and instability disrupt governance considerably. The policy challenge facing Lesotho, therefore, is to ensure a positive interface between its democratisation process and the maintenance of peace and security.

Secondly, and flowing from the above, democratic governance, peace, and security are likely to lead to stability and meaningful development. Although this may seem like stating the obvious, it is worth emphasising that governance should not be perceived as an end in and of itself, but rather a means to an end. The ultimate end of democratic governance ought to be meaningful and people-centered development. The policy challenge for Lesotho is thus to chart a development vision anchored upon sustainable human development, predicated on a market-friendly and state-driven development path.

Thirdly, although Lesotho's historical record points to long periods of both civilian and military authoritarianism, recent developments are positive in terms of nurturing and consolidating democratic governance. The most encouraging and, indeed, commendable progress has been made in the reform of the electoral system in order to deepen democratic governance, and security sector reform aimed at ensuring civil control and professionalisation of the security forces. Despite progress, major challenges still remain for Lesotho to reach a stage of democratic consolidation upon which sustainable peace and security can be firmly anchored. What the country needs to do now is consolidate the achievements thus far attained, while at the same time opening new arenas for deepening and broadening the democratic space, as well as promoting peace and security for the general welfare of the Basotho people.

It is abundantly evident from the discussion in this chapter that the primary actors in Lesotho's democratisation process include both external and internal forces. The key external actors are the bilateral and multilateral donor agencies and SADC, especially South Africa. The key domestic actors include the state, capital, labour, civil society organisations, and the churches. Policymaking on the issues of democratisation and security remains the domain of the executive branch of the state, overseen by the legislative branch, with a fairly minimal role for civil society organisations. Given that there is as yet no commonly shared vision or conception of national security, it may well be that the current efforts towards a national vision could bring about a positive change in this regard. What is encouraging, though, is that the democratic transition of the early 1990s has helped greatly in reducing tension among key actors regarding the conception of security. Thus, increasingly, the approach to security is bound to be much more consensual than has hitherto been the case.

Chapter 6

Mauritius

Gavin Cawthra

By one definition, Huntington's (1991) criterion of two turnovers of elected government, Mauritius is the only consolidated democracy in Southern Africa. While this is a highly contested criterion, it is certainly true that, with Botswana, Mauritius is one of only two Southern African states that have sustained democratic politics and democratic institutions continuously since independence.[1] It is also one of the wealthiest states in the region, and has the second-highest level of social development, as measured by the UNDP's Human Development Index, after Seychelles (UNDP 2002: 150). And it has managed to achieve this despite – or perhaps because of – the most complex ethnic and religious mix of all countries in SADC and few natural resources.

Evolution of democracy in Mauritius

At independence from Britain in 1968, Mauritius displayed many of the characteristics of other newly independent African countries: poverty and high unemployment; ethnic cleavages (about half Hindus of South Asian origin, a quarter Creole, 16 per cent Muslims of South Asian origin, and a small minorities of Chinese and European – mostly French – origin); reliance on a single export commodity (sugar); and a shortage of skills and experience. Shortly before independence, ethnic communal riots had broken out on the island and British troops had to be brought in to restore order. Within three years of independence the ruling Mauritian Labour Party (MLP), responding to the rise of a radical opposition party, the Mauritian Militant Movement (MMM), and to ongoing ethnic tensions and militant workers' strikes, had imposed a state of emergency, closed down opposition newspapers, imprisoned opposition leaders, and postponed elections (Lodge, Kadima, and Pottie 2002: 166). It looked like Mauritius was treading the well-worn path to authoritarianism.

However, thanks in part to sagacious political leadership, a turn away from radicalism by the MMM, and in part to the nature of the country's political system (of which more later), Mauritians were able to pull back from the brink and set about consolidating their democracy. There have now been seven free and fair elections since independence, resulting in three democratic transfers of political power, and the country can by any standards be regarded as a consolidated democracy, with an independent press, a vibrant political culture, a wide diversity of political parties, an independent judiciary, an active parliament, and a variety of state institutions aimed at enhancing and protecting democratic rights. Some analysts attribute this in a large part to the 'design of democracy' (Bastian and Luckham 2003) – the unique processes that have been put in place as a result of historic compromises crafted by a British commission (the Banwell Commission of 1966).

Political processes

During the independence negotiations, the various ethnic groups were naturally agitating for electoral systems that they thought would most benefit their group: the dominant Hindu-based MLP, for example, wanted a large number of single-member first-past-the-post (FPTP) constituencies, thus ensuring that the widely and fairly evenly spread Hindu population would win virtually every seat, while Muslims demanded separate voter roles and reserved seats to ensure representation.

After more than a decade of argument, the Banwell Commission settled on a Westminster model with important modifications. Instead of an FPTP system, it instituted a model in which three candidates with the most votes in each of 20 constituencies go to parliament. This has encouraged political parties to field multi-ethnic slates in each constituency in order to try to secure all three positions. Furthermore, all candidates are required to register their ethnic affiliation, and after the votes are counted, eight seats are allocated on an ethnically proportional basis to the 'best losers' (the candidates from specified ethnic groups who gained the most votes, but not sufficient to get into parliament) (Brautigam 1999: 145–46).

Although some analysts have argued that this system has entrenched ethnicity, it has also encouraged multi-ethnic party slates and has made it difficult for one party to win outright, thus encouraging coalition building and compromise, and ensuring that minorities are represented in parliament. The system rewards parties or coalitions that field candidates from all communities. However, unlike proportional representation (PR) systems, it tends to exclude tiny parties, so that politics is usually dominated by two or three coalitions (although these are very fluid). It also tends to lead to landslide victories for successful multi-ethnic coalitions, thus promoting strong governments, but ones that are very vulnerable to alternative coalition building. The modified Westminster system is 'parliamentary' rather than 'presidential' in nature – the prime minister is elected by the majority party, while the president has mostly symbolic powers. This has also helped to promote inclusivity – indeed, in September 2003 the post of prime minister was 'swopped' between the two parties in the ruling coalition to honour an electoral pact (*Mauritius News* 2003).

There is thus a strong case to be made that the 'design of democracy' in Mauritius has contributed significantly to democratic consolidation – although it is by no means clear whether the model would work in conditions where the ethnic proportions were radically different. Like all Westminster-based systems, however, it suffers from the distorting effects of the FPTP system. In the 1987 election, for example, although only 1.7 per cent separated the two major electoral alliances, this was translated into a 36.6 per cent gap in terms of parliamentary seats (Lodge, Kadima, and Pottie 2002: 170). In January 2002 a commission on constitutional and electoral reform put forward a number of sweeping recommendations, including moving to a system of PR at the national level and strengthening the powers of the president (in order to reduce the considerable powers of the prime minister). PR might radically alter the nature of politics, but it is unclear if it will be introduced, as the major parties fear its implications (Dassyne 2004; Morvan 2004).

Democratic design cannot be the only factor behind Mauritius's success, however, and analysts have put forward a number of other explanations, including:

- high rates of economic growth, achieved through successful application of the 'Asian Tiger' model (export-oriented industrialisation using cheap labour and moving from protectionism to liberalisation). There is probably a symbiotic relationship between economic growth and democracy, with the one reinforcing the other (although there is considerable disagreement about cause and effect), and because democratisation is more likely to be successful when there is enough money to spread around, to take the sting out of distributive conflict;
- political agency, in other words, the quality of political leaders and their willingness to sacrifice personal gain for the good of the country. This, like economic growth and perhaps also political stability, may in part be attributed to highly successful investment in education, which has taken priority since independence. A political culture of tolerance and compromise has been developed (Srebrnik 2002: 289); and
- a political consensus around the social dimensions of democracy, with successive governments investing heavily in education and social welfare and being willing to subsidise basic foodstuffs, fertilisers, etc. (Brautigam 1999: 156–57).

No doubt many other factors can be identified, including 'luck', i.e. changes in the external environment over which Mauritius has had little control, but which have benefitted it enormously, such as rising prices of sugar shortly after independence, and the Lomé Convention and the US African Growth and Opportunity Act (AGOA), which have allowed Mauritius to export its textiles and other industrial products under very favourable tariff conditions. Whatever the case, it is clear that Mauritians have been able, on the whole, to exploit 'virtuous' relationships among democracy, social welfare, economic growth, and stability and security.

But there have been many problems in the actual practice of democracy, not least the persistence of ethnic communalism and its periodic tendency to spill over into violence, and elite domination (Morvan 2004).

Democratic practice

Interest and participation in politics is high (in the last legislative elections, 80 per cent of voters turned out) and political contestation has hardly ever spilt over into violence. Although volatile, and characterised by shifting alliances, electoral swings, and coalition decay, many of the parties have been in existence since – or before – independence and are led by experienced politicians (Lodge, Kadima, and Pottie 2002: 171). However, there is a strong ethnic flavour to politics, although it is not necessarily reflected directly in parties, despite efforts by some political parties to promote class-based politics.

Minority groups have historically feared and resented perceived domination by Mauritians of Indian origin, and within the Indo-Mauritian community, Hindu–Muslim tensions have been a persistent concern. Radical electoral swings, brought about in part by the electoral system, cannot disguise the facts that Hindus dominate politics under the system of 'democratic majority rule', and that this is unlikely to change as long as Hindus make up more than half the population and other ethnic groups tend to be allocated roles as 'junior partners' in any coalition. As Srebrnik (2002: 289) puts it:

> For the past two decades, each election has been a competition between two Hindu-dominated coalitions, each vying to win support primarily from the Hindu majority. Even with the corrective of the 'best loser' system, Hindus have a guaranteed majority of seats in the National Assembly.

However, for the first time, a non-Hindu, Paul Bérenger (of European origin), became prime minister in 2003 (albeit as a result of an intra-coalition agreement), and while Hindus may naturally dominate by virtue of their numerical superiority, as noted above, the system encourages inter-ethnic coalition-building.

More worrying, perhaps, are signs of growing marginalisation of the Creole minority, many of whom (especially those of predominately African origin) form the poorest communities in Mauritius, and of radicalisation of some elements of the Muslim population. In February 1999 a popular Creole 'seggae' performer, Kaya, died in police custody, triggering four days of rioting in Port Louis and elsewhere, which resulted in the deaths of five demonstrators. Later that year, Muslim soccer fans rioted after their team had been defeated by a Creole one, and Muslim youths torched a Chinese gambling club, in which seven people died (Jaddoo 2002: 18; Srebrnik 2002: 283). A fundamentalist Muslim party, Hizbullah, was launched in the mid-1990s and continues to draw votes. These tensions may be exacerbated by growing unemployment and poverty, which especially affects the youth and Creoles, who tend to occupy the least-skilled positions. Mauritian labour is now relatively expensive, and thousands of jobs have been lost as companies have relocated elsewhere. Jobs have also been lost in the sugar industry, which faces an uncertain future (see below). This is only partly compensated for by Mauritian efforts to encourage high-technology industries, notably by building a 'cyber city'.

National security

Mauritius is unique among SADC states in that it has no defence force – indeed, it is one of the very few countries in the world that has managed without one.[2] This is a reflection in part of the perceived lack of external security threats, and in part of domestic political calculations.

External relations

Since independence, Mauritius has sought to maintain strong links with the major Western powers, as well as with Africa (through its membership of the OAU/AU, SADC, and COMESA), and the countries of the Indian Ocean rim (Mauritius is a founder member of the Indian Ocean Rim Association for Regional Co-operation). Given that half its population is of Indian descent, close ties have been retained with India, and increasingly with China (only 3 per cent of the population is of Chinese origin, but they dominate retail commerce). Relations with India are sometimes a source of domestic tension, as some minority groups resent the close links, seen most starkly, perhaps, in the fact that the Mauritian prime minister's chief security advisor was for many years a seconded Indian senior intelligence official.

Some strain has been put on relations with the former colonial power, Britain, over Mauritius's claims to the Chagos archipelago, including Diego Garcia, which was transferred from Mauritius to a new Indian Ocean Dependency by Britain shortly before independence. Subsequently, nearly 2,000 inhabitants were removed from the islands to allow for the construction of the US military base on Diego Garcia and were relocated, most to Mauritius and a minority to Seychelles. In November 2000 the British High Court of Justice ruled that the population removal had been unlawful, but applications by the Chagos islanders to obtain a right of return were refused in the British courts. The United States has strongly resisted any attempt to alter the status quo, as Diego Garcia is now a key base in the 'war on terror'. India has lent its support to Mauritian claims to the archipelago as part of its efforts to build a strategic alliance with Mauritius, but Mauritian governments have tended to hold back from pressing these claims too hard, lest Mauritius alienates its major Western allies. Mauritius also lays claim to the French-held island of Tromelin, about 500 km to the north-west, but this is a very minor irritant in otherwise good relations with France, which remains the country's main trading partner.

The post-11 September 2001 international security environment has put further pressure on Mauritius's international relations, given its strategic position as an offshore banking centre (and hence potentially for money laundering) and the presence of small militant Islamic groups such as Hizbullah. Legislation to control terrorism, introduced in February 2002, proved to be divisive, as Muslims saw themselves as the main target. As a result, the president (a Muslim) resigned, and some Muslims accused the government of using the issue of terrorism to clamp down on civil rights.

Generally, Mauritius has enjoyed a wide range of foreign interactions, which are mostly peaceful and constructive. It has managed to balance its interests in Asia, Africa, and the Indian Ocean rim with its need to maintain good relations with its major trading partners in Europe and elsewhere, and has played an active role in multinational and international organisations. However, growing strategic links with India may have unexpected domestic or international consequences in the long term, and the Chagos Islands issue remains a potential source of conflict. Like all small island states,[3] Mauritius is also extremely vulnerable to international market shifts, and tariff and other legislative changes in its main trading partners (Jaddoo 2002: 4). In particular, it suffered in 2004 from the higher oil prices arising from the US-led invasion of Iraq, and it faces substantial declines in revenue as a result of mooted EU reforms to reduce sugar prices, as Mauritius has long benefitted from preferential rates up to three times the global market rate. Mauritian sources estimate potential losses from EU sugar reforms of up to MUR 3 billion (USD 100 million) a year. With AGOA also up for future negotiation, Mauritius could be facing serious economic difficulties (BBC 2004; IRIN 2004).

Mauritius does not perceive that it is at risk from external attack – hence the decision not to develop a defence force. Its complacency in this regard is also shown by its apparent unwillingness to enter into 'treaties of guarantee' with any of the major powers.

Internal security

As noted above, Mauritian democracy has been remarkably peaceful, given the potentially volatile ethnic and class composition of the population. However, the violent events of 1999 – although mild by African standards – served to remind Mauritians that social exclusion and religious tensions could potentially breed conflict. The violence was initially sparked by allegations of police torture, and Amnesty International has continued to report public complaints of police brutality (Amnesty International 2003). However, some steps have been taken to address this.

Crime and corruption are also major internal security concerns. With its strategic position and modern offshore banking system, Mauritius has naturally attracted the attention of drugs cartels, money launderers, and – there is some evidence to suggest – also international terrorists, and this has had a corruptive effect. In the 1980s, three members of the legislative assembly were implicated in drug smuggling, and in 1988 and 1989 two attempts were made to assassinate the then prime minister, Sir Anerood Jugnauth, which were attributed to drug cartels. More recently, a series of corruption scandals have rocked the government. An Independent Commission against Corruption has been set up, but it remains to be seen how effective it will be (*Mauritius News* 2003).

To combat potential terrorism, and under US pressure, the government introduced new legislation in 2002, which included giving the authorities the right to extradite terrorist suspects to foreign states, denial of the right to political asylum, and incommunicado 36-hour detention without trial for suspected terrorists (Amnesty International 2003). As noted above, this was strongly opposed by some sections of the population.

Internal security is primarily the responsibility of the approximately 4,000-strong Mauritius police, an intelligence agency known as the National Investigation Unit, and a paramilitary Special Mobile Force (SMF), while protection of the 1.8 million square kilometre maritime economic exclusion zone is the responsibility of the small National Coast Guard (Library of Congress 2003).

The SMF is to all intents and purposes an infantry battalion trained and equipped for conventional military operations, with a focus on internal security (Mauritius Police Force 2003; Jaddoo 2002: 9). Its motto is 'We'll do it, what is it?', which presumably is meant to indicate that it will do whatever is required of it (it reports to the chief of police), but could also indicate that there is some uncertainty about its role. It is certainly not openly discussed in Mauritius that the SMF, with no conceivable external role, is essentially a counter-insurgency force that could be used to combat public disorder and prevent unconstitutional changes of government (it also has some disaster relief and socio-economic development roles).

Security policymaking

There being no ministries of police, intelligence, or defence, security policy is largely the preserve of the Office of the Prime Minister, as the prime minister is responsible, with the chief of police, for overseeing all security functions. This makes for a somewhat closed policy process, despite the active interrogation in parliament of major security issues, and its active role in legislation (e.g. over the 2002 terrorism bill). There are few public expressions of national security policy. The prime minister's national security advisor, until recently a seconded Indian military or intelligence official, also plays an important role (Mauritius requested this secondment after the attempted assassinations of Prime Minister Jugnauth in the late 1980s).

Mauritius in SADC

Despite its multifaceted foreign policy concerns, as a result of its history of colonialism and settlement, its position in the Indian Ocean, and its extensive global trade links, Mauritius has been a keen and active participant in the OAU/AU, COMESA, and SADC. It has from time to time offered its diplomatic services in resolving African conflicts, and it has played a leadership role, e.g. in the SARPCCO and by hosting meetings of SADC, and in August 2004 it took on the chair of SADC. It has also formed close political and trade relations with South Africa since 1994, supported reform of SADC and the AU, and played a leading role in the New Partnership for Africa's Development.

Although it is considerably nearer to the African continent than it is to any other, Mauritius's commitment to SADC and more broadly to Africa might appear to be counter-intuitive, given the Asian origins of most of its population, the close relations between its Hindu elite and that of India, its global trade, and the almost complete lack of strategic threats from the African continent. Its turn towards Africa is perhaps better understood as a perception of opportunities rather than threats, and a recognition that in Africa Mauritius is a relatively bigger fish in a relatively smaller pond than it would be in Asia. In Africa it can 'make its mark', and it perceives growing trade opportunities as a 'gateway to Africa' (not to mention the enormous benefits it gains from AGOA). Nevertheless, it is evident that Mauritius has little objective interest in the security concerns of the continental members of SADC – war in the DRC or conflict in Zimbabwe, for example, is hardly likely to impact on Mauritius.

With Seychelles having withdrawn from SADC (on the grounds that it cannot afford the fees), Mauritius and Madagascar are the only AU member states in the Indian Ocean that belong to SADC, making it difficult to envisage what sort of role Mauritius could play in the unfolding development of the AU's and SADC's security architecture – notably the proposed establishment of a regional rapid reaction capability.

Mauritius is also a member of the Indian Ocean Commission (IOC), which draws together the five islands of the south-west Indian Ocean – Mauritius, Réunion (France), Seychelles, Comores, and Madagascar. Formed in 1982, the IOC has involved itself mainly in trade and economic issues. Although it has a political mandate, little has been done in the field of security, and the islands are all very different and separated by vast expanses of ocean. It seems unlikely that the IOC will take on security functions in the near future (European Centre for Development Policy Management/IOC 1998), leaving it somewhat unclear where the various island states of the AU fit in terms of the evolution of sub-regional security structures such as SADC.

Conclusion: democracy and security

While most – although not all – international relations scholars subscribe to the 'democratic peace' thesis (that democracy leads to inter-state and, perhaps to a lesser extent, intra-state peace), and most development theorists determine a relationship between socio-economic development and democracy, issues of cause and effect are highly contested (see Cawthra, 'Comparative perspectives on regional security co-operation among developing countries', in this study). Is democracy a cause of economic growth, or vice versa? Is peace an output of democracy, or does peace create conditions in which democracy can thrive? Is peace a result of economic development, or vice versa? These questions are probably impossible to answer, and generalisations over time and place are always dangerous.

What is clear, however, is that Mauritius has found itself in a 'virtuous circle' where socio-economic growth (with a social democratic component); democratic politics and institutions; and internal as well as external stability, security, and peace appear to have been contingent and self-reinforcing conditions. This has been helped by an electoral system that appears to have resulted in the need to build a political culture of tolerance based on building multi-ethnic coalitions, and has led to regular changes of government. It has also been helped by a relatively benign international political and trading environment, in which Mauritius has been able to develop relationships with a number of global and Indian Ocean powers, and by bilateral and multinational agreements that have assisted the country in diversifying and expanding its economy. While politics remains ethnically based and Hindu-dominated, and there are growing social inequalities and exclusions, there still appears to be sufficient give and take in the system to accommodate all ethnic and social groups and classes. This may not always be the case, and the events of 1999 indicate that social tensions may erupt at any point, especially if economic growth slows, and unemployment and social exclusion increase.

Nevertheless, Mauritius is fairly unique among SADC countries in that its political regime appears to be secure and unthreatened. From this position of strength, it has been able to engage constructively with the SADC common security project, and play a leading role in its reform, less from existential need than from a calculation of opportunities.

ENDNOTES

1 South Africa could be included in this list post-1994.

2 Costa Rica and Panama are the best-known examples of states that have deliberately dispensed with their defence forces, while a number of mostly small island states have insufficient resources for armed forces.

3 With a population in excess of one million, Mauritius technically falls outside this category, but it nevertheless shares many of the characteristics of small island states.

Chapter 7

Mozambique

Anicia Lalá

The vibrant and dynamic process of democratisation in Mozambique, despite its wide appraisal by the international community as having been successful, has strikingly demonstrated the feebleness of the celebrated 'end of history' thesis and has revealed the shortcomings of the triumph of the market economy.

The democratisation process that Mozambique is undergoing is proving to be a complex one, characterised by deep feelings of uncertainty as a result of the intertwined nature of multilayered transitions. In a country ravaged by 16 years of war (1976–92) between the Frente de Libertação de Moçambique (FRELIMO) government and Resistencia Nacional Moçambicana (RENAMO) rebels, the drivers of democratisation are found at various levels. At the international level, the end of the Cold War meant that the sources of support to the belligerents would be strained and that a generalised discourse on liberalisation of the economy would be strengthened in a context of democratisation. From a regional perspective, the fall of the apartheid regime in neighbouring South Africa, which constituted the major cause of destabilisation in Southern Africa in the late 1970s and throughout the 1980s, was a real catalyst. Thus, the removal of the source for aggression in the region, and of the major source of support for RENAMO, as well as the related events of democratisation in South Africa and the independence of Namibia, generated positive stimuli for the establishment of democratic systems elsewhere in the region. On a national level, the exhaustion of the belligerents, the intense internal public demands for the end of the war, and declining state legitimacy constituted crucial factors for the Rome Peace Agreement that provided for the restructuring of the political system.

The evolving situation from a centralised economy to a market economy (which started in 1987), the transformation from a one-party rule to a multi-party system, and the change from war to peace became key determinants that shaped the democratisation process.

The economy: quo vadis social development?

The economic discourse in the immediate period after the war increasingly emphasised the need for privatisation, the attraction of foreign direct investment, and the attainment of a strong macro-economic balance, as essential requirements for a strong and vibrant economy. Massive injections of external aid in the past decade have contributed to the celebration of high growth rates, on average 8 to 9 per cent from 1995 to 2001 (UNDP 2002: iii), and increasing economic recuperation. These macro-economic benefits, commended over time by the International Monetary Fund, including the increasing ability of the country to repay its debts (as a result of its enrolment as a heavily indebted poor country) and to control the level of inflation, do not seem to be matched in the micro-economic arena, nor do they seem to have improved ordinary people's daily lives. In any case, studies show that the trend in the economy is to recede. The Composed Indicator of Economic Activity in Mozambique shows that from 1991 until the end of 1995 the real economic activity of the country was boosted as a result of the end of the war, the relocation of people, the emergency rehabilitation processes, and the recovery of the normal activity of its enterprises. But the same did not hold from 1996 onwards. Even with a strong movement towards privatisation, which in turn swelled the numbers of the unemployed, the economy stagnated until 1999 and after that. The figures for foreign direct investment in 1999 amounted to USD 1.706 billion, against only USD 294 billion from national investment (Grobbelaar and Lalá 2003: 27). This reveals the weakness of national financial capacities, made worse by difficult access to credit with high interest rates, and thus leading to a situation in which the bulk of business activity is controlled by external capital (*The Economist* Intelligence Unit 2003: 10).

It is revealing that the Mozambican political elite are reacting by associating themselves with major projects, transforming themselves into a business elite through partnerships they are allowed to make due to their decision-making power over investment and the economy. The same conditions for 'self-empowerment' (!) are unfortunately not created at the level of medium and small enterprises, which are declining due to a low level of entrepreneurship trust (Ratilal 2002: 253) and are increasingly getting pushed into the informal sector, while the economy is mostly dominated by monopolies and oligopolies.

Nonetheless, government policy priorities have been to reduce poverty, and, in order to achieve that, the Action Plan for the Reduction of Absolute Poverty, 2001–2005 (Republic of Mozambique 2001) was adopted in April 2001, on the basis of the poverty reduction strategy paper developed in conjunction with the World Bank. Available data shows that 69.4 per cent of the population lives beneath the poverty line (UN 2000: 16). The human poverty index of the south of the country is 39.8 per cent, while at the centre it is 60 per cent, and in the north 64.3 per cent, revealing that there is a long way to go in addressing inequalities (UNDP 2000: 32). However, the sectors of investment priority have been education and health, and data reveals that the human development indicators are, surprisingly, rising, despite the hardships of the economy and the impact of the 2000 floods. But the figures still remain among the lowest in the world, with the country rating a human development rank of 170 among 173 countries (UN/Republic of Mozambique 2002: 4). Also of extreme concern is the impact of HIV/AIDS, which is expected to reduce life expectancy from 50.3 years to 36.5 by 2010.

The data presented above lead us to a panorama in which exclusionary tendencies between Mozambicans and foreigners, as well as within Mozambican society, and regional differentiations will increase the overall level of mistrust in society. Despite the government's commitment to poverty reduction and achievements in human development, the adoption of neo-liberal policies seems to have been accompanied by high levels of criminality and rampant corruption, contributing to the rise of human insecurity and, overall, pushing Mozambique in the direction of a more conflict-prone society.

Democratisation: the institutional framework

The democratisation process started with the adoption of a new constitution in 1990. This paved the way for multi-partyism and for the inclusion of different interests in the political system.[1] The first elections were held in October 1994, with over 88 per cent participation by the population, leading to a parliament constituted of 44.8 per cent seats for RENAMO and 55.2 per cent for FRELIMO. This was followed by an extensive process of country-wide consultation on various legislative matters (financed by the international community), and work towards the revision of the constitution, particularly to reduce presidential powers. Paradoxically, the major proponent of change – RENAMO – did not support the adoption of the constitution, as the second elections were approaching and its belief in victory led it to prefer to preserve the status quo. The first attempt to change constitutional rule into one more reflective of the general will of the country, while taking into account the concerns of minorities, was thus deemed to be a failure.

The country's electoral system does not enable further political inclusiveness. The system of proportional representation, with a threshold of 5 per cent of votes at the national level to hold a seat in parliament, in reality has become a bipartisan one. An additional layer, where more pluralism could be tolerated, is the decentralisation process. Through decentralisation, municipalities were instituted and local elections conducted. In 1998 the municipal elections took place with a low level of voter participation and amid a boycott by RENAMO.

The parliament, as the highest institution for governance oversight and for conflict resolution, is failing. Illustrative of this have been the developments since the second general election held in 1999, in which FRELIMO captured both the presidency and parliament, notwithstanding protests from RENAMO. After this, RENAMO almost rendered parliament non-operational with its boycott throughout the year 2000. The mostly low level of education, preparation, and experience of members of parliament for parliamentary tasks detracts from their capacity to carry out their functions. This in turn results in a stronger executive with ever more legislative power, and limited public access to information. The fact that this is an emergent democracy with deficits in democratic practices implies that parliament will take a long time to develop.

The non-parliamentary opposition is active in the social arena, trying to lobby the government and the head of state on certain matters. Recognising its role, former president Joaquim Chissano encouraged an informal network through which it was consulted as regards the country's major projects, such as in the pre-1999 constitutional revision, the land tenure discussion, or even Agenda 2025 (the project aimed at creating a national development vision for the country until 2025). This the government decided to leave in charge of a group of notable personalities from various religious, academic, political, and civil society organisations.

Socio-political dynamics and governance performance

A decisive element of the trajectory that the democratisation process will take is how state policies generate, maintain, and reinforce their legitimacy. Since democratisation is also about people's empowerment and their perception that the structures and institutions work towards the achievement of a common good, governance also comes into the picture. Mozambique's capacity is very limited, with few people with higher education qualifications in the state apparatus, and with low salaries that lead to corruption throughout the state bureaucracy. Efforts to transform this situation are being made. However, this implies a reduction in jobs, in a society with very weak social welfare safety nets, and without correspondent improvement in the delivery of services.

Although the education and health sectors are making progress, in the police, justice, and penal sectors the main deficits remain, contributing to the decline of state legitimacy and increased feelings of insecurity. Problems are related to lack of police effectiveness in the face of rising criminality, and organised transnational crime and corruption, compounded by a lack of qualified personnel, inefficiency, and chronic delays in the resolution of cases. More strategically relevant is the lack of an integrated vision of the whole judicial sector, which clearly needs to work in a co-ordinated manner. Profiting from these weaknesses, criminal and corruption networks seem to have taken root in society. Political will towards change in this state of affairs needs to be high, and measures such as the dismissal of the attorney general and six of his senior staff related to fraud allegations (US State Department 2001), although important, represent only 'the tip of the iceberg', since strong allegations exist that the major beneficiaries of these criminal networks are linked to the higher governmental and party structures. The controversial investigation and trial in November/December 2002 of the accused murderers of Carlos Cardoso, a journalist who uncovered a major corruption scandal in the banking sector and was murdered in November 1999, was seen as a key attempt to re-establish the dignity of the criminal justice system. Despite the openness of the trial to the media, the fairly competent way in which the process was handled by the judges, and the conviction of the accused, the perception that those ultimately responsible for the crime were not found or punished prevails in Mozambican society.

The media

Crucial to the development of governance practices is the role of the media as a watchdog, but also as an actor engaging in the dissemination of information and constructive dialogue in society. Democratic pluralism has been helpful, and the Mozambican media has grown steadily, both in numbers and in its capacity to intervene in society. The media has been vibrant in raising debate about the most controversial economic and political aspects of Mozambican society and fostering a diversity of ideas. However, sometimes the debate degenerates into extremist positions that contribute to polarising society.

After the events referred to above, media professionals were constantly harassed and threatened when reporting on these and other corruption-related events, but they kept an informative and challenging posture, not becoming intimidated. However, a major challenge still persists, which is that of improving the quality and depth of coverage, for which there are allegedly not many incentives due to meagre salaries and lack of adequate training (IRIN News 2002). Constraints on the impacts of the media are the high level of illiteracy and the limited circulation of newspapers in the rural areas, making the radio the most effective means of information. Nevertheless, overall the country seems to rate well in terms of press freedom, being one of the few in Southern Africa with empowering legislation (Pereira, Davids, and Mattes 2002: 6).

Civil society

A major positive development in the socio-political life of the country is the role played by movements from within civil society in deflecting tensions. These movements constantly appeal for and take initiatives to encourage dialogue when political crisis emerges or when political leaders make public suggestions using violent imagery. Also noticeable is the role of NGOs in coping with various socio-economic community activities and political issues such as civic education, which remain beyond the state's limited capability. Despite the controversial financial and ideological nature of some of these NGOs, and some of them being regarded as defending external interests, the facts that they were able to organise themselves into a network, LINK, and that they have been working in a more co-ordinated way with the government are improving the level of trust.

The role of religious institutions and traditional authorities in solving conflict at the community and local levels has been remarkable, with its multiplying effect on the wider societal process of reconciliation. Their recognition by the state after a decade of exclusion constitutes a new source of partnerships for the state and reinforces its legitimacy.

Notwithstanding the progress made by these three actors – civil society organisations, NGOs, and traditional authorities – a national survey shows that a gap exists between the interests of urban civil society and the majority of the rural-based population. The survey shows that NGOs partially face a problem of recognition, as people stressed that they rarely consult the communities; and that there are differing views concerning the attitude of traditional chiefs consulting their communities (UEM-CEP 2002: 41–43).

National security: the context for change

The transition from war to peace constituted the ground on which changes would be pursued in the national security arena. The country was faced with the major challenge of reconciliation and the implication at the time that this should be underpinned by the armed forces retreating from their prominent role in the country's affairs – a role held because of the war, not because they were out of the control of the political elite. The armed forces as the main instrument and actor of the war became the object of stigma and negativism from both society and the country's major donors.

Thus a major feature of the post-war period, rooted in the General Peace Agreement (GPA) (Republic of Mozambique 1993), was strong donor conditionality as regards the restructuring of the defence sector. Protocol IV established that the armed forces should not have more than 30,000 men, regardless of future threats that could arise. The fact that the major regional threat had disappeared led donors and some nationals to think that the armed forces did not have a strong role to play in peace time.

Priorities had to be set in relation to the reconstruction of the country, and combating poverty provided the discourse that would lead the way. The national elite was therefore left with very limited room to manoeuvre: the country needed massive injections of aid to stimulate economic take-off. Also, IFIs' expectations of the country were high. A structural adjustment programme had been in place in Mozambique since 1987, but the war had not allowed for any progress. The IFIs were also very reluctant to see any role for the armed forces, and the prescription was to downsize and cut the latter's budget, without any concern as to how the restructuring ought to be done. On the other hand, there was an extreme polarisation between the concepts of human security and state security and the notion that one could only be obtained at the expense of the other. This way of thinking prevailed in society, despite the fact that in the history of the country, the development of its armed forces had always been linked to the formation of the independent state, and during the struggle for liberation and in the immediate post-independence period, the armed forces had been seen as the guarantor of the nation and had organic ties with the people. This image was completely eroded when the armed forces stopped being able to offer protection to the people during the war, often relying on the latter's food provisions in order to survive.

Amid this environment and in the face of the fact that the armed forces, after the demobilisation of all troops, had to be rebuilt to comprise, on a 50-50 basis, men from both the guerrilla forces and the government troops, the political elite reacted by adopting the argument that the army should be built, albeit with reduced numbers, into a highly professional and efficient force. However, the elite security concerns in the immediate post-war phase, in a situation where the country was nearly dispossessed of any sovereignty due to the strong presence of the UN, remained unaddressed. These concerns might have been aggravated by regional developments, with the negative impact of the results of the elections in Angola in September 1992, which returned to war. This factor fuelled insecurity, especially taking into account RENAMO's threats to boycott the process throughout the period that led to elections in 1994. With the state of affairs in the new armed forces – Forças Armadas de Defesa de Moçambique (FADM) – the decision was taken to transfer to the police force the best of the operational commanders and soldiers from the former government troops who had decided to remain in the security forces, and the few operational weapons that existed at the time.

This short-term security concern moulded the framework that subsequently became the basis for the reshaping of the security sector. Despite this, there was already an acknowledgement of the need to concentrate on internal security, as the police had remained a marginal force throughout the war, and would now be faced with the task of providing a stable environment for the country, above all in order to attract foreign investment.

Constitutional and legislative provisions

The foundation of the new security sector is the constitution of 1990, which establishes the goals of national defence as being to defend national independence, preserve the country's sovereignty and integrity, and guarantee the normal functioning of institutions and the security of citizens against any armed aggression (Republic of Mozambique 1990: art. 59). It determines that the armed forces respect the constitution and the nation as a basic principle of democratic control of the armed forces.

The constitution defines the president as the commander-in-chief of the armed and security forces (Republic of Mozambique 1990: art. 117.4), and invests him with the powers to declare a state of war and its termination, a curfew, or a state of emergency; to sign treaties; to declare general or partial mobilisation; to preside over the National Defence and Security Council; and to appoint, exonerate, or dismiss the chief of general staff, the police commander, the branch commanders of the armed forces, and other superior officers of the defence and security forces (Republic of Mozambique 1990: art. 122). In order to establish checks and balances, the National Assembly must sanction the declaration of a curfew and a state of emergency; ratify international treaties; and define defence and security policy, once presented by the National Defence and Security Council. It also oversees the defence and security budget.

The establishment of the National Defence and Security Council (Republic of Mozambique 1990: art. 158) is also a positive factor, as it provides the president with a consultative organ to support him with informed and professional advice for decision making. The presence of representatives from all the security forces in the same organ, apart from providing accurate information about the situation on the ground, ensures that issues will be considered from various perspectives, and will, in principle, lead these forces to co-ordinate.

However, from the time of the peace agreement in 1992 until the elections in 1994 there was no clear policy direction on the armed forces, apart from the GPA and its rather general provisions. Indeed, it was only in 1997 that further legislation was approved creating the pillars for the defence and security forces. The Defence and Security Act 17 of 1997 determines the main principles as being: prohibition of political affiliation; priority for prevention of and negotiated solutions to conflict; commitment towards peace; reversion to force only in cases of legitimate defence; and contributing to a peaceful and secure climate in the region, the continent, and internationally (Republic of Mozambique 1997a: art. 2).

The act also outlines the restructuring of the sector according to the new roles and missions that are now separately defined: an external orientation for the armed forces and an internal one for the police. In summary, the defence forces are responsible for the integrity of national territory and sovereignty, the liberty of the citizens, securing the means of the nation's development, the protection and rescue of populations in case of calamities or accidents, participation in peacekeeping, and the maintenance of peace and respect for international law (Republic of Mozambique 1997a: art. 10).

Public order functions, on the other hand, include the assurance of public order and respect for the law, prevention and combating of crime, and border patrolling (Republic of Mozambique 1997a: art. 13). The act also covers the intelligence sector, and defines the State Security Agency's responsibilities as the compilation, research, production, analysis, and evaluation of information to assure the security of the state. Additionally it refers to its roles of preventing acts against the constitution and the functioning of state organs, and combating espionage, sabotage, and terrorism (Republic of Mozambique 1997a: art. 15). The act is supposed to precede sector legislation from each of these areas, but the defence sector is the only one to have produced such legislation.

The positive aspects of these advances in legislation are considerable in the context of Mozambique, since the country had previously not had any legislation to guide the sector, as all orientation and command in the past had come exclusively from the commander-in-chief.

Institutions

The new framework implied the creation of a MoD, detached from the military and as part of democratic oversight over the FADM. The FADM is thus subordinate in administrative and legal matters to the MoD. The minister of defence has to account for the sector, being responsible to parliament and the public for the performance of the armed forces. He/she is responsible for chairing the Defence Council, which comprises the chief of general staff and the commanders of the three services (army, air force, and navy). The armed forces are left with the operational aspects, namely the preparation for and execution of their missions. As a new structure, in its civil role the MoD is still confronted with serious capacity-building challenges in terms of management, recruitment, and maintenance of skilled personnel. Also, its articulation with the FADM and especially with the general staff headquarters needs to be improved. The process of clarifying the dividing lines between the daily activities of the organs of the MoD and the departments of the general staff headquarters has taken a long time, perhaps revealing a need for a major revision of both structures and respective competencies.

The National Council for Defence and Security started convening only in 2002, and that only because of the need to decide upon the participation of the FADM in the Burundi peace mission. This reveals that co-ordination among the institutions of the security sector is very weak, and that the discussions that should be evolving about improving the sector as a whole are dormant, or exist partially only between the head of state and the relevant minister.

The parliamentary committee for defence and public order constitutes only an embryonic organ for the further cultivation of accountability, since the average MP has to deal with the need to educate himself/herself about the functioning of a democracy, about parliament's own role and general parliamentary procedures, and only then about the specific issue for which he/she is responsible. Those who work on this committee also have another disadvantage, which arises from the fact of the security sector being a closed area about which information is difficult to obtain. Notwithstanding these disadvantages, the committee generates caution in the executive, as the latter knows it can be called to account.

Probably the most significant achievement in restructuring is that the ruling party no longer controls the armed forces. They comprise an independent institution which, so far, has remained true to democratic rule, never attempting to reverse the constitutional order.

Developing a national security policy

There is no evidence of a major vulnerability, threat, and risk analysis having been consistently done in order to inform the policies on defence and security. The policies were conceived on the one hand because the sector institutions were performing in a legal vacuum, and on the other because there was a need for a framework in which to start restructuring the sector. The acts were drafted mostly with the support of foreign advisors.

The initiative for the laws came from the executive, in spite of the constitution empowering the parliament with that task. This shows the weakness of the parliament in terms of its main legislative task, but the positive contribution was that it refused to pass the Defence and Armed Forces Act 18 of 1997 (Republic of Mozambique 1997b) before having a general policy on national defence and security. This, however, instead of being drafted through a wide consultative process involving all relevant state institutions, was left to the MoD. It would have been wiser to have involved the Ministry of Foreign Affairs, since the external missions assigned to the military are supposed to derive from political foreign policy objectives. In practice, it was probably counter-productive to wait for any contribution from the Ministry of Foreign Affairs, which is overstretched in terms of time and resources. Civil society made hardly any contribution to the act. The consultation process was very weak, and there was only one major seminar, organised by the MoD with the support of the African–American Institute, that allowed for discussion about security and defence in post-war Mozambique. It has to be recognised, however, that over time a culture of secrecy on security issues has been built in Mozambican society. Mozambican civil society, being itself under construction, either had a limited understanding of the issues or felt constrained. Its willingness to participate and debate defence-related issues was revealed to be limited, despite its necessary role as both a watchdog and as a contributor that could serve as a channel to express the needs and views of the people.

Since then, it seems that not much has evolved within the policy formulation arena in the MoD. The Ad Hoc Working Group established in December 1994, comprising representatives of the services and civil servants at the MoD, which prepared the draft of the acts on defence and security policy, defence and armed forces, and military conscription, seems to be in need of revitalisation. The group was apparently tasked with drafting the first-ever defence white paper, but so far this has not been completed. This is a necessary step, however. Once a proper threat analysis has been developed, there will be a basis on which to formulate the missing strategic defence concept (which once again should merit contributions from other ministries), so as to elaborate a military strategic concept and a strategic plan for institutional development for the MoD.

Policy implementation and performance

The concept of national security in the Defence and Security Act (Republic of Mozambique 1997a) was not widely contested. It has been the implementation process that has brought outrage from the general public, especially with regard to the incapacity of the police and the criminal justice system to deal with daily criminality and organised crime. Indeed, the shape, training, and quality of information of the police have been questioned in the light of the mounting threats linked to the drug trade and trafficking, money laundering, trafficking of human body parts, smuggling of goods, vehicle theft and bank robberies, organisation of assassination groups, penetration of the state and business by criminal networks, obstruction of justice, and corruption by criminal networks. How these threats are to be dealt with, when, and with which resources is still to be clarified, as there is not yet an integrated criminal justice system and correspondent policy. Nonetheless, the Ministry of Interior has developed the Strategic Plan for the Police of the Republic of Mozambique, 2003–2012 (Republic of Mozambique 2003), which was approved by the Council of Ministers in May 2004. People involved in the process revealed concern for the order of priorities, as all the work done hinged on the missing public order act. There are, however, current reassurances that the latter is in the pipeline. On the other hand, the justice sector also produced an integrated strategic plan, which was approved in 2002, but reveals only a minimal level of co-ordination between the police and the justice institutions concerning criminal justice.

Common to the process of policymaking is the fact that personnel are absorbed by daily tasks (which are in themselves emergencies, given the nature of the sector), and do not have time to complete the policy process. This is compounded by the fact that the intelligence sector has also not presented its act, leading to a reinforcement of the public image that the security sector remains a closed arena.[2]

Public discontent was also noticed in 2000 when major floods hit the country and the FADM did not have the capacity or organisation to intervene effectively, requiring massive support from neighbouring countries' military forces to deal with the situation. This raised major questions about the general state of the defence and armed forces sector, and appeals were made for the government to provide minimal resources for the operability of the FADM, especially taking into account its new tasks such as disaster relief, peace-support operations, assistance in fishery protection, and coastal patrol. Although government programmes in the two post-war mandates said very little about defence issues, they did mention them. The problem was that no decisions followed as to the medium- and long-term composition, equipment, training, and deployment of the FADM, or about the resources it needed to perform its missions.

Currently efforts are under way to implement the new organisational restructuring of the MoD, to finish the defence white paper, and to elaborate a strategic plan for the defence sector. Among other major projects are those to improve conditions in the military academy and to prepare troops to participate in peace-support operations.

Mozambique in the SADC project

Due to its recent history of armed conflict, and successful achievement and maintenance of a peace agreement, other countries have seen Mozambique as a credible intermediary in conflict situations. Mozambique has been involved in the Burundi peace process, acted when the Comores crisis erupted, and participated in the easing of tensions in Madagascar and in connection with the Zimbabwean crisis, among others. Its devotion to the regional project originates from an historical legacy of strong engagement as an active member of the FLS. The country was also deeply involved in the creation of SADCC and in the latter's transformation into SADC. Recently, Mozambique has been committed to the development of SADC's OPDSC. The country held the OPDSC presidency in 2002–03 and engaged in furthering the institutionalisation of its structures, including the elaboration of SIPO.

Mozambique has also taken an active part in the other mechanisms of SADC dealing with security issues, such as the SARPCCO, and has participated in regional peacekeeping exercises that took place in Zimbabwe and South Africa, 'Blue Hungwe' (1997) and 'Blue Crane' (1999), respectively.

Mozambique has also acceded to SADC's Mutual Defence Pact, viewing it as a way of deterring major outbreaks of violent armed conflict in the region, despite an understanding of the need to improve procedures.[3] A major question that could be raised is the extent to which Mozambique would be able to meet and maintain its commitments within the pact, should such need arise, since it possesses weak armed forces. Surprisingly, this does not seem to constitute a major problem for the government. Officials have indicated that Mozambique's contribution does not necessarily have to entail the deployment of forces, but that it can be made from a political standpoint, or in areas such as communication and command. The pact should also be looked upon as an opportunity for the country to start reorganising its forces in order to meet regional commitments.[4]

The decision to participate in the AU mission to Burundi is an indication that the country feels the need to have the capacity to engage in peace missions. The fact that Mozambique went through such pacification and is undergoing a democratisation process in a peaceful way has prompted international and, especially, continental pressure for the country to be visibly represented in peace missions in order to share its experience and to encourage the mission recipient country. Nonetheless, from the point of view of sustainability, it was questionable whether the country was really ready to engage in a mission such as the one in Burundi. Mozambique has previously sent observers to the DRC and had a small military police unit in East Timor, these being the only prior such engagements. The latter happened with the external logistical support of Portugal and, in the case of Burundi, this support came from the United Kingdom. The successful participation of the Mozambican contingent in the Burundi mission indicates that the country stands ready to engage its troops in similar missions, provided that financial and logistic support comes from external sources.

Concerning the impact that a country's domestic process of democratisation may have on its regional role, one senior Mozambican official argued that the strength of a country's image is proportional to its internal political developments, including its institutional management capacity and the guarantee of the liberties of its citizens. These constitute major factors in a country's credibility, especially as regards its involvement in conflict resolution.[5] In his view, the fact that various countries, such as South Africa, Namibia, and Mozambique, are undergoing democratisation processes is a positive regional indicator. This supports the building up of the perception that it is impossible to escape such a process, thus helping to forge the need to create common values. However, situations such as that in Zimbabwe and the trends in Swaziland show that the positive impact is limited, insofar as each country is following its particular way within different understandings of democracy. Such analysis is helpful to explain resistance to the consolidation of SADC structures – as the state-building process is occurring simultaneously along the lines of contested democratisation transitions, governments are very wary of discussing domestic security issues. The outcome is a situation where either the countries do not want to be confronted with a regional discussion on their domestic situation, or they want to bring it to the forefront of the agenda to legitimise and attain regional support for a pre-determined cause, which is often linked to the maintenance of a certain elite in power.

Conclusion

Democratisation in Mozambique reveals a highly exclusionary process, both from the political and economic points of view. The way out of the creation of an extremely polarised society lies in increased pluralism and tolerance of competitive views and interests in order to develop a more integrated, equitable, and cohesive society.

The impact of democratisation upon national security perceptions led to a total reorganisation of the security sector, by conceding priority to public security imperatives. Also, democratisation required the introduction of new practices for the oversight of the security forces by democratic institutions, although this needs to be strengthened, particularly as regards non-violent means of conflict management and resolution. The improvement of security sector management, the provision of adequate resources, and the enhancement of performance remain challenges, since security must be treated as a public good to be delivered to the people. This approach, embracing both state and human security, should be anchored in a national security policy. Its implementation, along with the consolidation of the practices of transparency and accountability, and the improvement of democratic control structures, will constitute a major achievement in the movement towards the democratic governance of the sector, so far embryonic.

The end of the internal war, the reformulated national security conception, and the historical commitment of the country towards integration in the region have led to the present situation where regional issues rate high on the country's agenda. Mozambique is totally committed to the regional co-operation goal, and its achievements during its presidency of the OPDSC demonstrated that it can assume a pivotal position, despite not being a regional power. The extent to which the country's devotion to the regional agenda might be curtailed seems to be only a remote scenario, created either by a most unlikely halt of the internal democratisation process through a new armed conflict, or by a power change resulting in a less politically and technically capable government that is unable to deal with its regional counterparts. The changeover from the Chissano to the Guebuza regime at the end of 2004, however, suggested that this is also most unlikely and that, if anything, Mozambique's ability to play a regional role is likely to increase.

INTERVIEWS

Official in the Ministry of Interior, April 2003.

Senior official in the Ministry of Interior, Maputo, 26 April 2003.

Senior official in the Ministry of Defence, Maputo, 4 April 2003.

Senior official in the Office of the President, Maputo, 22 April 2003.

Senior official in the task force working on the presidency of the OPDSC, Maputo, 3 April 2003.

ENDNOTES

1 Lalá (2002: 27); Ostheimer (1999: 3); Rocca (1998); Schneidman (1991).

2 Author's interview with Mozambican government official, April 2003.

3 Author's interviews with senior Mozambican government officials, Maputo, April 2003.

4 Author's interview with senior Mozambican government official, Maputo, April 2003.

5 Author's interview with senior Mozambican government official, Maputo, April 2003.

Chapter 8

Namibia

Bill Lindeke, Phanuel Kaapama, and Leslie Blaauw

Namibia has achieved a widely respected democratic political process following decades of apartheid oppression and military occupation. Repeated multi-party elections, good governance, a generally free media, respect for the constitution, and rule of law characterise 15 years of independence. On the human security side, Namibia has sustained modest economic growth with a strong spending bias toward human capital development in health and education. Extreme inequality and persistently high poverty and unemployment remain the most important challenges, complicated by very high levels of HIV infection, although good state and civil capacities are being brought to bear on these problems.

In respect of traditional state security issues, independent Namibia has had only brief encounters with violent threats to peace and security. The most serious problem involved the spill-over violence of Angola's civil war in a portion of the far north-eastern border area. Namibia also sent troops to the DRC (August 1998–September 2001) in defence of an embattled government there. However, despite being situated in such a 'bad security neighbourhood', the country has been remarkably tranquil since independence.

Democratic contributions from the transition to independence

In many ways, Namibia epitomises a successful transition for African human and common security (Forrest 2000; Bauer 2001). Following a protracted armed struggle for independence that drew in several countries, and extensive cross-border violence, negotiations took place in 1988, leading to a Tripartite Agreement that allowed a peaceful transition to independence for one of Africa's very last colonies. These negotiations directly involved the superpowers of the day, the immediate neighbouring countries that were part of the conflict, and the UN. However, the Namibian parties to the conflict were not included at this stage. These latter players had been part of the negotiations a decade earlier and became the grand architects of their own destinies after UN-supervised elections under UN Security Council Resolution 435, which took place in 1989.

Except for an initial spasm of violence in which People's Liberation Army of Namibia (PLAN) combatants were killed inside Namibia, the transition proceeded remarkably smoothly. Several thousand UN operatives serving in the UN Transition Assistance Group (UNTAG) oversaw the withdrawal of South African troops, the disarmament and demobilisation of PLAN fighters, the voluntary repatriation of Namibian exiles, the registration of voters, the electoral campaign, the conduct of the election itself, and the eventual transition to independence.

The South West Africa People's Organisation (SWAPO) – the UN General Assembly's declared 'sole authentic voice of the Namibian people' – captured 57 per cent of the vote from an incredible 96 per cent voter turnout in the seven-day-long voting for a 72-member Constituent Assembly. The South African-backed Democratic Turnhalle Alliance gained 27 per cent, and five out of the many other smaller political parties split most of the rest. These seven parties drew up a democratic constitution that was adopted unanimously to govern the newly independent country. As with other 'pacted' transitions, Namibia's elites were able to construct a consensus with the consent and co-operation of a multitude of external forces. This process launched one of the most successful transitions in Africa and among all democratic transitions of the 'Third Wave'.

As a result of the election, Namibians, through their elected representatives in the Constituent Assembly, were able to construct a widely admired democratic constitution, adopt and pursue a policy of national reconciliation, merge the previously warring armies, and create a stable democratic political system that became one of Africa's leading models according to a variety of standard criteria (Keulder 2003: 35).

Peace and stability

Namibia's new dispensation combined several features that account for the widely acknowledged success. The end of the war and of apartheid were both a cause and a consequence of the transition. The commitment to democratic practices and a mixed economy created a common agenda for moving the society forward. The policy of national reconciliation created the political environment to begin afresh to build a more just society. Finally, the policies of affirmative action and inclusion guaranteed that the new society envisioned would be dramatically more inclusive than the apartheid past.

Among the most important accomplishments of the new government has been the ending of decades of military occupation by colonial troops. Even today, more than a decade later, especially in the northern regions,

Namibians continue to credit SWAPO with the end of the military violence of occupation, and some indicate that they would continue to support the ruling party for this reason alone.

The first democratic accomplishment was the writing and adoption of the constitution by unanimous consent in the Constituent Assembly. Following general principles that were negotiated more than a decade before, the assembly was able to complete its work in a matter of weeks. The results drew widespread praise from all quarters. The constitution blended various institutional elements from different democratic societies and entrenched guarantees of human and civil rights.

One of the critical policies in helping to achieve this peaceful condition was that of national reconciliation. This policy had already been anticipated in meetings outside the country between SWAPO leaders and various internal elements of Namibian society. In particular, President Nujoma and many of his colleagues were instrumental in pushing the reconciliation agenda. During the first administration, opposition politicians were regularly included in deliberations and governing tasks (e.g. as the ombudsman and the auditor-general, and in cabinet and other posts), and an important participatory pattern was established that underpins Namibian democracy.

In the early phase of the 435 process, South Africa's last administrator-general in the territory issued a general amnesty for all politically related offences up to 1990, thus legally neutralising the issue of past actions for all sides. Since SWAPO had its own problems with the very large number of its own members imprisoned and tortured in the dungeons of Lubango, Angola (Leys and Saul 1995), all sides seemed to have a stake in moving forward rather than revisiting the past. This reconciliation policy repeatedly aimed at preventing the country becoming bogged down in recriminations over the past, and gave momentum to the necessary development of the society as a whole.

Democratic assessment

With the end of the Cold War, certain choices were closed to Namibians (returning to the bush with diminished international support), while others became all but inevitable (acceding to democratic practices and adopting a mixed economy). SWAPO embraced the new challenge enthusiastically, with the support of many old and new international allies. Namibia has retained strong international support in the form of larger donor assistance than average for African countries, in the large number of foreign embassies (more than 40) and international agencies (more than 12) present in such a small country, and in the leadership role that it has played in the numerous regional and international bodies where it is represented (more than 50 budgeted international memberships).

Free and fair elections subsequent to 1989 demonstrated that Namibia was capable of running its own democracy and abiding by the rule of law. Indeed, free and fair elections have been a hallmark of Namibian democracy. After the 1994 elections, in which the president was elected independently and SWAPO gained a free hand with over a two-thirds majority in the National Assembly, a discernible change was evident, with less concern for the involvement of other political players in governance. Such a change in attitude was only partial, but saw the emergence of less tolerant forces and tendencies within the ruling party. However, the overall democratic project has remained intact, and some democratic practices, forces, and institutions have become more mature and embedded in the political system. No dramatic overhaul of the constitution has ensued from the ruling party's two-thirds majority.

Among the highlights of institutional development is the increasing effectiveness of parliament. Although the absolute dominance of cabinet in the National Assembly weakens its critical checking and balancing roles, committees have become important access points for the public and oversight centres for parliamentarians. These committees comprise opposition members and SWAPO backbenchers. The Public Accounts Committee is led by an opposition member, and has become very effective in bringing budget and spending issues to public and parliamentary attention. Namibia plays a very active role in international parliamentary bodies and seems interested in adopting best practices whenever it is feasible. The National Council, representing the 13 regions with constituency-elected councillors, has taken its oversight role seriously by becoming an effective check on cabinet. Several pieces of important legislation have been sent back for reworking or have been rejected outright by the council, which has developed a less partisan working style.

Other constitutional and statutory bodies (auditor-general, Public Service Commission, Judicial Appointments Commission, Ombudsman's Office, and the higher courts) have also developed effective oversight capacities. Government has acceded to the findings of these bodies when it is found to be at fault, which is an important measure of the rule of law for a democratic society.

Civil society has several access points to influence policy beyond the ballot box, but has yet to regularise the practice. During the liberation struggle, civil society had been a strong 'substitute opposition' and it went into eclipse as the new government assumed many of the functions and personnel from pre-independence social opposition. Although people regularly express complaints through the radio call-in programmes, the most common public practice remains a pervasive self-censorship toward the ruling party, the military, and the national leadership, bordering on fear. Nevertheless, some sectors such as those concerned with legal rights, gender inclusion, and the environment do have strong and sustained inputs to the political system. Access to local government seems to be stronger than access at the national level at present. Hence it is hoped that the current extensive decentralisation exercise at the regional and local levels will increase public access and effectiveness.

Government does listen to the wider public, but many SWAPO leaders remain wedded to the liberation movement heritage of distrusting potential rivals. They seem to have an obsession with control, and to fear civil society becoming a 'shadow opposition' to the ruling party, especially in conjunction with external sources of support. In part, the strong support for the government of Robert Mugabe in Zimbabwe follows from these sentiments. Often, the inclusion of civil society is only *pro forma* or token, rather than substantive.

One area in which SWAPO and other interests in society have clashed is that of media freedom. SWAPO publishes a newspaper of its own (*Namibia Today*), established and controls the government paper (*New Era*), and controls the Namibian Broadcasting Corporation, whose radio service reaches by far the largest audience. Nonetheless, it has had several confrontations with the media over disliked coverage. This is true for the independent media and government-owned press as well, but the daily press, owned by whites, has been especially subject to criticism, and to the banning of government advertisements and government-paid subscriptions. Such a policy does not seem to have intimidated or harmed the media up to this point. Despite the coverage biases of incumbency and control over government media, most Namibians have many opportunities to be well informed.

In sum, it seems that Namibia has made the necessary policy and performance adjustments to continue the process of 'developing democracy', in Diamond's (1999) terms. Perhaps democracy is not yet consolidated in Namibia, but it has been sustained and advanced to some considerable degree of maturity. This has been greatly assisted by the generally prevailing peace and stability of the country since independence, the government's adherence to the constitution, and the policies of reconciliation and inclusion.

This assessment of Namibia's democratic performance is generally supported by international measures of various aspects of important democratic features and by the general level of social peace and satisfaction as measured in opinion surveys. In its *Human Development Report 2002*, the UNDP (2002) has assembled some of these measures, as has the African Development Bank's (2002) *African Development Report 2001.* One of the evaluations comes from the conservative Freedom House, which has regarded Namibia as 'free' since independence, based on policy and performance on a number of issues that the organisation regards as important. In the area of civil liberties, Namibia has rated a 3, and on political rights it has fared even better, at 2 (scores of 1, 2, and 3 are considered 'free', a designation achieved by only nine African countries). These scores have been consistent since 1991. In press freedom, Namibia rates a bit lower, due to the government's attitude indicated above.

On other measures, such as corruption, 'voice and accountability', law and order, government effectiveness, and gender inclusion, Namibia scores very positively – often second or third in Africa, often vying with its neighbours Botswana and South Africa (UNDP 2002). In sum, Namibia is consistently at or very near the top in Africa in measures of democratic performance. Furthermore, the country has done better than average in economic growth (achieving positive real per capita growth since independence, albeit modest compared to Botswana), and has stayed out of the debt traps and other financial difficulties that plague so many African countries.

This positive outcome can also be traced in the attitudes of the Namibian people. As measured in the Afrobarometer surveys, Namibians are among the most satisfied in the region – and in Africa – with the performance of government and trust in leaders. The most disturbing opinions among Namibians are related to the lack of general appreciation for democracy, and lack of strong opposition to anti-democratic actions. Keulder, an Afrobarometer researcher, claims Namibia seems to have a greater supply of democracy, from the constitution and the current political leadership, than there is a demand for it from the public. This is especially true of the main SWAPO base of support in the northern Oshivambo-speaking rural areas, and even more marked among rural Oshivambo-speaking youth. Higher education levels and more income are positively related to democratic values, which could mean improving conditions in the future due to Namibia's high levels of education spending (over 20 per cent of the budget), high literacy rates (82 per cent), and relative economic success (Keulder 2002).

Additional deficits and challenges to democracy and stability include both economic and political issues. On the economic side, Namibia continues to have one of the most unequal distributions of income and wealth in the world. Specifically, a very large body of relatively uneducated and unskilled people remain unemployed. Although the younger unemployed are likely to have more schooling, they are not appropriately trained for employment opportunities, especially given the high proportion of employed workers who have low-level skills. As in other developing and developed countries, unskilled work is not a high growth sector of the economy. Since independence, unemployment has been a source of social unrest (though isolated), especially among youth and former combatants. This issue has regularly generated some of the largest public demonstrations and marches to State House to attract the symbolic attention of the president, to whom everyone looks for solutions.

On the political side, Namibia has passed through the succession stage of transferring peacefully from the first independence leader to the next, with the retirement at the end of 2004 of President Sam Nujoma. However, like its neighbours to the south and east, Namibia is not likely to see a change of governing party any time soon, which is taken as an indication of democratic consolidation and maturity by some political scientists.

On the economic side, modest growth has failed to cut deeply into poverty and inequality. The modest growth rate in job creation from the private sector has put pressure on the government to grow its employment at an unsustainable rate. Inequitable distribution of land remains a major challenge, and there is some popular pressure on SWAPO to act on this issue. Thus far the land issue remains manageable under the current policy regime, though it will need increased resources and attention.

Despite success in extending education and primary healthcare, inequality remains a danger to peace and stability. This is especially true in terms of the crime and domestic violence that have accompanied Namibia's independence transition. However, the government has sound economic policies in place and there are good growth prospects in the medium term, while the concentration of the poor in low-density rural areas, coupled with strong support for the ruling party, reduces the political risk of inequality and poverty. Nevertheless, as in most Southern African countries, food security is a vital issue for the rural poor. Climate changes or recurrent droughts frequently put many households at risk. In 2002–03, hundreds of thousands of people were on food assistance programmes as a result of both drought and flood.

Finally, the impact of HIV/AIDS is an ever-present challenge to human and state security. Each sector of the economy must feel the impact – in education (teacher mortality and orphans in classes), in the workforce (shortages of key skills and high cost of replacements), and the general disruption of the society as people become ill and family life is threatened (ECA 2003: 49). The high point of the crisis is expected in the next few years, which gives little time to make adjustments. Namibia has been a bit slow and late in rolling out the treatment phase of its response, but has the advantage (like Botswana) of good infrastructure and a small population that makes it more affordable. Namibia's HIV/AIDS policy framework is well developed, giving some advantages in dealing with the pandemic.

Security legacies of colonial rule

Contrary to the assertion by Arlinghaus (1984: 17) that during the period of colonial rule in Africa the indigenous societies were largely demilitarised, some parts of Namibia under South African rule experienced the trauma of high militarisation. This reality is especially true for the area in and around the northern war zones, which experienced massive and prolonged direct military occupation. Apartheid military perceptions at times saw Namibia as a fifth province, and at others as a buffer against the African onslaught.

This state of militarisation was possible due to the various provisions of the South African Defence Act 44 of 1957, which tilted the scale of civil–military relations in favour of the colonial military's institutional interest. There were also other pieces of draconian security legislation, which bred a war psychology and whose application caused immeasurable hardship and suffering to ordinary Namibian citizens. These included the Terrorism Act 83 of 1977, which provided the security apparatus with extensive powers, including arrest without a warrant, trial, or legal representation (Ruppel 1987: 229; SWAPO Department of Information and Publicity 1987: 107).

As a result of the intensification of the war of liberation, the provisions of these laws were ruthlessly enforced by the colonial troops, who became active agents of coercion. This was manifested by the dusk-to-dawn curfews and the requirements that all persons above the age of 16 should carry identification documents at all times. Worse was the discretionary power given to the military arbitrarily to detain and interrogate a civilian accused of 'subversive political activism', as well as those suspected of concealing information on the whereabouts of PLAN combatants. Ruppel (1987: 227) described this state of affairs as the regime resorting to security laws to suppress legitimate opposition and 'to make up with institutionalised violence for what it lacked in legitimacy'. This could hardly have been expected to lay the basis of democratic or civilised norms.

Security legacies of the liberation movement

PLAN was established in 1966, based on a classic Maoist guerrilla army model (Brown 1995: 20). From its inception, PLAN was a political army that was required to maintain strong party–army interpenetrations. This posed a number of challenges for the SWAPO leadership in their quest for asserting control over the army. Hence the system of political commissars was introduced: such officers were not only responsible for approving military plans, as well as other operational functions at each level of the organisation, but were also tasked with the building of an ideological army with civilian dominance.

Therefore, in addition to waging a war of attrition, during their missions into the country, the combatants also had the responsibility of mobilising civilian support for their cause. The latter, according to Brown (1995: 29), helped the operations of PLAN in many ways – for instance, 'ammunition, grenades, mortars and landmines no longer had to be carried on human backs into northern Namibia, but could be loaded onto cattle or vehicles provided by business people'.

With the view of undermining the party through infiltration, the South African regime made various attempts at planting its agents both within the rank and file of the liberation movement membership and in the army. The pinch of these plants was felt by SWAPO from 1981, when both the PLAN command structure and the general SWAPO leadership came to the realisation that the enemy had extremely accurate knowledge of their movements and intentions. This led to the establishment within SWAPO of a specialised SWAPO Security Organisation (SSO) as the curator of internal party political order, with the absolute power to act against perceived threats to the party, as well as the ensuing identification of friends and foes of the party and its course. Given this high-profile and politicised security role, the organ quickly became an essential core of the liberation struggle, as it took on the mission of securing the party from both external and internal threats.

This culminated in the infamous and highly controversial spy drama, which was epitomised by the detention and systematic torture of hundreds of SWAPO members in prison camps in Angola in the 1980s, most notably at Lubango (Leys and Saul 1995: 6). This was, however, perpetuated not only for the strengthening of the party, but also to satisfy the preservation instincts of those constituting this security organ, and subsequently led to what Lamb (2000: 105) terms a severe civil–military imbalance in favour of SSO. Despite earlier insistence by the SWAPO political leadership that it had overall control of all military and political activities executed under the banner of the movement, the effective autonomy of the security organ was later recognised (though not widely) by some SWAPO leaders, such as Theo Ben-Gurirab.

Institutional restructuring in the post-colonial era

The implementation of Resolution 435 required prioritising an effective programme for the process of the disarmament, demobilisation, repatriation, and reintegration of ex-combatants, as initiated by UNTAG. Later, after independence, the new combined military was trained under an agreement with the British government, which supplied the British Military Assistance and Training Team (BMATT), thus giving additional professional reinforcement for civilian control.

Although issues of defence mainly remained a direct prerogative of the various organs of the South African government in Pretoria and Cape Town throughout the period of South African colonial rule over Namibia, on the ground South Africa created a number of military and quasi-military structures in its fight to retain control over the territory. For example, the notorious Koevoet, a police counter-insurgency unit, was formed in 1977 (Brown 1995: 23). Another such structure was the South West Africa Territorial Force, which, according to Cawthra (1986: 201), was conceived by South African military planners with a long-term role in mind, in particular that it would provide opportunities for indoctrination of recruits, who would then constitute the nucleus for the armed forces in the post-independence dispensation.

Of all these, only the South African Defence Force members were withdrawn back to South Africa. Therefore at independence Namibia was faced with the challenge of transforming and integrating security apparatuses that were inherited from the previous political dispensation, in order to bring them into line with the newly established political and constitutional order, although in practice only about 10 per cent of the Namibia Defence Force (NDF) came from the former military units allied to South Africa, the vast majority being from PLAN (Preston 1993).

Entrenching civil supremacy

As the defence and security establishments are entrusted with the responsibility for executing the important functions of national defence and security, there is a need to define the parameters for managing relations between armed forces on the one hand, and the broader interest of society, as represented by those elected and/or appointed to hold public office, on the other.

This reality provided the basis for civil supremacy, which requires the armed forces to exert their bureaucratic bargaining powers, while also requiring them to accept policy directives of elected political office bearers in general, and in particular that of the office bearer entrusted with the defence functions (Lamb 2000: 100). These principles strengthened the liberation tradition and were reinforced by the BMATT just after independence, when the different armies were consolidated into a common national military, the NDF.

Civil supremacy principles in Namibia derive their legal basis from article 1.2 of the constitution, which vests state power in the people and stipulates that this shall be exercised on their behalf by the democratic institutions of the state. These principles, together with other articles of the constitution, provide the mechanisms for effective subordination of the armed forces to civilian political control, by entrusting political office bearers with the overall policymaking prerogatives, including those relating to foreign and defence policies.

Further delineation of the defence force's professional competence, together with the limitations of its direct involvement in the political policymaking terrain, is provided for in the Defence Force Act 20 of 1990. The act distinctively allocates the respective institutional roles and identities of a civilian-led MoD on the one hand, and an army composed of a professional and politically sterile corps of professional soldiers on the other. According to these provisions, the ministry is responsible for instilling the relevant civilian expertise through its various support services, including the exercising of political authority. The armed forces are tasked with defending Namibia's territorial integrity and national interest.

Civilian dominance is complicated by the fact that, between the years 2000 and 2003, 61 per cent of the members of the National Assembly were either directly or indirectly members of the executive branch. This created a perception that the legislature is dominated by the executive. This has important implications for parliamentary oversight over public institutions in the security sector, as a cornerstone of good governance in the sector and for the transparency of security sector planning, management, and budgeting.

While it is appropriate that some information about the security sector is confidential, most of it can be made public without fear of compromising state security. A lack of transparency invariably undermines a country's long-term economic and political stability more than transparency damages its security. Namibia's liberation tradition of secrecy and closed command conflicts with the open democratic system that is being created: these two approaches remain contradictory and a cause for concern.

One indicator of the national perceptions of security is found in the allocation of public resources to security agencies in relation to other public institutions and functions. Table 1 provides outlines of such allocation in the 2004 budget to three agencies of state operating in the security sector: the NDF, the State Security Agency (SSA), and the Special Field Forces (SFF).

Average allocation to the security sector (defence, state security [intelligence], and the SFF [a kind of gendarmerie]) as a percentage of the country's GDP since independence has been nearly 3 per cent, peaking at 4.5 per cent in 1999. Increases in defence spending can be seen as running parallel to slight declines in health and education budget shares, despite improved state security conditions after the end of the civil war in Angola.

Table 1: Public sector expenditure on the security sector

Year	Total public sector expend-iture	Allocation to the MoD		Allocation to the SSA		Allocation to the SSF		Alloca-tion to the security sector as % of GDP
	NAD millions	NAD millions	As % of national budget	NAD millions	As % of national budget	NAD millions	As % of national budget	
1990	2,175.7	119	5.5	0	0	0	0	1.9
1991	2,897.5	188	6.5	0	0	15.4	0.5	2.8
1992	3,382.0	190	5.6	0	0	17.9	0.5	2.5
1993	3,386.3	180	5.3	0	0	14.6	0.4	2.0
1994	3,738.5	214	5.7	17.6	0.5	10.9	0.3	2.0
1995	4,380.0	275	6.3	19.5	0.5	18.0	0.4	2.4
1996	5,325.1	382	7.2	17.5	0.3	28.3	0.5	2.8
1997	5,778.3	414	7.2	25.9	0.5	48.2	0.8	2.8
1998	6,446.2	521	8.1	28.7	0.5	80.1	1.3	3.3
1999	8,009.3	789	9.9	22.1	0.3	150.0	1.9	4.5
2000	8,761.9	785	9.0	41.2	0.5	219.6	2.5	4.2
2001	10,492.0	905	8.6	38.6	0.4	233.0	2.2	4.3
2002	11,477.5	935	8.2	41.2	0.4	267.0	2.3	4.0
2003	12,256.7	879	7.2	46.6	0.4	193.8	1.6	3.2

Note: In the 2004 budget speech and documentation, these trends continued with slight declines in personnel countered by slight rises in spending (Ministry of Finance 2004). There were 16,091 funded positions in the NDF, while NAMPOL had 12,508. Defence spending totaled NAD 1,087,888,000, up by NAD 94 million on the year. The SFF had over 6,000 positions with more than NAD 265 million budgeted. National Intelligence received over NAD 45 million. No changes in existing trends were indicated, e.g. before the 1999 presidential election, thousands of new security sector jobs were created largely through the establishment of the SFF.

The NDF received on average 7.2 per cent of the national budget between 1990 and 2003. The allocations rose gradually until 1999, when they peaked at close to 10 per cent. Overall, defence has been the fourth-largest spending vote after basic education and culture, health and social services, and finance (Sherbourne 2001: 1). Defence spending is also often favoured in the additional budgets midway through the fiscal year, when the allocations receive less attention.

Security institutions

The overall staff component of the MoD for the NDF in 2003 consisted of 17,441 positions, of which only 15,834 were filled. This compares with the Namibian Police Force (NAMPOL), which was allocated almost the same number of positions in its establishment (17,034), of which only 11,656 were filled (Republic of Namibia n.d.: 18). As recently as 1998, the figures were half this number. The war in the DRC and an attempted secession in the Caprivi sparked a significant increase in military spending and presence in the country. The addition of expensive air and marine wings have also had budget implications. Older equipment will need future replacement and updating as well.

Apart from its engagement in regional and international peacekeeping operations, the NDF has maintained an active peacetime role of complementing various efforts of civil authorities and communities alike. These included protection of the Namibian territorial waters in collaboration with the Ministry of Fisheries and Marine Resources, and undertaking joint operations with NAMPOL. It has also undertaken emergency and rescue missions, including the combating of bushfires, and most importantly de-mining operations in the northern regions of Kunene, Omusati, and Ohangwena, where hundreds of unexploded mines from the war were left scattered.

A company owned by the MoD, called August 26th, with a board comprising senior uniformed and civilian officials in the defence sector, has emerged in recent years as a significant new player. It has some important roles that are not yet clearly defined. In the investment portfolio of this company is the ownership of a diamond mining concession allocated to the Namibian government by the then government of the DRC, as compensation for the cost of Namibia's efforts to save the regime at a critical moment. Although the costs of these military activities were born by the state revenue fund, the accruals from this venture filter to the coffers of a state enterprise owned by the MoD rather than to the general government revenue that bore the burden of the initial expense. The diamond mine issue has attracted questions in parliament by the opposition, but with little follow-up.

Although it remains difficult to establish the operations and structure of the National Intelligence Security Agency (located in the Office of the President) due to a dearth of reliable data on its operations, expenditure, and staff component, the lump sum allocations are reflected in the national budget documents. According to the figures provided in these documents, the allocations to the intelligence agency have never exceeded 0.5 per cent of the national budget, and from 2001 to the present they have been on a slight decline. The agency had a budget of NAD 46 million (USD 4.6 million) in 2003. However, the taxpayers and the general public remain in the dark regarding the actual role of this agency and how the funds appropriated to it are being used and accounted for. Staff numbers probably range between 200 and 400 if other ministries with similar budgets can be used as a measure. These are over and above the VIP security troops, who now outnumber the police involved in crime fighting! Allegations of the intelligence agency monitoring political figures surface from time to time (*Windhoek Observer* 2003), but neither the Caprivi incident nor the *Uniao Nacional para a Independencia Total de Angola* (UNITA) incursions from Angola in the north-east seem to have been anticipated in any effective way by any of the intelligence community.

A final security structure to consider is the SFF, which was established as a division of NAMPOL just before the presidential elections in 1999. It was formed as one of the employment strategies that resulted from sustained public demonstrations and job protests by the war veterans. The SFF's primary responsibilities are those of preventing crime and the maintenance of internal security and law and order and, more specifically, the suppression of illegal civil disturbance. It provided the personnel to saturate the north-east in response to the Caprivi incident and UNITA cross-border violence. It has come in for serious criticism for its lack of training and professionalism, and over the years several brutality charges have been laid against its members. The allegations are summarised in the annual reports of the Namibia Society for Human Rights, a controversial self-appointed watchdog NGO.

Civil society

Creating a climate in which civil society can actively monitor the security sector and be consulted regularly on defence policy, resource allocation, and related issues is essential to the process of fostering common ground on what constitutes a threat to national security or how to go about the promotion of national interests. In Namibia the security sector, perhaps with the exception of NAMPOL, is largely detached from the scrutiny of civil society and the general public.

In fact, the relationship between the media and the NDF (and the MoD in particular) reached boiling point in 2001, when the defence bill was presented and debated by parliament. This resulted from three sections of the bill that were seen by media practitioners as having been designed to muzzle them. These sections codified restrictive measures that rendered the disclosure of unauthorised security information or information calculated or likely to endanger national security or the safety of the members of the NDF a punishable offence (MISA 2002: 77).

Namibia's role in regional security

Namibia at independence was well positioned to lend scope and provide guidance to achieving regional objectives made possible by the end of both apartheid and the Cold War. Indeed, the Statement on Defence Policy (Republic of Namibia 1993) reflects the state's perception and approach to regional security by emphasising that

> Namibia's foreign and defence policy is founded on the principles of peaceful coexistence and cooperation with other countries and in operation of international law. The day-to-day guarantee of security lies in the maintenance of international order and, in particular, in regional stability. Defence relations with neighbours and the international community as a whole are good, and the Ministry of Defence and Namibia Defence Force will extend military co-operation and links as far as is practicable. Prospects for regional stability and co-operation in the 1990s are encouraging, but despite this, and the assessment that the threat is low at present, defence policy must be based on the premise that Namibia may face a regional security threat in the future (Republic of Namibia 1993: 6).

This statement is underpinned by constitutional principles that outline Namibia's foreign relations. Article 96 of the Namibian constitution states that

> [the] State shall endeavour to ensure that in its international relations it
>
> - Adopts and maintains a policy of non-alignment;
> - Promotes international co-operation, peace and security;
> - Creates and maintains just and mutually beneficial relations among nations;
> - Fosters respect for international law and treaty obligations;
> - Encourages the settlement of international disputes by peaceful means.

The Namibian government has concluded various bilateral defence and security agreements with Southern African countries. It signed a Protocol of Understanding with its Botswana counterpart on defence and security in Windhoek on 26 July 1990 (Republic of Namibia. Office of the Prime Minister 2000). Namibia also concluded a Joint Permanent Commission on Defence and Security with Angola, and a Joint Permanent Commission of Co-operation with Zambia (Du Pisani 2001/2: 18) and with Tanzania (Du Pisani 2000). It also signed an agreement with its South African counterpart on cross-border policing, aimed at combating drug and arms smuggling, and vehicle theft. Details of an agreement with the DRC on bilateral security co-operation remain a closely guarded secret (Cilliers 1996).

Namibia was also successful in peacefully settling its dispute with South Africa over Walvis Bay, the country's principal port, and the Penguin Islands off the Namibian coast: at independence South Africa retained control over both of these. The 1999 ruling by the International Court of Justice that peacefully resolved the dispute between Namibia and Botswana over the Kasikili/Sidudu Island in the Chobe River is a positive sign for the prospects for peaceful resolution of conflicts in the region (Blaauw 1995). The attitude of the leaders and people in general with regard to the court's ruling was, in the words of Anne Mutelo of the Ministry of Foreign Affairs, 'to agree to disagree, but this did not lead to the outbreak of conflict'.[1] In fact, the two countries embarked on a mutual collaboration to demarcate the rest of their boundaries in a joint exercise, completed in late 2002 and ratified in the following year.

Namibia is also actively involved in the region's security co-operation practices, and the NDF has participated in several joint regional exercises. The country's concern with regional peace and security is further reflected in the active role it has played in UN peacekeeping efforts in Angola (Du Pisani 2000). During its tenure as a non-permanent member of the UN Security Council, the country left its imprint on the international stage, with important initiatives and actions in respect of various international conflicts, such as those in Angola, Burundi, the DRC, Ethiopia and Eritrea, Liberia, and Sierra Leone. In addition, Namibia drafted and piloted a resolution that acknowledged that aggression had been committed against the DRC by its neighbours (Rwanda and Uganda), and drew a distinction between invited and uninvited forces in the DRC. The country has furthermore insisted that human rights and humanitarian assistance be included in the mandate of the UN peacekeeping force in that country.

Namibia played a similarly active role in advancing peace in Angola. In 1999, it was part of a panel of experts, under the leadership of Sweden, which was tasked with the responsibility of tracking violations of sanctions that were imposed by the UN against UNITA (Du Pisani 2001/2: 18). Arguably, these achievements have contributed to enhancing the prestige of the country as an important role player in improving regional security. The country also ratified the UN Convention on Transnational Organised Crime, which deals in part with trafficking in people (*Mail and Guardian* 2003).

Since the end of the 1990s, Namibia's regional security policies have been increasingly scrutinised for the controversial decisions that accompanied its decision to become militarily involved in both the Angolan and DRC conflicts. To Anne Mutelo of the Ministry of Foreign Affairs, the protection and enhancement of national interest were the primary factors that motivated Namibia's involvement in the DRC. She claims that

> Namibia's involvement in the DRC was indeed due to the protection of our national interests. Had Namibia not become involved together with its allies, the chaos brought about by the conflict in that country would have engulfed the whole Southern African region. Due to Namibia's proximity to Angola, the conflict in the DRC would have resulted in refugees fleeing that conflict coming to Namibia, since Angola was also still in conflict. This would have meant stretching our national resources to the limit leading to social and economic problems.[2]

Yet Namibia's involvement in both Angola and the DRC received severe criticism. Such criticism stems in part from the fact that the issue of who the primary determinant of foreign policy is has not yet been resolved. In this regard, Du Pisani (2000: 299) posits: 'In the case of new States such as Namibia, presidents and the executive often dominate aspects of their countries' foreign policy.' Yet, the controversy that Namibia's involvement in the DRC evoked also serves as a reminder that '[t]here are, indeed, competing bureaucratic and personal interests involved in the making and conduct of foreign policy' (Du Pisani 2000: 307).

To Tsie (1998), it was the absence of a functioning SADC security structure that prompted Angola, Namibia, and Zimbabwe to assist the Kabila government in the DRC. More poignantly, Du Pisani (2001/2: 17) reminds us that '[r]egional or sub-regional security regimes may help to keep non-democratic governments in power and to protect fragile governments that might otherwise have imploded. The conflict in the Democratic Republic of Congo … is a good illustration of this.' It also demonstrates that the disposition of SADC member states remains important in determining the state and character of regional security. At the 2003 summit in Tanzania, SADC heads of state signed the Mutual Defence Pact, which commits member countries to act (in some fashion) in the event of external or internal aggression against a member state. It is hoped that this pact will provide the vehicle for SADC to link to the AU's peace and security mechanism.

In the final analysis, what Namibia's involvement in both Angola and the DRC demonstrates is that the military has become politically more influential. Yet Namibia has a functioning democratic system in which there is considerable public input. In this respect, the perceptions of the Namibian population that the threats to its security may be more related to social, health, and economic issues than military threats are being expressed. The question then becomes whether a political system so thoroughly dominated by one political party will listen to these concerns.

Political transition

The year 2004 may be known as the year of elections for Namibia. Three sets of successful elections were held: first, the local council elections in May, then parliamentary and presidential elections in mid-November and, finally, regional council elections in late November. In addition to the continuity of the election results, featuring huge SWAPO majorities with fragmented opposition parties still surviving, the most important change was the smooth succession process that unfolded. President Nujoma kept everyone guessing until the last moment concerning a possible fourth term, but successfully engineered a transition process, filled with drama, that guaranteed continuity of leadership and political stability.

Newly inaugurated President Pohamba has generally pursued a policy of continuity, yet he has also attempted to heal the election wounds within SWAPO and established an anti-corruption emphasis to mark his distinct style as president. He has rotated some security sector leadership, but has not altered the basic policies in place thus far.

Conclusion

The attainment of independence by Namibia was an important development in fostering an environment for the promotion of regional peace and security. Both governmental and non-governmental actors in an independent Namibia have been expected to play an active role in the reduction of tension and the promotion of mutual security. Namibia has made an important contribution not only to the enhancement of its own safety, but also to the promotion of regional security.

As the scene of one of the most successful transitions to peace and democracy in Africa, the country could perhaps have done more in terms of reinforcing the regional processes for multilateral confidence building and balanced civil–military relations. A greater focus on human and common security is both a Namibian and a regional need. As a successful democratising country characterised by peace, stability, and development, Namibia should be both a role model for its neighbours and a catalyst for the spread of its success.

ENDNOTES

1 Personal communication to the author, 3 June 2003.

2 *Ibid.*

Chapter 9

Seychelles

Anthoni van Nieuwkerk and William M. Bell

Seychelles, one of the world's smallest nations, comprises 115 islands, all of which were uninhabited until 1756, when French planters and their slaves settled. Possession of the islands alternated between France and Britain several times during the French Revolutionary and Napoleonic periods, until finally France ceded Seychelles to Britain in 1814 in the Treaty of Paris. Britain administered Seychelles as a dependency of Mauritius, from which the islands received little attention and few services, although they were gradually granted increasing administrative autonomy. In 1888 separate nominated administrative and executive councils were established for Mauritius and Seychelles, and in 1903 the islands became a crown colony separate from Mauritius. The involvement of Seychellois in their own political affairs began in 1948 after World War II, when Britain granted suffrage to approximately 2,000 adult male property owners.

In 1964 two parties emerged on the political scene: the Seychelles People's United Party (SPUP) and the Democratic Party (DP). Both were determined to improve local conditions and to develop popularly based local politics, but they differed in substantive ways. The SPUP had a socialist ideology, favouring worker-oriented policies and pressing for complete independence from Britain and a non-aligned foreign policy, while the DP took a more capitalist approach, and wanted to continue the association with Britain and to allow British and US military bases on the islands.

Continuous and mounting demands from the Seychellois for an increased share in running the colony's affairs prompted Britain to enact a series of constitutions for Seychelles, each of which granted important new concessions. The first universal suffrage election took place in 1967. In 1970 Britain set up a ministerial form of government and gave Seychellois the responsibility to administer all but external affairs, internal security, the civil service, and the government's broadcasting service and newspaper. The opening of an international airport on the east coast of Mahé in 1971 improved contact with the outside world. The end of the islands' relative isolation led to an expansion of tourism and concomitant booms in foreign capital investment and the domestic construction industry.

Finally, Britain granted the colony complete independence, and on 29 June 1976 the Republic of Seychelles became a sovereign nation.

Governance and democracy

After independence in 1976, Seychelles was ruled for less than a year by Sir James Mancham as president. With the support of Tanzania's Julius Nyerere, France-Albert René, the prime minister, led an armed coup in 1977 that toppled Mancham and sent him into exile (Franda 1982). The new president, René, a Marxist, pressed ahead with quite radical socialist programmes, including state control over all sectors of the economy. In 1978, the SPUP became the Seychelles People's Progressive Front (SPPF). This was followed in 1979 by the institutionalisation of the one-party state system. A new constitution was adopted in that year, which provided for a strong executive headed by the president, and a legislature of 23 elected and two appointed members. The government proceeded with its programme to set minimum wage levels, raise government salaries, improve housing and health facilities, broaden educational opportunities, provide social security coverage, and generate employment in agriculture and fisheries. The socio-economic indicators improved markedly. During the 1970s and 1980s several coup attempts were made, including one launched from South Africa in 1981, inducing the René government to become more autocratic.

In 1989 René was elected (in a poll in which he gained 96 per cent of the votes cast) for a third five-year term. He was selected by his party as the sole candidate. His domestic position therefore appeared secure. However, external factors forced a change. The collapse of communism in Eastern Europe meant that he lost his powerful Soviet protector. At the Commonwealth heads of government meeting in 1991 he came under considerable pressure from the British and other governments to introduce democratic reforms. The Government of France, a major aid donor, made it clear that it expected political changes – President Mitterand had visited Seychelles in 1990 as part of an Indian Ocean tour. It became clear that Seychelles would find itself increasingly isolated if it continued to pursue uncompromisingly socialist policies. As Bennett (1993) argues, other countries in Africa were dismantling one-party states in the face of the new winds of change blowing across the continent – a further incentive for the regime to modify and adapt its mode of governance. Finally, René could no longer ignore economic factors. In 1991 Britain and France, the main donors, cut aid to a trickle. That year, for the first time since 1983, Seychelles registered a negative economic growth rate, largely due to the fall in tourist numbers during the Gulf crisis.

In December 1991 René caused surprise when he called an extraordinary congress of the ruling SPPF. He announced a complete reappraisal of policy and the introduction of a pluralist political system, inviting all exiled Seychellois to return to play a responsible role in the affairs of the state.

There were three phases in instituting the new constitutional dispensation. The first involved the setting up of a constitutional commission; the second was the drafting of a constitution to be tested in a referendum; and the third, multi-party elections (Bennett 1993: 363; Hatchard 1993). A constitutional conference was convened, the composition of which was based on support obtained by popular vote. Seven newly established political parties participated in the process, and members of the public were also invited to provide their input. The first draft of the constitution failed to receive the required 60 per cent majority in a referendum. The new and current constitution was approved by 73.9 per cent of the voters in a referendum held on 18 June 1993 in a relatively smooth process. This was followed by the first democratic elections in July 1993. The SPPF gained 57 per cent of the vote, and 27 of the 33 seats in the National Assembly (Lodge, Kadima, and Pottie 2002: 280).

The constitution limits the president to three five-year terms of office. And, in contrast to past practice, it now requires the president to make appointments to public offices from a list of candidates proposed by an Independent Constitutional Appointments Authority or from the existing civil service. With regard to membership of the National Assembly, nominated members were replaced with a system whereby elections are held on both a constituency basis and by proportional representation. A charter entrenches fundamental rights and freedoms in the 1993 constitution. This charter defines a democratic society as a pluralistic one in which there is tolerance, and proper regard for the fundamental human rights and freedoms and the rule of law, and where there is a balance of power among the executive, legislature, and judiciary (Hatchard 1993: 608). Regarding the declaration of a state of emergency, the 1993 constitution imposes strict safeguards.

As elsewhere, the development of multi-partyism in the Seychelles has seen the launch of competing newspapers (all in Victoria, the capital) – most new publications support one or the other opposition party. The 1993 constitution requires the state to ensure that the state-owned/controlled broadcasting service operates independently and affords 'opportunities and facilities for the presentation of divergent views'.

Having somewhat improved its image abroad, René's administration relied on a robust economy, a relatively high standard of living, and a generous welfare system to catapult itself and the ruling party to a landslide victory (67 per cent of the vote) in the March 1998 general elections. While partiality and intolerance contributed to the electoral landslide, a divided opposition without a clear strategy was no match for the SPPF, particularly with its dominant control over local administration facilities and the welfare budget, which may have played a decisive role in the outcome of the election.

The electoral system makes provision for funding of political parties through the Political Parties (Registration and Regulation) Amendment Act of 1996. Funding is based on the percentage of votes obtained at the preceding general election. The SPPF thus obtained a significantly greater share of budgetary resources, which was coupled with its strength in access to district council administration facilities and local district SPPF administration support facilities.

Early presidential elections were held in September 2001 and National Assembly elections in December 2002. In both instances the SPPF won, although the Seychelles National Party (SNP) candidate captured 44.95 per cent of the 2001 presidential votes, as opposed to 54.19 for the SPPF presidential candidate, René. This was despite the latter's ability to tap into the comprehensive SPPF party machinery and his access to greater budgetary resources.

On 24 February 2004, during his state of the nation address, President René indicated his intention to resign the presidency. On 14 April 2004 he resigned, and nominated his appointed successor, James Alex Michel, formerly the vice president of Seychelles (since the introduction of the office of vice president in 1996). The presidential transition was peaceful, with discontent limited to the opposition SNP. The international community, by and large, applauded the peaceful leadership transition. René retains the influential position of president of the SPPF, and will attempt to breathe new life into declining party support and rejuvenate the party machinery. Immediately upon taking office, the new president set about establishing his own credentials. He began with a programme of consultation and dialogue, in an effort to re-establish the confidence of the business community. This was quickly followed by further liberalisation of the trading regime, removal of stringent import licensing controls, and the gradual reduction of the state monopoly on imports enjoyed by the government parastatal, the Seychelles Marketing Board (SMB). A review was conducted of government ministries, and these were effectively streamlined in an effort to reduce budgetary expansion and improve the level of service and efficiency. The consultation dialogue was widened to include grassroots communities, with meetings held in all districts in an effort to re-establish confidence within the community. This community participation exercise has resulted in government becoming more aware of the grassroots concerns of the population at large, giving it sufficient time to make the necessary administrative and developmental changes before the 2006 elections.

In some senses, the ghost of Seychelles's one-party past lingers on. According to observers from the Francophone Community and the Commonwealth, the 1998 elections were free and fair. However, they noted that the results could have been unduly influenced by the payment of social security benefits through accelerated means testing just before the election. Consequently, the group recommended a bipartisan review of the separation of state and party political functions. Furthermore, the president's array of powers (head of state, head of government, commander-in-chief of the armed forces, appoints ministers, personally in charge of several ministerial portfolios, titular head of the ruling party) gave René uncontested influence in two of three branches of government. His victory in 1998 was also due in part to his overwhelming political advantage at the local level. All seats on the 23 elected district councils – formerly SPPF district branch committees – were held by ruling party members. And indeed, the ruling SPPF continued to dominate the Seychelles political party landscape, as it has done during 27 years of uninterrupted rule. Today, under a new president, the power arrangements remain.

Democratisation or liberalisation?

Various factors impact on the political landscape of the Seychelles. The population comprises people of African, European, Indian, and Chinese origin. Racial identities, especially Chinese and Indian, play an important role in the formation of political alliances. While successful elections in Seychelles have become commonplace, it is a young democracy with significant centralising tendencies, and still faces many challenges of democratic institution building and the cross-fertilisation of the political roles of the judiciary, the legislature, and the still very strong executive. However, the single largest political issue facing Seychelles is the implementation of its economic liberalisation programme, as the government continues to control nearly 70 per cent of the economy, largely through the SMB.

The fourth phase of Seychelles' transition to a liberalised democracy began effectively in June 2003, with the introduction of the Macro-economic Reform Programme (MERP), which was launched during an SPPF extraordinary congress. The MERP is designed to tackle many of the issues that have marked much of the criticism levelled at the SPPF over the years since the introduction of multi-party politics. It has received the conditional support of the IMF and the World Bank, and has been well received by Seychelles' bilateral partners.

The thrust of the MERP is to correct the fundamental macro-economic imbalances in the economy, so as to provide a platform for economic recovery. It impacts on all economic players, with the emphasis on government budgetary and fiscal restraint in order to achieve budget surpluses from 2003, supported by a reduction of ministerial budgets of between 10 and 15 per cent over three years, the cessation of budgetary subventions to parastatal organisations, and a reduction in capital expenditure. Measures have been taken to remove excess liquidity in the system, with controls maintained over inflation and interest rates.

The MERP has involved the introduction of a goods and services tax, coupled with a gradual reduction of trade import tariffs, in keeping with the call for a liberalised tariff-free trade regime promoted by the regional trading blocs, particularly COMESA and SADC.

The MERP also includes a more liberalised trading regime with a gradual reduction in the SMB monopoly on imports of essential commodities, a review of the exchange rate mechanism, increased privatisation of state assets, a review of the existing social sectors, and a restructuring of the civil service. Seychelles representation abroad has been the first casualty of the restructuring process with the closure (or suspension) of embassies in London, Kuala Lumpur, and Pretoria.

The MERP has to date achieved a key objective, the mopping up of excess liquidity. However, the latest central bank report indicates that the budgetary containment has not been successful. Inflation has increased and the availability of essential commodities has decreased, largely due to unexpected impacts on the price of oil commodities on world markets and the disturbing impact of the tsunami of 26 December 2004, followed a few days later by torrential rain.

The projected economic performance for 2005 suggested a negative growth rate of 4 per cent. Tourist arrivals were expected to decline by 10 per cent in 2005, while fishing and agriculture were also projected to decline. Inflationary pressures were expected to increase, with consumer prices rising by 12 per cent. The balance-of-payments gap in 2005 was projected at USD 45 million (7 per cent of GDP). Reserves were at about USD 33 million, or less than a month of imports, and were thus unable to absorb the negative current-account shock. This was further compounded by the accumulation of arrears on external debt payments, at the rate of approximately USD 40 million a year, over the previous two years. The vulnerability of the external position of the Seychelles highlights the need for grant financing to fill the gap. A Paris Club unconditional moratorium on debt payments for 2005, although useful in slowing the accumulation of arrears, was not expected to provide fresh resources to fill the gap. The external debt stood at an unsustainable 200 per cent of GDP in 2005.

Crucially, the MERP is effecting a realignment of Seychelles representation in international organisations, with an emphasis on strengthening ties with those organisations from which Seychelles is likely to derive the greatest benefit. Seychelles ceased its membership of SADC in 2004, and has done the same with the Indian Ocean Rim Association for Regional Co-operation. It is expected to strengthen its relationships with the World Bank and IMF, African French-speaking countries, the Indian Ocean Commission (IOC), and COMESA.

Security conceptions

In the period immediately after the 1977 coup, internal security concerns, as well as the wider Cold War climate and strategic Indian Ocean environment, dominated the political scene. As Franda (1982: 65) remarks: 'Having come to power by force and with the assistance of Tanzania, René and his government were acutely aware of their own vulnerability.' The ruling elite became obsessed with survival, and this led to a particular interpretation of security – further informed by the shape of the post-coup government: revolutionary, socialist, and one-party. Throughout the 1970s, rumours of counter-coup attempts persisted, and in 1981 a group of South African-led mercenaries was foiled in an attempt at overthrowing the government (Arnold 1995). In reaction, the René government instituted a series of controversial measures aimed at promoting public security. Press censorship, a lack of privacy in the mail, the curtailment of judicial freedoms, preventive detention, schools for enforcing discipline, forced exile of political opponents, and the creation of an armed militia produced an atmosphere of fear and suspicion.

Not surprisingly, the government rejected the notion that the army should be apolitical or politically neutral. Politicisation of the military meant that that 'our troops are trained to defend the interests of socialism' (Franda 1982: 71). The government devised a number of ways to keep the military subservient to the government and the party, ranging from administrative to political party controls.

The move away from the one-party socialist system resulted in changing understandings of security by government officials.

Security policymaking

Franda (1982: 69–72) notes that the 1977 coup in the Seychelles was 'particularly interesting' because it was carried out in a country that did not have an army. In any event, the Seychelles People's Liberation Army was established shortly after the coup. The core of that army was made up of 60 Tanzanian-trained guerillas who had taken up arms against the Mancham government. Since the coup, Tanzanian and Indian officers have played a major role in training the army. The basic structure of the military was established in December 1980, with the enactment of two laws detailing a legal procedure for disciplining soldiers and providing for separate commands for the army, navy, and air force. The principal tasks of the navy and air force have been defined as maritime defence – i.e. detecting foreign vessels fishing or otherwise operating in the Seychelles economic maritime zone. The army is obviously intended to maintain domestic order. The first group of soldiers entirely trained by Seychellois officers was turned out in April 1981.

The bulk of Seychelles' military expenditures were previously directed towards internal and presidential security. The army consisted of one infantry company and one supply unit. Of the 450 members of the armed forces, 300 served in the Presidential Guard. The paramilitary forces included 250 active-duty national guardsmen, of which 200 were assigned to the coastguard. Today, the security sector is made up of approximately 800 people: around 400 in the Seychelles People's Defence Force (SPDF), 300 in the police, and 150 in the National Guard.[1]

Currently, the country's defence and security functions are governed by the constitution and the Defence Act. The president is the commander-in-chief and minister of defence, and can choose to send soldiers into battle. If he/she is unable to exercise these duties or incapacitated, the vice president deputises. The chief of staff of the SPDF and police commissioner are the accountable officers and responsible for administrative affairs. The National Defence Council, comprising these persons, meets regularly (and often informally) to consider defence and security matters. It is unclear how the intelligence function currently operates. There is no department of defence. Parliament plays a small, and somewhat marginal, oversight role in defence and security matters, and the National Assembly annually considers the defence budget. A variety of parliamentary mechanisms now exist (including questions, motions, and ad hoc committees) to allow for a more robust engagement with defence and security matters. There is no evidence to suggest that civil society organisations and the media exert significant influence in defence and security matters.

Understandings of security

During a training course for senior representatives from the security sector, including parliament, course participants identified Seychelles' threats, as indicated in Table 1.

Table 1: Seychelles' threat perception

Internal	External
Non-military • Poaching • Trafficking in illegal arms • Illegal immigrants • Unemployment • Political unrest • Drug abuse • HIV/AIDS	**Non-military** • Illegal fishing • Oil washing from tankers • Illegal poaching • Violation of the economic exclusion zone • Money laundering • Health threats • Environmental disasters • Cyber crime • Drug trafficking
Military • Possibility of terrorist attacks against visiting US military personnel	**Military** • War in Iraq (external shocks such as high oil prices, drop in tourism)

The group identified a number of strategies to manage aspects of these threats, including enforcement measures (regarding illegal activities and immigrants), better training of officials, education on the effects of threats such as HIV/AIDS, adoption of appropriate legislation, and collaboration with regional partners and institutions.

Regarding civil–military relations, the course participants acknowledged the legacy of the one-party system and agreed that healthy relations were a continuous process that needed to be maintained. The group identified a number of steps that could be taken to achieve that objective, including a well-trained and -equipped SPDF public relations officer; a well-thought out media programme; more interaction with members of the National Assembly; an information campaign focusing on schools; more transparency in policy planning, implementation, and evaluation; and a clearer definition of the roles of the military and the police.[2]

Perceptions of regional security

The Indian Ocean region, in which Seychelles is located, is vast and features a range of widely differing security challenges. Most countries of the Indian Ocean are of developing status and face a common set of issues and problems ranging from nation state building to human development and national security (Singh 1995). In a study of Indian Ocean security building, Mills (1998) identified non-traditional security issues to include resource scarcity (concern over the environment, including marine living resources, population growth, and migration); transnational crime and policing (drugs, narco-terrorism, and light-weapons proliferation); and global economic challenges (globalisation, poverty, currency fluctuations, and weak implementing agencies). Traditional security concerns, according to Mills, include disarmament (particularly nuclear), the Indian–Pakistani dispute, increasing Chinese military power, involvement of non-Indian Ocean powers, security of oil supplies, religious tensions, and border disputes. More recently, one might add to this list the threat of local and global terrorism and the impact of unilateral US military interventions.

In a discussion of new security threats in the Indian Ocean region, Lauseig (1999) argues that drugs, weapons proliferation, corruption, and crime syndicates are consequences of the weakness of the state and the worldwide expansion of criminalisation. He also identifies two additional factors that are as important as the state's measure of weakness: the economic sub-stratum (banking system, internal market) and geographic influence (communication infrastructure, diversified transport networks).

It is difficult to determine accurately the official Seychelles position or response to these concerns, partly because of a particular political culture and style of public-policy decision making, which does not allow for easy access from the outside. However, judged by the threat perceptions of senior security officials, one can conclude that the Seychelles government is well aware of the new security threats in the Indian Ocean region, and also has a sober realisation of the human and financial resource constraints that seemingly prevent the country from adopting more elaborate and ambitious foreign security policies.

Seychelles has for the most part followed a policy of non-alignment in international affairs. It also supported an initiative to create a 'zone of peace' in the Indian Ocean. For example, it attempted to deny all naval vessels with nuclear weapons docking rights in Seychelles. However, realpolitik predominated and US and other navy vessels dock in Seychelles on a regular basis. The government of Seychelles relies on a 'you don't tell us, we won't ask' policy in relation to nuclear weaponry on board US, Russian Federation, and other visiting vessels. The United States used to have a satellite-tracking station on the island of Mahé, but, due to US spending cuts, it was removed in 1996. Seychelles has relied heavily on its relationship with France, although development assistance from the French government has steadily declined over the years. As a result of its non-aligned policy, Seychelles was able to forge effective relationships with both sides during the Cold War. The 'tracking' facility was in fact linked to the global network of the US nuclear capability. The former Soviet Union, on the other hand, desired to maintain a close watch and a counterbalance to US interests in the Indian Ocean region. To a lesser degree, the Chinese, Libyan, Indian, and Cuban governments supported Soviet intervention in the region. The tracking station was ultimately closed because of the decline in the Cold War, the upgrading of technology within the US facility in Diego Garcia, and, as mentioned above, the tightening of US budgets.

As Ellis (1996) has argued, the Seychelles' strategic location in terms of US–Soviet rivalry in the Indian Ocean, as well as South Africa's regional policy of destabilisation during the 1980s, led to attempts to influence the island's government by bribery and force. More-powerful governments and business interests as far afield as Italy also manipulated Seychelles' status as a sovereign state 'in order to perform various transactions of dubious legality' (Ellis 1996: 166), and there is some evidence that the islands were used for financial transactions by arms dealers and as a staging post for drug trafficking. These past practices undoubtedly impacted on the quality of governance, and might still have lingering effects.

Not surprisingly, during its one-party socialist phase, the government of the Seychelles was quite vocal in its foreign relations. The end of the Cold War era saw the decline of the influence of the communist and socialist countries, and with it came Seychelles' relative isolation. Unsure of where to turn, and maintaining a certain amount of revolutionary nostalgia, it reluctantly considered its regional options. Seychelles joined the most significant of the regional organisations, SADC, in 1997, only to withdraw in 1994 because of economic considerations. Seychelles is a member of the AU, but is not particularly active.[3] It has remained in COMESA, which focuses more on trade than political issues. The strategic calculation, from the Seychelles perspective, is whether the benefits of regional co-operation outweigh the costs and duties associated with membership of these organisations. The mere fact that it finds membership fees a large burden is an indication of its limited resources and foreign policy reach. Consequently, it concentrates on areas of functional co-operation such as through the IOC. Given that tuna processing constitutes Seychelles's only significant export, it has participated in the Western Indian Ocean Tuna Organisation, the Indian Ocean Tuna Commission, and the Indian Ocean Marine Affairs Co-operation Council. In 2001 it participated in an initiative to develop a memorandum of understanding on regional co-operation (with countries from East Africa) regarding the establishment of a regional search-and-rescue centre.

Because of its small size, Seychelles' security objectives can be achieved only in co-operation with others, and regionalism offers the country a way forward in this area (Bell 2003). At present there are serious deficiencies in the collective security arrangements of the Indian Ocean region, which are ad hoc and largely comprise bilateral, as opposed to regional, agreements on military co-operation, supported by bilateral joint training exercises and senior officer exchanges.

In the Indian Ocean area, states can begin their own comprehensive regional security strategy by developing a framework that establishes a common definition of security, which was a stumbling block with the Indian Ocean Zone of Peace. They can then move towards establishing a regional forum with the specific aim of dealing with political and military issues.

In particular, practical co-operative measures to be explored include developing a conflict resolution capacity and an early warning system, and establishing a confidence-building agenda with greater transparency and understanding of strategic perceptions and defence planning. These can be expanded to include common issues such as maritime search and rescue, delimitation of boundaries, territorial surveillance, resource management, marine scientific research, safety of shipping, immigration, drug trafficking, piracy, poaching, illegal fishing, illegal arms, and natural disasters.

Over time, specific non-aggression pacts with common defence policies could be concluded, supported by practical measures such as unified operational procedures, training, and military curriculums to accomplish inter-operability, a military communications network for early warning, joint training exercises, personnel exchanges, and peacekeeping capacity (Bell 2003: 13).

Conclusion

Seychelles has taken its first bold steps in establishing itself within the international community as a state that recognises the fundamental importance of maintaining democratic institutions and good governance. Its current direction follows the path that many effective democratic states have successfully trodden. However, it must be understood that the country's faltering economy is a consequence of both internal and external factors. The current economic reform phase, intended to correct years of unsustainable social policies, will involve some sacrifice and hardship to the Seychelles population. On the external front, the global security arena after the attacks in the United States of 11 September 2001 has had severe consequences for the Seychelles: unavoidably, an economy dependent on upmarket tourism and one export product (tuna) was bound to be damaged by the global economic and security turmoil.

The 2003 war in Iraq had an even bigger impact on the Seychelles. As Baregu (2002) has commented, the implications of the American 'war on terror' are twofold: Africa is likely to experience intensified interference in its internal affairs, including direct efforts to monitor terrorism; and African governments will have to demonstrate that their defence policies are designed and organised in such a way as to enhance American strategic interests and national security goals. These implications are unavoidable for all of Africa, and small, developing island states have virtually no manoeuvring space. Seychelles is currently experiencing this tightening of the policy menu, and has to find a way of maintaining balanced relations with the key external players. It has to take into account the role of the IFIs, the tourist market, the commercially driven French presence in the Indian Ocean region, an assertive Indian presence in the same region, a growing commercial and political South Africa, and the unavoidable military dominance of the United States.

Global turmoil has also impacted on the country's relations with its more immediate environment, including SADC. There is a strong belief among senior government officials that SADC failed to provide the Seychelles with much benefit, relative to the financial and human resources required to remain a member. In that sense, a simple cost-benefit analysis pointed the way forward. What most officials fail to admit, however, was Seychelles' reluctance to adopt SADC's economic rules, particularly the requirements with regard to its free trade agreement. Until the adoption of the MERP, the country was simply not ready to liberalise its economy in order to harmonise with that agreement. Regarding security, it remains to be seen whether the Seychelles will be able to replace SADC's embryonic security umbrella with arrangements closer to home.

The survival of the SPPF government will depend on how effectively it manages these upheavals, particularly over the next three to four years. Traditionally, governments that have initiated the bold changes are not those that benefit politically, although Seychelles may prove to be an exception.

ENDNOTES

1 Interview, senior member of the SPDF staff, March 2003.

2 Based on a training course run by the Southern African Defence and Security Management Programme in 2003.

3 Seychelles is a member of the UN, the Commonwealth, the AU, the African Development Bank, COMESA, and the International Organisation for Francophonie, and is a member of the Africa-Caribbean-Pacific–EU relationship. In January 2002 Seychelles was one of 20 members barred from voting in the UN General Assembly because of unpaid arrears to the organisation.

Chapter 10

South Africa

Maxi Schoeman

Even before South Africa joined SADC in 1994, the Southern African region had played an important role in the country's national security considerations. During the apartheid era, the activities of the FLS and countries such as Angola, Botswana, Lesotho, Mozambique, Zimbabwe, Zambia, and others that provided the liberation movements with support were a primary concern of South Africa's national security. The South African government's regional destabilisation policy of the late 1970s and the larger part of the 1980s was a result of the perception of the apartheid government that the region posed a serious threat to the country. Destabilisation caused large-scale damage and loss of life to the states and people of Southern Africa, and together with South Africa's economic dominance of the region, resulted in a large measure of insecurity and a lack of trust.

These perceptions have not necessarily changed significantly since the end of apartheid (see, for example, IPA 2001: 31).[1] South Africa's membership of SADC resulted in the region remaining a priority for the country's national security, though threat perceptions changed dramatically, as did the way in which the region is perceived by policymakers.

Whereas the 1970s and 1980s, the era of 'Total Onslaught', saw the militarisation of the South African state and society, the 1990s became an era not only of demilitarisation, but also of attempts to civilise the military. These initiatives were part of the transformation and democratisation process that reached its height during the Mandela presidency and included a fairly large civil society[2] input into new thinking on security that took place during the 1990s.

Structural support for democracy

A range of institutions were created after April 1994 to safeguard, support, and promote constitutional democracy, with the most prominent being the public protector, the South African Human Rights Commission, the Commission for Gender Equality, the Truth and Reconciliation Commission (temporary), the Commission on the Restitution of Land Rights (temporary), and the Constitutional Court.

Within the realm of defence and security, the most prominent structure is the Defence Secretariat (DS), which, with the South African National Defence Force (SANDF), falls under the minister of defence and the Department of Defence (DoD), with the SANDF concentrating on operational issues and the DS on strategic and general defence policy issues.[3] The primary aim of the DS is to provide civilian oversight of the military, and in this capacity it serves as policy advisor to the minister of defence and as monitor of compliance of the SANDF as far as policies and directives issued by the minister are concerned. The establishment of the DS as a civilian oversight body is a direct result of the democratisation and demilitarisation process in South Africa. In its Strategic Business Plan, the DoD (Republic of South Africa. DoD 2003: vi) spells out the objectives of the DS as follows:

> The Defence Secretariat, which is largely a civilian component, is responsible for formulating policy and strategic direction to ensure alignment between the DoD and Government policies, the financial administration of the DoD, and ensuring adherence to legislation, Government policies, instructions and regulations. Furthermore it is responsible for managing the acquisition of armaments for the SANDF.

South Africa in SADC

In August 1992 the SADCC was transformed into SADC, not only as a response to a changing international environment and new demands on the region,[4] but also and not least in preparation for the imminent membership of a post-apartheid South Africa. The addition of South Africa in August 1994 radically changed the structure of SADC as a region, if not (immediately) of the organisation itself. From 1980 until 1994 Zimbabwe was the uncontested leader (though informally) of the regional formation, and together with Botswana it was economically and militarily the strongest state in the organisation (Angola was militarily powerful, but its forces were tied up in the war against UNITA rebels). South African membership changed these dynamics dramatically – there could be no doubt about the country's military superiority; its economic giantism (it accounts for 75 per cent of SADC's GDP); and its very high status, standing, and level of popularity internationally. In all spheres, South Africa eclipsed the region and in particular Zimbabwe, with Zimbabwe's President Mugabe relegated to the sidelines as South Africa's Mandela became the favourite in international circles.

Yet South Africa's very strength soon proved to be its biggest challenge. The end of apartheid did not translate into an immediate sense of trust and confidence in the new SADC member. Despite South African declarations of the priority of the region for the country's security and foreign policies (see following section), it found it difficult, right from the start, to find its 'place' within SADC. South Africa was careful not to impose itself as a 'big brother' on its neighbours. Its neighbours, on the one hand, continued to be suspicious of South African intentions, and on the other hand, accused the country of not playing a dominant enough role in regional affairs, but privileging relations with the First World, and in particular with Europe.

At a very practical level, South Africa, at the time of a democratically elected government coming to power, also faced a host of very practical problems that would impact on its security relations with the region. The country became a preferred destination for large numbers of migrants in the region (and further afield) who were looking for economic opportunities and better lives. An estimated 2–8 million illegal immigrants were in South Africa by the mid-1990s, placing a heavy burden on the country in terms of the provision of basic services and the cost of repatriation.[5] At the same time, and in line with developments in the rest of the world, a much more open South Africa also became a preferred destination and operational base for drug trafficking and other forms of organised crime (including the illegal trade in light weapons), its fairly open borders contributing to its attraction.[6] As is the case in many other countries, the new democracy has also become a target for 'all sorts of dubious and nefarious enterprises, including intelligence infiltration' (Khanyile 2003).

Conditions within South Africa have also influenced its security relations with the region. Two of the biggest challenges facing the country were (and still are) that of the eradication of widespread poverty and underdevelopment, together with the related objective of wealth creation. Within a context of balancing its internal obligations with regional obligations – finding the right balance between these separate yet related demands – South Africa also had to redefine its security concerns, including undergoing a conceptual transformation of its military. These redefinitions of security and transformation were not only based on the changing regional landscape and the demands of a 'new' South Africa, but were also influenced by international trends, including a new security paradigm (see, for example, Ayoob 1995; Buzan 1991; Job 1992) that gained ground in the aftermath of the end of the Cold War and a general downsizing of militaries and military spending worldwide.

By 1999 the defence budget had been cut by almost 57 per cent (SAIRR 2003: 461): in 1989 defence accounted for 15.64 per cent of total government expenditure, but by 1999 it had fallen to 7 per cent. In the 2005/6 budget announced in February 2005, only 5.8 per cent of total revenue was allocated to defence, and this was set to decline to 4.9 per cent by 2007/8 (SAIRR 2005: 6). Although these declining figures may indicate the country's move away from its militarised past, one cannot help but feel some concern when taking into account that 70 per cent of the defence budget is spent on personnel, whereas the international best practice is that this percentage should be in the range of 40 per cent (*Beeld* 2005b).

In 1994 the full-time component of the (then) SADF was 100,000 strong, and 36 000 liberation fighters had to be incorporated as part of the defence transformation process. By 1999 the SANDF had been downsized to 87,000; in February 2003 the figure was 75,300 (*Beeld* 2005b); and by 2004/05 it was 73,000. The aim is that this figure will stabilise at 70,000. The composition of the SANDF is fairly representative of demographic realities in the country (see Table 1), though in gender terms the figures are still disproportionately high in favour of males: 85 per cent of SANDF members are male and 15 per cent female.[7]

Table 1: SANDF racial composition (%)

	2004/05	**Proposed**
Black	62	65
Coloured	12	10
Asian	1	0.75
White	25	24

Source: GCIS (2005: 468)

As part of the movement towards greater civilian control over the military, the DS was created through national legislation and based on section 204 of the constitution. The DS is, among other things, designed to enhance parliamentary oversight and civil control by the minister over the DoD.

Drivers of democratisation

A number of internal and external factors contributed to the end of apartheid and the onset of democratisation in South Africa. These factors in many instances contributed to the demise of apartheid and not automatically to democratisation.[8] The latter was the path chosen, partly through negotiations, by adversaries – the then National Party government, the various liberation movements and domestic resistance movements (such as the United Democratic Front [UDF]), and other stakeholders who eventually participated in the negotiated settlement. Although a distinction is drawn here between internal and external factors for change, the distinction is not as clear-cut as implied: in some instances it is difficult to assign a specific driver to the categories 'internal' and 'external', as will become evident in the following discussion.

Internal drivers of change

The stark realities of numbers, with blacks outnumbering whites; the huge influx of blacks into supposedly 'white' cities; and the persistent deterioration of the 'homelands' and obvious failure of the policy of creating 'national states' for the various ethnic groups could not but have made the government of the 1980s aware of the fact that it would not in the long run be able to maintain apartheid. Already in the 1970s, the regime began a reform process (however limited and constrained) attempting, albeit largely within the confines of apartheid dogma, to initiate some reforms of the system, in effect and unwittingly opening up opportunities for increasingly radical demands from, and political action by, resistance movements within the country (the Wiehahn Commission on black trade unions, for example).

Within the business sector, awareness of the importance of such a potentially large black consumer class resulted (together with the 'bite' of economic sanctions) in pressure being put on the government for change. The economic recession of the 1980s, together with the lack of foreign direct investment and the sheer cost of continuing the extravagant apartheid system, also undoubtedly contributed to the demise of apartheid. To reap benefits from the emerging global economy, with its emphasis on post-industrial economic sectors, export-led growth, and value-added economic activities, demanded a restructuring of the economy, which in turn demanded external assistance in the form of technical know-how and investment – resources denied the apartheid government.

The heavy price the country was beginning to pay for apartheid (and its continued presence in Namibia and involvement in the Angolan civil war) from 1985 onwards led many South Africans to start to explore alternatives, and white academics, business people, the clergy, and even sports administrators started seeking contact and dialogue with the African National Congress (ANC). Interestingly enough, it was also in 1985 that the government tentatively initiated contact with the banned ANC (Louis le Grange, minister of law and order, met with the ANC in Zambia in 1985), and in the same year President P. W. Botha offered in parliament to free Mandela, provided he and the ANC renounced violence as a political instrument.

In large part, internal resistance to apartheid and to the National Party government, gaining strength after the Soweto riots of 1976, played a crucial role in the fight to end apartheid. Of particular importance here were the roles of trade unions (particularly the Congress of South African Trade Unions and its affiliates) and the UDF, which gained in influence in the 1980s, especially after the constitutional reforms of the P. W. Botha government. Although aimed principally at the struggle against apartheid, these mass movements adopted and promoted democratic strategies right from their inception, and it is perhaps worthwhile to remember that the anti-apartheid struggle was as much for genuine democracy as it was against racism as embodied in the apartheid state and its policies.

A crucial driver of change was, of course, the ANC itself, which played a role both internally and externally. Its internal role was to some extent symbolic (it was, after all, a banned organisation, branded 'terrorist'), but especially after the 1976 Soweto riots the organisation became increasingly prominent in domestic politics, influencing the trade union movement and the UDF, bringing together the components of the 'national democratic revolution', and conducting a sustained armed struggle within the country, even though the latter was also largely symbolic.

During the period of negotiations (1990–94), the ANC retained and strengthened its role as a driver of change, keeping a wide range of popular organisations united and committed to a process of change that would not alienate the white community: in fact, the ANC, through the idea of the 'rainbow nation', managed to extend its nationalism to include and, importantly, attract sections of the white population who had not traditionally supported the organisation.[9]

External drivers of change

The extent to which external sources influenced the process of democratisation, especially in terms of the demise of apartheid, remains debatable. However, there is general agreement that the international sanctions campaign did play an important role, as the state of the domestic economy (see above) was directly influenced, and negatively so, by economic sanctions (particularly in the form of 'disinvestment'), and became an important driver for change. Raising international awareness on the need for using sanctions as a tool to force change in South Africa was perhaps one of the most important roles of the ANC in exile. It waged a highly sophisticated and successful campaign – especially in Western capitals – to increase pressure on the South African government, and by the end of the 1980s it had more diplomatic missions across the world than the government.

No matter, though, how successful sanctions had been, it would be wrong to view the South African example of the 'success of sanctions' as a possible recipe for 'encouraging' other states to democratise. Sanctions worked in South Africa not only because of the extent to which and the way in which the country's economy was integrated into and dependent on the world economy (a product of its level of economic development), but largely because of the racial bias in the political and economic inequality that characterised South African society during the apartheid era. An overview of the use of sanctions against African countries will show that sanctions are seldom successful and often have the opposite effect to what is intended.

Apart from economic sanctions, a number of other external drivers also propelled the country in the direction of democratisation, based on the principles of a market economy. These factors can be summarised as follows:

- South Africa's perceived military defeats in Angola in the late 1980s, together with the financial burden of its involvement in Namibia and Angola, put an additional burden on an already strained fiscus and had important psychological effects.
- South Africa's comprehensive international isolation across a spectrum of dimensions, including the cultural and sports dimensions, divided the country internally, and increasingly whites came to believe that the price to pay for the continuation of apartheid was just too high.
- The end of the Cold War, the collapse of the Soviet Union, the success of the Namibian peace process, and the general support for and recognition by the international community of the need for a settlement also played a role. This not only pushed the apartheid government towards change, but also the ANC – with the Soviet Union collapsing, it was losing an important source of power and support, and Western countries, after the Namibian settlement, were also beginning to put pressure on the liberation movements to move towards negotiations.

Character of democratic practice

Democratic practices in South Africa are formally framed within the country's constitution, and the bill of rights (backed up by the Constitutional Court) provides mechanisms and protection for citizens to participate in public debate and in formal political processes, such as elections. Whereas the period 1990–94 was an 'opening-up' period, with a myriad of processes under way and a myriad of voices being heard, the post-1994 period has been characterised by a formalisation of democratic processes, with much of what had formerly come from civil society now being absorbed into the country's legislature, with 'hard-core' discussion of pertinent issues often taking place in parliamentary portfolio committees.

These committees serve as a good example of the claim that democratic practices have increasingly been formalised. Parliamentary portfolio committees, and in this case more specifically the Portfolio Committee on Defence, provide an opportunity for civil society to participate to some extent in, at least influencing formal decision making, if only in the sense of being heard on certain issues. These committees often invite members of or groups from civil society, mostly the NGO sector, to address them on issues related to the mandates of the committees. Whether such inputs are necessarily taken into account when actual policy formulation takes place – and whether these committees necessarily influence policymaking – is less clear. However, the portfolio committees are arenas where decision makers and civil society meet and interact. As far as the parliamentary Portfolio Committee on Defence is concerned, there seems to be a general feeling that this committee is more important and influential than the others. According to Brigadier-General Ntsiki Motumi, the portfolio and parliamentary committees do influence policy 'in the sense that government administrators (Defence Secretariat) prepare draft policies, engage with parliamentarians and thereafter changes are made if necessary, before promulgation'. She cites the example of the NSF Special Pensions Act and the DoD 2010 Human Resources Strategy (Motumi 2003).[10]

It is rather doubtful whether the Portfolio Committee on Defence originally had much influence. The committee's former and long-serving chair, Thandi Modise, complained in 2003 (with reference to problems surrounding grievance procedures and protocols, and the ongoing transformation in the SANDF) that '[o]ur committee has been trying to get noticed for two years' (*Beeld*, 2005c). At the same time, two unions representing SANDF members, as well as a member of the opposition Democratic Alliance party, complained that neither the portfolio committee nor the DoD had responded to requests for meetings in order to address problems related to transformation in the SANDF, and all parties alleged that they had been trying to arrange such meetings for longer than a year (*Beeld*, 2005c). However, under the new chair, Professor Kader Asmal, it would seem that things changed, and that the committee played a much more active role of oversight than used to be the case. According to a newspaper report in March 2005 (*Beeld* 2005a), Asmal was infuriated by the strategic business plan for the SANDF submitted to the committee and instructed the defence secretary to rewrite and re-submit it. Clearly, he planned a much more active role for the defence committee.

There is little if any indication of any move towards increased militarisation in South Africa or of an 'excessive' role for the military. In fact, relative to the size of its population and economy, South Africa now has the fourth-smallest defence force on the continent. Problems seem to be located more in the realm of politics, particularly party politics. It would seem that most of the problems currently associated with the SANDF have their origin in complaints about the downsizing of the institution (in terms of personnel and other resources). Moses Khanyile of the DS's policy and planning division argues (2003) that in certain instances the portfolio committees on defence and public accounts are 'very powerful', and he cites the example of the country's controversial arms deal.

As far as the formalisation of democratic practices is concerned, one can detect a movement over the past years (since 1994) from participatory, to consultative, to what can perhaps be termed procedural democracy. If the era surrounding the formal negotiations leading up to 1994 and for some time after the inauguration of the first democratically elected government saw fairly large-scale participation in the processes leading up to a settlement (though the formal settlement was an elite pact in many respects), the Mandela era, in particular, was characterised by a measure of consultative democracy, if one takes into account the extent to which civil society was 'roped in' to provide advice on policy formulation. The Mbeki era, though, increasingly sees a move towards limited civil society participation, compared with the previous era. Participation is specialised and mostly of a technical nature, focused on the particular expertise of outsiders in cases where 'inside' expertise and capacity are not readily available. For example, Khanyile (2003) has pointed out that NGOs often have more 'current' information on the peace support environment, and therefore are of assistance to the DoD, especially 'in the early stages of policy-formulation, because of their specialised knowledge and involvement in this environment' (Khanyile 2003).

The above claims need to be unpacked briefly. When referring to the role of civil society, two broad functions can be identified. The first is the function of civil society (including the NGO sector, as this is an important element of civil society for the purpose of this overview) to interact with the state in order to influence government policy, usually for the purpose of benefitting the interest groups represented by the particular elements of civil society engaging with the state. Such interaction is not necessarily solicited by the state, but is normal practice in democratic societies.

A second function of civil society is engagement with the state with a view to influencing state policy on issues that have a broader or 'national' character. Part of this kind of interaction is engagement solicited by the state where specific inputs are needed in cases where the state does not have expertise to deal with issues. Such inputs can also serve the purpose of engaging with civil society in order to legitimise policies and build support for government actions – in short, achieving 'social consent'. This process has been very evident in the various round-table discussions hosted by the Department of Foreign Affairs (DFA) on a range of policies, including the 1998 white paper on peacekeeping and various aspects related to the New Partnership for Africa's Development (NEPAD) and the establishment and development of the AU and its organs.

What is striking about the role of civil society in South Africa, with particular reference now to issues related to defence and security and, more broadly, foreign affairs (to the extent that foreign affairs often encompass aspects of defence and security policy, especially when it comes to regional and African policies) is that two types of civil society 'actions' can be identified. The first is a critical stance regarding government policy, coming mainly from the (white, English) media, which is mostly aimed at defence expenditure, and more particularly defence procurement package agreements, including both the nature and cost of the equipment, and subsequent indications of corruption or dishonesty involved in the granting of contracts. Particularly on questions pertaining to former Deputy President Jacob Zuma's alleged benefits deriving from the various arms contracts, the procurement package received wide coverage in the media. Such criticism, though, has little to do with engagement between the state and civil society – in fact, government (and especially the Mbeki government) does not take kindly to criticism.

It would seem that initially, in the period 1990–94, various forms of civil society participation in the transformation process were rife, and debates on a wide range of topics raged in the news media, including issues such as the transformation of the military and the nature of a post-apartheid security and defence. A host of NGOs were involved in policy issue areas, to the extent that policy was often developed without the appropriate oversight by and accountablility to parliament and the executive.

After the 1994 elections, this vibrancy in society was gradually formalised and 'the voice of the people' was captured in the importance attached to parliamentary oversight and the various measures adopted to assure such oversight, e.g. the parliamentary portfolio committees. But this era (roughly 1994–99, or the Mandela era, though one should be careful not to place too much importance on the person of the president in each era, as structural constraints and opportunities also go a long way in explaining differences) still saw a lot of civil society participation, with the military establishment and DFA often engaged in discussions with various groups in civil society on the formulation of policy and the development of legislation. The white papers on defence and on peacekeeping operations were fairly comprehensively 'workshopped', as was the defence review. And in the post-1999, or post-Mandela era, the Defence Act of 2001 was drawn up not only by experts from the Departments of Defence and Justice and legal experts, but also by other 'experts' from civil society.

A number of points should be made here. The first is that civil society participation has become increasingly confined to the services that research NGOs in particular can provide to government; in a way, therefore, civil society participation is largely narrowed down to engagement with the NGO sector and to some extent academic institutions with strong research capacity. An early explanation for this is offered by Jakkie Cilliers of the Institute of Security Studies (ISS):

> We can look at every sector of South African society, including the areas that we engage in [security], where government has been so weak and has been so mistrustful of its own people and particularly of the old guard that government almost laid itself bare to policy influence on anything from land reform to security issues (quoted in Le Pere and Vickers 2001: 68).

But the new government grew in confidence and capacity, and increasingly it seems, civil society inputs have become of a technical nature rather than, first and foremost, offered by or solicited from an ethos of idealistic views of 'people's participation'. In the words of Motumi (2003), 'the Mandela era appeared more consultative because it was characterised by the development of policy frameworks. During the Mbeki era the challenges are around policy implementation and service delivery.'

Mbeki's integrated governance system has meant a huge increase in the size of the presidency, concentrating technical expertise in the office of the president and providing a lesser role for skilled civil society (read NGO) inputs. As part of the Integrated Governance and Planning Framework for Government adopted by the cabinet *lekgotlas* (informal meetings) of July 2001 and January 2002, five clusters comprising the directors-general of the relevant government departments were established to provide strategic policy direction and 'monitor performance' (Motumi 2003) in all areas of governance, including the identification of gaps and critical challenges, and the pulling together of cross-cutting issues. The SANDF is represented in the justice, crime prevention, and security cluster, as well as in the international relations, peace, and security cluster (with the latter also including, among others, the DFA, the National Intelligence Co-ordinating Committee, and the South African Secret Service).

Furthermore, under Mbeki, one also sees the end of the period during which large-scale (new) policy formulation was needed to reflect the character of the 'new' South Africa, and the move has been increasingly towards delivery and implementation, partly explaining the diminished role of civil society (Motumi 2003). A last point to be made is that research-oriented NGOs and academic institutions (in the realm of security and defence issues) continue to play a prominent role in articulating positions and opinions on these matters, and to participate in debates and contribute their skills. The Africa Institute, for instance, is very active in the promotion of NEPAD, at times also in the critiquing of the NEPAD process (though maybe inadvertently so), and the ISS in the development of viewpoints and recommendations regarding the AU and its various organs and protocols. Discussions hosted by these institutes are frequently well attended by officials from the DFA, the DoD, and other relevant government bodies. Very often, though, these officials are from middle-management level and not necessarily the real decision makers, but rather the people who need to implement decisions and who need expert advice and ideas on the practicalities of policy.

Civil society, in its critique of the continental process or of security policy and developments within the Southern African region can, of course, play a useful role, articulating what the government can perhaps for reasons of political sensitivity not say. However, and when all is said and done, civil society participation is to a very large measure supportive of government policy, and is aimed at contributing to the building of a democratic South Africa and of the necessary capacity, skills, and knowledge for the country to realise its domestic and international objectives. A good example is also the fact that the DoD solicits civil society inputs through the various advisory boards it has established, among these the Equal Opportunity Board, Military Veterans Board, and Military Arbitration Board (Motumi 2003).

National security concept

There is a clear distinction between national security at the domestic level, which is largely the responsibility of the South African Police Service, and that of regional (and external) national security, which is mainly the task of the SANDF.

South Africa's orientation to its external national security has changed from an explicitly offensive strategy (as characterised by the 'Total Strategy' approach of the 1970s and 1980s) to that of a defensive approach. According to the 1996 white paper on national defence,[11] the 'objectives of security policy include the defence of the sovereignty, territorial integrity and political independence of the South African state and the promotion of regional security in Southern Africa' (Hough and Du Plessis 2000: 65).

Security is defined in broad terms, in line with current international thinking. In a document entitled 'Ready to govern: ANC policy guidelines for a democratic South Africa', adopted at its national conference in 1992, the ANC identified lack of security in terms of underdevelopment, poverty, and an absence of democratic values as promoting conflict within and between states. Therefore, 'national and regional security should not be restricted to military, police and intelligence matters, but as having political, economic, social and environmental dimensions' (Hough and Du Plessis 2000: 16–17).

The Southern African region forms an important focus of South Africa's national security doctrine, policy, and thinking. In an input into the National Growth and Development Strategy (1996), the DFA argued, with reference to the country's national external security strategy, that 'the emphasis should be on the security and long-term economic and political stability of the entire sub-continent, since South Africa's national security cannot be sustained in an unstable and insecure region' (Hough and Du Plessis 2000: 69).

External national security is based on advancing the principles of collective security, non-aggression, and the peaceful settlement of disputes, while some of the transnational threats identified are the proliferation of weapons of mass destruction, international terrorism and extremism, organised crime and narcotics trafficking, and issues related to environmental degradation.[12] The defence white paper of 1996 implies the recognition or perception of a number of threats that are related to the economic, political, and societal dimensions of a broad definition of security:

- the spread of disease;
- the burden of refugees;
- civil war in some SADC member countries;
- regional instability; and
- chronic underdevelopment.

The above threats could result in inter-state disputes, tensions, and conflict in the region, with the possibility of extra-regional interference and intervention that might make it 'necessary to deploy the SANDF in multi-national peace support operations' (Hough and Du Plessis 2000: 79–80). Significantly, the white paper also refers to the possibility that inter-state disputes could arise in relation to trade, foreign investment, natural resources, and previously suppressed territorial claims.

The crux of South Africa's orientation in terms of its regional security perceptions and relations is captured in the 1996 white paper as follows:

> South Africa has a common destiny with Southern Africa. Domestic peace and stability will not be achieved in a context of regional instability and poverty. It is therefore in South Africa's long-term security interests to pursue mutually beneficial relations with other SADC states and to promote reconstruction and development throughout the region (Hough and Du Plessis 2000: 80).

The basic premise, according to the 1998 South African defence review, is that 'Southern Africa is a region of allies' and that South Africa as a member of SADC participates in common security arrangements under the auspices of this organisation and its various organs and committees (Hough and Du Plessis 2000: 82). Another aspect of South Africa's approach to regional security that needs mentioning at this point is to be found in its assertion in the 1998 white paper on international peace missions that 'participation in international peace missions is a secondary function of the armed forces' (Hough and Du Plessis 2000: 111).

Who makes security policy?

There is no doubt that civil society – or, more specifically, research-oriented NGOs and academic institutions – does (still) to a greater or lesser extent influence security policy, but this does not mean that one can assume direct causality between the inputs of these groups (through seminars, workshops, conferences, and publications) and the actual making of security policy. Foreign affairs and security policy have always and in most countries been a realm in which heads of state or government play a large role (the role of Tony Blair and George Bush during the Iraq war of 2003 is a case in point). In apartheid South Africa in the 1970s, P. W. Botha combined the portfolio of defence with his role of prime minister, and up to the mid-1950s South Africa did not have a minister of foreign affairs – this portfolio was part and parcel of the prime minister's duties and functions.

Under Mbeki, who is a technocrat, an integrated system of governance has been developed, giving the president a bird's eye view of foreign policy, and security and defence issues, and his governance and management style leads one to believe that he is definitely in charge of security policy, though perhaps not to the extent to which he participates in and is responsible for foreign policymaking. Although defence policy is made by the DoD, with the DS also playing an important role, there is still political control at the highest level (the Office of the President). The DFA, because of the nature of peacekeeping operations, also contributes to the making of defence policy.

Regional security co-operation

From the start of its membership of SADC, South Africa has indicated a willingness to participate fully in and assist in the development of security co-operation practices in the region, particularly through the building of security structures.

The SANDF has participated in several training exercises with fellow SADC member countries. The official version of South Africa's involvement in Lesotho in 1998 is that it was a joint SADC operation, and the SANDF has provided humanitarian and disaster relief to a number of its SADC neighbours and to countries further afield, including:

- shipments and airlifts of food and medicines to Rwandan refugees;
- assistance to flood victims in Mozambique and Tanzania;
- assistance during the ferry disaster on Lake Victoria in 1999;
- assistance to Lesotho during an exceptionally cold spell in the winter of 1999; and
- de-mining operations in Angola and Mozambique.

It would be difficult to ascribe South Africa's participation in regional security co-operation practices as directly or even necessarily related to democratisation and democratic practices. Many SADC members, not all of them democracies, participate in these exercises or assist neighbours during times of crisis. However, South Africa's participation is obviously directly attributable to the end of apartheid and its commitment to regional co-operation, security, and integration.

South Africa also participates actively in the security institutions of SADC, not least in terms of institution- and capacity-building. South Africa is deeply involved in the activities of the ISDSC and SARPCCO, which are regulated through the Protocol on Politics, Defence, and Security Co-operation.

An area in which South Africa does play a very active role is that of conflict resolution in the region. This role is directly related to the country's perception of itself as a democracy in which human rights are of paramount importance, and can perhaps be traced to the nature of its own transition to democracy – a peaceful one. The idea that conflicts can be solved through negotiation is one strongly adhered to by South African policymakers, and much time, energy, and resources have been spent on conflict resolution efforts in the DRC and Burundi in particular, including the contribution of troops to peacekeeping operations in both countries.

However, in terms of regional security institutions and arrangements all is not plain sailing. From 1996, with the inception of the SADC OPDSC, until 2001, no agreement could be reached on its operationalisation, particularly given the stance of Zimbabwe, its first chair. However, the stalemate was broken and a Protocol on Politics, Defence, and Security Co-operation was signed during the Blantyre summit of August 2001. Mozambique became the new chair and handed over responsibility for the OPDSC to Lesotho in 2003, to be followed by a term for South Africa. The Mutual Defence Pact was signed at the 2003 SADC summit, though by the end of 2004 only four countries had ratified the pact, perhaps pointing to the difficulties in finding common ground in the face of divergent approaches to security, ranging from 'hard-core' political–military security preoccupations to member states privileging human security. Although the pact is in a way a watered-down version of the original, which would have obliged states legally to come to the aid of a member suffering a military attack by internal or external forces,[13] it does, in the words of Ngoma (2003), reflect 'an unmistakable intention by its members to establish a security community'.

Nevertheless, the pact could widen existing rifts, and its impact on regional co-operation and good relations (at the very least) should be carefully monitored. One of its biggest dangers might be its reorientation of SADC's initial 'new security' approach, which de-emphasised military–political security and any form of violence as a solution to conflicts, towards a more traditional approach in which state security, military–political issues, and external (military) threats are given priority. South Africa's deputy foreign minister, Aziz Pahad, was quick, though, to point out that the pact would not demand 'immediate response' from member countries in the case of an attack on a fellow SADC country, but that it allowed for states to respond 'according to their possibilities' (*Mail & Guardian Online* 2003). It would seem that South Africa's decision to enter into the pact has more to do with promoting good relations in the region than with a firm belief that it will actually have much practical impact. The pact is a symbol of the belief that with the (albeit still early and tentative) end of civil wars in Angola and the DRC, the region might, at long last, be moving towards an era of peace and stability.

Conclusion

Is there a clear link between democracy and the type of security paradigm in which South Africa operates internally and regionally? A firm conclusion can probably only be reached once the country has been compared to its neighbours. Comparing contemporary South Africa to apartheid South Africa, the answer would be that since the early 1990s the role of the security establishment in South Africa, in particular the role of the defence force, has changed dramatically. One reason is that the country has been democratised, a process that opened up space for politicians, political society, and civil society to debate and determine the nature of security, and the structure and role of the security system. Whether the system thus created is delivering the results initially envisaged is not clear. The events in America of 11 September 2001 have brought military security approaches to the fore again, while under the influence of economic globalisation and the drive for 'investment efficiency', the SANDF, like many other modern defence forces, has been forced to scale down significantly. The two are not necessarily compatible, and an 'open' security policy and structure that allow for genuinely regularised inputs from civil society may not be viable in an environment determined largely by capacity level (i.e. the capacity available to transform theory into practice).

ENDNOTES

1 However, in written comments received from Brigadier-General Motumi of the SANDF (2003), she expressed the opinion that South Africa is no longer viewed as 'Big Brother' by its SADC neighbours because it has 'played ball by strengthening its relations with other countries through the signing of defence pacts, trade, tariffs etc.'

2 This is a somewhat sweeping statement and will be refined in a later section.

3 I would like to credit the input received from Moses Khanyile from the policy and planning division of the DS (interview with the author, 8 September 2003), though any factual mistakes are mine, as are interpretations and analysis.

4 The SADC Treaty is a good example.

5 For an overview of the problems related to illegal immigration, see Solomon (1998). It should be noted, however, that there is little agreement on the numbers of illegal immigrants in the country. The *South Africa Survey 2001/2002* (SAIRR 2002: 142) quotes the Bureau of Market Research's report stating that 'claims of the number of illegal immigrants ranging between 2m and 8m [are] unsubstantiated and exaggerated'.

6 As in the case of illegal immigration, there is a burgeoning literature on these issues. Some indications of the magnitude of the problems are to be found in Rotberg and Mills (1998).

7 Figures taken from a parliamentary briefing statement by the (then) minister of defence, J. Modise (1999); additional information from *South Africa Yearbook 2004/5* (GCIS 2005: 468).

8 For an early, but good analysis or explanation of the reasons behind the demise of apartheid, see Geldenhuys (1991).

9 The 'rainbow nation' concept did not indicate a new direction within the ANC – non-racialism has always been an important principle of the organisation – but it has served to give a practical and visible content to the idea and ideal of non-racialism.

10 Also the opinion expressed in the author's interview with Moses Khanyile of the DS, 8 September 2003.

11 Unless otherwise indicated, all quotations from official documents (e.g. white papers or the South African constitution) are taken from Hough and Du Plessis (2000).

12 National External Security Strategy input, Hough and Du Plessis (2000: 71).

13 The adopted version of the pact only obliges member countries to participate in 'such collective action in any matter it deems appropriate'. The full text of the pact is available on the SADC web site: http://www.sadc.int.

Chapter 11

Swaziland

Joshua Bheki Mzizi

Swaziland has been described as the last country with an absolute monarch in Africa. The notion of absolute monarchism can be traced to early European thought that held that the universe was a grand empire, founded upon principles of divine *logos* (Harding 1976). Judeo–Christian beliefs underscored the centrality of royal authority and the notion of the divine appointment and nature of kings. Royal absolutism, therefore, implied that kings were God's representatives among nations, commanding unsurpassed authority. In Europe today such notions are no longer tenable. On the other hand, it should be recalled that when European powers colonised Africa, one of their priorities was to weaken traditional forms of governance by locating the locus of power and social control somewhere in Europe. Traditional forms of governance were thus secondary.

The eventual 'death' of African traditional authority suited the colonial masters. When Africa's people began to call for democracy around the middle of the twentieth century, the primary question was, with what should colonial governance be replaced? The idea of reverting to the glorious past of African kingdoms and chiefdoms as edifices of power was not an option, because the colonial masters still wanted to perpetuate their interests in Africa. British Africa was thus channelled to adopt the Westminster model of parliamentary democracy, while in French Africa, colonialism was effectively continued. Neither worked for much longer.

This study will locate the problems of democratisation Swaziland has faced since 1968 in the context of a monarchical political regime. Swazi kingship is not absolute in the sense that Western thought holds, but has a rigid structure of checks and balances, although these are meant to consolidate power in the monarch. It is this conceptualisation of the centrality of the monarch that explains the nature and fundamental function of security in Swaziland.

Triumph of tradition

Swaziland's dominant cultural text is characterised by an ideology of traditionalism (Mzizi 2002), which is the cornerstone of the attempts to consolidate the modern superstructure. This ideology, according to Macmillan (1985), started to emerge in the 1920s and 1930s as Swazis were trying to come to terms with the social dislocation created by colonialism. Traditionalism as an ideology seeks to recover symbols of the past in the economy of legitimating modern systems in the socio-cultural and political community. While in agreement with Macmillan that, like culture, traditionalism – which is culture's functional expression – is dynamic in both form and content, Mzizi (2002: 168) argues as follows:

> This [dynamism] is a natural phenomenon true of all social facts, but the uniqueness of the Swazi scenario lies in the fact that the Swazi cultural reality falls into the trap of being used by the dominant group to legitimate the status quo. The most dangerous scenario is when the gullible masses are unaware that what they have always held to be culture and tradition are being used to subjugate them in whatever form. In this scenario, traditionalism falls into the trap of social class, serving the whims of the dominant class in their agenda of power wielding and self-preservation.

Swazi kingship survived through the hardships of colonialism owing to formidable and gallant attempts first displayed by Queen Regent Labotsibeni Mdluli, and later King Sobhuza II, her grandson. The queen regent, while sensitive to the inevitable processes of change, asserted a strong regency that prepared the new king, Sobhuza II, to fit into both the old and the new worlds with an agenda to either strike a balance between the two or employ elements of the old to dominate the new.

The colonial government had recognised Swaziland as a chiefdom under a paramount chief, as was common throughout British Africa. Sobhuza was thus allowed by British colonial practice to be in charge of all traditional institutions, except for matters that fell within the jurisdiction of the resident commissioner, the British crown's representative. Sobhuza II used this leverage to consolidate his power base, fighting off all colonial tendencies that threatened traditional institutions. In the 1950s and 1960s, however, the struggle for political independence led to tension between the new emerging ideology of party politics favoured by the British and the traditional ideology (Mzizi 1995: 172). Sobhuza had warned in 1959 that if the British were championing a constitutional dispensation that would undermine traditional authority, a constitutional crisis would result (Van Wyk 1965: 16).

It was the element of one-person-one-vote that Sobhuza saw as a threat to traditional authority. His attempts to win independence on the sole ticket of the monarchy failed, hence he was pushed to establish a royal political party, the Imbokodvo National Movement, in 1964. The power base of this movement was the monarchy, and its institutions were represented in the charismatic personality of Sobhuza himself, who commanded unquestioned allegiance from the entire population. He contested power at the independence elections and emerged with a sweeping victory, as if to prove a point to the colonial detractors that kings in Africa had inherent powers. To the British, kingship was to be constitutionally entrenched, but not to be politically contested, and to be confined to the traditional superstructure. To Sobhuza, kingdoms could not be half republics and half kingdoms. The authority of the king could in no way be compromised. This view was to have far-reaching consequences.

Political parties, especially the Ngwane National Liberatory Congress (NNLC), led by a medical doctor, Ambrose Zwane, espoused a pan-African ideology. Its appeal to the working class threatened the dominance of the king's party in the 1972 elections. However, it won a meagre three parliamentary seats, signalling the end of multi-partyism in Swaziland, and the beginning of a long-drawn-out process of constitution making. Seeing that the independence constitution had admitted political pluralism, and that this scenario could in the long run jeopardise the dominance of the monarchy, Sobhuza banned political parties on 12 April 1973. By using extra-legal traditional powers, he thus succeeded in asserting himself in the position of political as well as traditional leader (Wanda 1990). In a well-prepared proclamation, he reasoned as follows:

- the constitution has indeed failed to provide the machinery of good governance and for the maintenance of peace and order;
- the constitution is indeed the cause of growing unrest, insecurity, dissatisfaction with the state of affairs in our country and an impediment to free and progressive development in all spheres of life;
- the constitution has permitted the importation into our country of highly undesirable political practices alien to, and incompatible with the way of life in our society and designed to disrupt and destroy our peaceful and constructive and essentially democratic methods of political activity. Increasingly this element engenders hostility, bitterness and unrest in our peaceful society (Kingdom of Swaziland 1973a: secs. 2(a), (b), and (c)).

The constitutional crisis that Sobhuza had predicted in 1959 had indeed come to pass. To him, full freedom and independence could not be realised until a home-grown constitution that would guarantee peace, order, good governance, happiness, and the welfare of the Swazi nation was crafted.

It has been argued that actually Sobhuza II had the best of intentions in 1973. Kuper (1978: 336–37), his official biographer, sees the 1973 events as a turn from

> nominal political independence into a full sovereignty under a leader who had proven his wisdom and moral courage over the years, a man ready to listen to all sides before making a decision, a King who was not a tyrant, a King inspired by ideals of the best in a traditional African monarchy in which there was the interplay of councils and the King [was] the mouthpiece of the people.

Kuper's highly positive remarks are based on the traditional role of Swazi kings that had no concept of absolute authority (Booth 1983; Hlatshwayo 1994), since various councils (*emabandla)* were put in place to check and balance the powers and decisions of a king. These councils were established on the principle that they were representative. Hence selection into their membership was not arbitrary.

But in 1973 the king assumed supreme powers that made him both the centre and circumference of the entire political machinery. Clearly he had taken charge of every facet of Swaziland's political life, both in the traditional domain and in the modern governance sector. He assumed all executive powers previously granted to the prime minister and cabinet. He could act now at his own discretion, consulting whomsoever he wished without being bound by law. He gave himself power to detain without charge for a renewable 60 days any person he deemed was a threat to the peace, and the courts had no jurisdiction to listen to cases of detention. Meetings of a political nature, including processions and demonstrations, were to be controlled by the commissioner of police (Mzizi 1995: 176).

Sobhuza recreated himself into an absolute monarch who, until 1978, ruled the country with a council of ministers that, according to the legislative procedure order of 13 April 1973, had no final say on any legal bill, but were limited to drafting it and handing it to the king to pass as a king's-order-in-council (Mzizi 1995: 177).

The Umbutfo Swaziland Defence Force (UDF) was formed during the turbulent 1973 crisis with the sole mandate of defending the institution of kingship against internal challenges. *Umbutfo* is a siSwati word for 'regiment', and by tradition regiments are established and named by a king for the purpose of protecting kingship. Regiments in the traditional sense must undergo a period of royal training that involves painstaking discipline, a ritual from which they graduate with an insignia of special beads called *simohlwana*. While undergoing the initiation process, they must demonstrate unflinching love for and loyalty to the king and country. The expression they use after graduation is, *tsine sigane iNkhosi* (we are married to the king). Thus it was the case that the first 600 recruits into the UDF were drawn from strong, able-bodied young and middle-aged men who had passed the traditional initiation at different times. They were now ready to defend the king, not with the traditional shield and battle-axe, but with rifles and modern artillery.

Towards a homegrown constitutional dispensation

In the aftermath of the 1973 events, Sobhuza II set up the Royal Constitutional Review Commission. Membership and the terms of reference were wholly determined by him. The terms, which were never gazetted, included a provision to inquire into the broad parameters upon which Swaziland's constitution should be based (Kuper 1978: 338). The report of that commission, including its *modus operandi,* was never made public. But a logical assumption is that King's-Order-in-Council 23/1978, which established a parliament, was a consequence of that royal commission. The order not only established the procedure for election, but also retained the powers of the king to make laws by decree and cemented the 1973 proclamation as the supreme law of Swaziland, subject only to amendments or repeal by the king after a 'new Constitution for the Kingdom of Swaziland has been accepted by the King and the people of Swaziland and brought into force and effect' (Kingdom of Swaziland 1978).

Making educated observations on the tensions Swaziland has experienced since 1973, Khumalo (1996) says:

> One reason for the escalation in the nature of the constitutional tensions arising from the dual system operating in Swaziland ... has been the manner in which this system attempts to consolidate traditional authority structures within a predominantly modern system of government. Prior to the repeal of the constitution in 1973, the traditional structures were given recognition, but at a separate level of the administration. In this way, although some tensions were inevitable, they were much more confined than they have been since 1978. The question which arises, therefore, is how can we address the tensions in view of the fact that there

will always be some interaction between the traditional and modern sectors?

The search for a truly Swazi philosophical framework was itself a plausible idea, but it was how to go about the project that seemed to complicate the exercise, and perhaps derail its focus. The male-dominated commission was made up of staunch royalists. It would appear that the motive behind such a selection was to put together a team that would carry out an already predetermined mandate. The commission did not entertain the issue of multi-party politics, but instead focused on laying the groundwork for an electoral system that would be controlled and superintended by chiefdoms, and ultimately by the king, through royally appointed committees. When the Establishment of the Parliament of Swaziland order (Kingdom of Swaziland 1978) came into force, it was apparent that elections were to be conducted for the purpose of establishing an electoral college, which was the body that elected members of parliament. Nominations for parliament were made in secret. Quite clearly, this was a way of ensuring that parliament comprised candidates who would enhance the power and prestige of the monarchy. Although Sobhuza II had indicated that the 1978 reforms were still an experiment, the executors of the experiment believed otherwise, i.e. that it was a permanent arrangement to be safeguarded by hook or by crook. There was much national consternation on the unrepresentative nature of parliament and the seemingly unsophisticated methods of selecting candidates for the electoral college. Members of the electoral college, for instance, were voted for by the public in *tinkhundla* centres through an open single-file method, in the manner of cows bound for a dipping tank. Defenders of the experiment held that it was the most traditional way of doing things. But one thing was certain: the power of the monarch over the modern political process remained intact. This was considered the primary motif that would hold the nation together and ward off so-called foreign ideologies.

Sobhuza died in 1982 during the first phase of the experiment that was already showing signs of political corruption and abuse in the name of the king. The Liqoqo, or Royal Council, was announced as the supreme council of state soon after Sobhuza's demise. It started by amending the Sedition Act of 1938, coming up with the 1983 Sedition and Subversive Activities Amendment Act. Opposition to the Liqoqo was considered a seditious act and carried a maximum prison term of 20 years. The regency left by Sobhuza was thrown into turmoil, as the Liqoqo wielded unbridled power in creating self-serving legislation.

The final showcase of the Liqoqo was the dethronement of the queen regent for failure to accede to some of the fast-lane innovations. But internal power struggles weakened members' resolve, and by 1986 the Liqoqo had disintegrated.

Mswati III, Sobhuza's successor, has made three major attempts at reform. The methodology he employs, for good or bad, hinges on the doctrine of consolidating royal power. Instead of taking a neutral position and letting Swazis debate the nature of the monarchy they desire, the king has been in control of all the efforts in the same manner as his father was. Mswati III set up the first commission in 1990 as an outgrowth of his traditional kraal meetings, dubbed 'the peoples' parliament' by the media. A senior prince who had served in Sobhuza's cabinet was appointed to guide the commission's activities. This commission had a loose structure and an informal mandate, hence its report was only verbally presented at the royal kraal without the expected setting of officialdom and circumstance. The king must have learned his lesson from this loose structure, as people talked about anything under the sun, and the media were there to report on every public meeting. For that reason, he set up the Tinkhundla Review Commission (TRC) by Decree 1/1992, but more to focus on the electoral system, and not the constitutional question as such.

Once again the normative factor was injected in section 3(b)(iv) of the terms of reference. The commission's mandate was to receive views regarding

> the way in which Customary Institutions in the Kingdom of Swaziland should and/or could be accommodated in the political system of the Kingdom of Swaziland in view of their important constitutional and social role in terms of Swazi Law and Custom (Kingdom of Swaziland 1992).

Khumalo (1996: 9) remarks as follows on the limitations imposed on the commission:

> First, the investigation into the structural arrangement of the constitution was necessarily limited. The monarchy, for instance, and its role in the constitution was presumed to be beyond question .... Second, the initial presumption appears to be that the customary institutions must be accommodated in any future constitution.

According to Khumalo (1996), the question of monarchical support should have been put to the public litmus test. Had this route been followed, different opinions would have emerged and a fresh conceptualisation of the monarchy would have been possible in a new constitutional dispensation. Secondly, the reference to customary practices was a clear mandate to expand and refine the *tinkhundla* philosophy of 1978.

The commission reported that Swazis had rejected the return to party politics (Kingdom of Swaziland 1992b). Executive authority was to be vested in the king, who should continue to appoint a prime minister and a cabinet in consultation with the prime minister. Two innovative elements were recommended on electoral procedure: that election to parliament should be direct, and elections should be by secret ballot. These two elements were incorporated in the Establishment of Parliament Order, 1992 (Kingdom of Swaziland 1992c). But again the supremacy of the monarchy over the executive and everything else was spelt out in section 55, as follows:

> The King may require the Prime Minister and other Ministers to consult with him on any matter relating to the Government of Swaziland, and the Prime Minister shall keep the King fully informed concerning the general conduct of the government of Swaziland and shall furnish him with such information as he may request in respect of any particular matter relating to the government of Swaziland.

In addition, section 51(2) stipulates that the king may remove the prime minister or any other minister from office at any time, and is not obliged to give reasons for his actions. The king's decision cannot be challenged in a court of law. Although the TRC report (Swaziland 1992b) recommended that Swaziland must craft a constitution with a bill of rights, four years were to pass before a Constitutional Review Commission (CRC) would be set up. Like all previous commissions, the CRC was directly stage-managed by the king through a prince.

There was an attempt, as had been the case in the 1992 effort, to appoint a broad-based commission. But the non-representative clause in the terms of reference fuelled obvious suspicions to the extent that, and in addition to other precipitating factors, it led some progressive and enlightened commissioners to abandon the exercise. The subsequent 1996 commission was very large in size, composed mainly of a cocktail of individuals perceived to be supporters of the monarchy, but with no knowledge of the task before them. Many of the commissioners, while taking glory in the fact that they had been royally appointed, saw their new task largely as an employment opportunity.

Deviating from its original mandate to produce a draft constitution within two years, the commission managed only to come up with a shoddy report three years after the deadline, in 2001. On the role of the king, the CRC (Kingdom of Swaziland 2001: 77, 82) states:

> All powers of governing (ruling) and reigning over the Kingdom must remain entrenched in the Ngwenyama, according to Swazi law and custom and existing laws; if the King is not there, in the Ndlovukazi, and if both are not there, in the Authorized Person ... The nation further insists that the King's Office must be established, be autonomous, be strong and be a microcosm of the various government ministries, departments and sections ... Parliament must work to perpetuate the *Tinkhundla* System of Government.

As was the case with the 1992 TRC, the CRC made a comment on the question of multi-party politics:

> An overwhelming majority of the nation recommends that political parties must remain banned. They do not want political parties in the kingdom. There is an insignificant minority which recommends that political parties must be unbanned. The recommendation is that political parties must remain banned in the Kingdom. The existing laws regarding this position must be enforced (Kingdom of Swaziland 2001: 95).

The CRC report was subsequently presented to the constitution-drafting committee as an important reference document that contained the views of the nation on some highly contentious issues. The new constitution of Swaziland, which was assented to by the king on 26 July 2005 and was due to come into force in January 2006, has been viewed correctly as centralising power in the monarchy and underscoring the pervasiveness of tradition over modernity. Both the TRC and CRC reports favoured an executive monarch with far-reaching powers, which is the spirit of the 1973 King's Proclamation to the Nation. The constitution has captured these sentiments and enshrined them variously throughout the document. The dual legal system is recognised by the constitution, and all matters that are subject to Swazi law and custom are prohibited from being adjudicated under common law. The constitution does contain a bill of rights, albeit with the usual claw-back clauses. But the freedoms of assembly and association that purport to open up the political space for political pluralism are limited by the imposition of the *tinkhundla* system, which was declared democratic and inclusive. Below are the relevant sections that illustrate the material contradictions on this point (Kingdom of Swaziland 2005):

> Section 58(1): Swaziland shall be a democratic country dedicated to principles which empower and encourage the active participation of all citizens at all levels in their own governance.
>
> Section 58(6): The State shall promote among the people of Swaziland, the culture of political tolerance and all organs of State and people of Swaziland shall work towards the promotion of national unity, peace and stability.

These provisions should be contrasted with the following:

> Section 79: The system of government for Swaziland is a democratic, participatory, *tinkhundla*-based system which emphasises devolution of state power from central government to *tinkhundla* areas and individual merit as a basis for election or appointment to public office.
>
> Section 80(3) The *tinkhundla* units or areas, inspired by a policy of decentralisation of state power, are the engines of development and the central pillars underpinning the political organisation and economic infrastructure of the country through which social services to the different parts of the Swazi society are facilitated and delivered.

Although the constitution appears to favour political liberalisation, there is a strong bias towards maintaining the status quo insofar as political agitation and organisation are concerned. If political parties are to make any impact on matters of governance, they must needs conform to the philosophy of *tinkhundla*. This is, of course, a far-fetched, ambitious expectation, especially for the NNLC, which espouses a pan-African ideology, and the People's United Democratic Movement (PUDEMO), which upholds a socialist democratic model of governance.

Finally, the new constitution of Swaziland was eventually signed by the monarch after all the clauses he had a particular interest in were changed to conform to his whims and tastes. The direct influence of the Swazi National Council Standing Committee could not be discounted as the debates gained momentum. While this was not in contradiction with the terms of reference of either the CRC or TRC, many observers felt that the king's interventions towards the close of the exercise could be seen more as political interference than meaningful dialogue with the nation. The future of the constitution of Swaziland is yet to be judged.

That being said, the reality remains that Mswati III's attempts at reform have been marred by a litany of problems. Internal pressure, although officially ignored, continues to be disruptive of the royal agenda for how change should be managed. The dissenting voices are heard far and wide, thanks to the international media and access to the internet. Faced with these realities, the king has landed himself in further trouble by assigning to himself the prerogative to manage change virtually on his own terms. This *modus operandi* creates problems of legitimacy, because of the inherent vested interest in the outcome of the process. Holding unequivocally to the strategy and philosophy of his late father, Mswati III desires to see a constitutional dispensation that will endorse him as an unbridled superintendent of all the modern and traditional socio-cultural and political institutions.

His commissions, because of their chronic failure to demonstrate objectively how they aggregate public opinion, can be seen as tools for repeating at best what they perceive he wants to hear, or at worst what he tells them in the closed regular consultative meetings. The normative factor, namely, the immanence of traditionalism, receives reasoned configurations and, with little regard for the complexities of the implications, imposes the traditional factor on every facet of Swazi life. This has caused problems in governance and the rule of law. On the question of individual liberties and fundamental freedom, the CRC reported:

> The nation recommends that rights and freedom which we accept must not conflict with our customs and traditions as the Swazi nation. Agreements with other states and international organisations which deal with rights and freedoms must be submitted to the nation (at *Tinkhundla*) before such agreements become law in the Kingdom (Kingdom of Swaziland 2001: 83).

The state of the opposition

The banning of political parties in 1973 in effect meant that any organised opposition to the operation or processes of government was circumscribed, killing the ethos and spirit of opposition politics so vital for emerging democracies and good governance. Dr Ambrose Zwane, leader of the NNLC, was detained and harassed, eventually seeking refuge in Tanzania. Zwane's escape did not please Sobhuza, who still wanted to be viewed as a nationalist supporter of Africa's liberation. Besides, Zwane's ancestors and other close relatives were traditionally connected to royalty, playing very significant leadership roles and functions. The king therefore reverted to diplomacy to secure Zwane's return on condition that he would not again be disruptive of the status quo, while Sobhuza himself made an undertaking never again to detain him. Zwane returned to the kingdom already a sickly and frail man. The ordeal had taken its toll on him, and Sobhuza's resolve to kill off the NNLC had been achieved.

During the Liqoqo era, PUDEMO was launched by a group of university students who were responding to the widespread violation of human rights in general, and the deposition of the queen regent in particular. PUDEMO's programme expanded from these primary concerns to address the core of the problem, namely, the absence of an official opposition. The law was invoked to deal with PUDEMO malcontents, but their voices were heard far and wide because their concerns resonated with popular public sentiment. A 1994 letter to the king (Mzizi 1995: 188–89) clearly spells out PUDEMO's demands:

- The 1973 State of Emergency and all other representative laws should be repealed;
- The unconditional return and indemnification of all political exiles should be gazetted;
- An interim government to administer the process of democratic change should be established;
- The *Tinkhundla* government is squandering public funds and further fails to properly manage the country's economy … [It is a] government that is not democratic, transparent and accountable to the masses but is controlled and directed by secret cabals. A government where those government officials who were found guilty of corruption and treasonable acts are rewarded with promotions. A government which does not listen to the voices of the toiling masses.

Apart from issuing statements and organising marches, PUDEMO has not embarked on an aggressive strategy that would force government to the negotiation table. Police torture and harassment, including the relocation and demise of the original leadership, succeeded in killing the initial enthusiasm. Through its youth wing, the Swaziland Youth Congress, PUDEMO has continued to exert pressure by appealing to external forces to join in the call for the democratisation of Swaziland. The Swaziland Solidarity Network, operating from Johannesburg, South Africa, is one such effort that continues to make periodic attacks on the Swazi government.

Alongside PUDEMO, the Swaziland Federation of Trade Unions (SFTU) has also made calls for democratisation, using both internal and external mechanisms. The SFTU's policy document indicates a resolve to fight for citizens' rights; human rights; and political, cultural, and economic rights.

The SFTU has exploited its status in the International Labour Organisation (ILO) by comparing oppressive laws in Swaziland with corresponding ILO conventions. Police harassment of the SFTU and other workers is carefully documented to support the charges. As a result of the SFTU's sustained complaints, the ILO has deployed three missions since 1998 to review the situation in Swaziland. As this is usually very embarrassing for the government, the SFTU has been charged with advancing a secret agenda to overthrow the state (Mzizi 2002: 210–13). However, this strategy has kept the Swazi government on its toes, as the repercussions of losing export benefits through the Generalised System of Preferences and other import/export privileges are too great to countenance. Swaziland's textile industry and the sugar export trade can only be sustainable if these trade benefits exist.

Other formations that have been calling for democratisation include the Council of Swaziland Churches through its Peace and Justice Department, the Human Rights Association of Swaziland, Lawyers for Human Rights, and the Swaziland Democratic Alliance. Each of these formations has made its voice heard at various stages, but they have all been systematically ignored by the establishment. However, a landmark process first mooted in the late 1980s by government finally saw the light of day in 1997, when various stakeholders were assembled by government to craft a 2025 vision statement for Swaziland. The result was the National Development Strategy (NDS) (Kingdom of Swaziland 1997).

Chapter 8 of the NDS is entitled 'Governance and public sector management'. The opening paragraph underscores the progressive notion that good governance is a collective responsibility of the entire society. Making direct reference to the effect of the 1973 events, the NDS states:

> The separation of powers between the three arms of government, particularly the role of the judiciary was compromised. The lack of a participatory process, specifically in the political sphere, led to the progressive erosion of a national set of values and vision around which the citizens could be mobilised (Kingdom of Swaziland 1997).

Although appearing after the CRC had been set up, the NDS suggested some strategic objectives that would make the envisaged constitution widely acceptable. According to the NDS, a constitution

> will be the supreme law of the land, ensuring the separation of powers of the three arms of government (the executive, legislature and judiciary), defining the universally accepted tenets

> such as a Bill of Rights guaranteeing freedom of association and speech; rule of law; freedom of the press; protection of disadvantaged groups; equality and protection against all forms of discrimination (Kingdom of Swaziland 1997: 66).

The NDS recognised that a viable constitution-making process should take place in an enabling environment where free political expression is guaranteed and mechanisms for wider representation are respected. It recommended the establishment of 'structures for promoting broad participation in the politics of the land to ensure full participation of all social formations in the formulation of a constitution or set of national conventions' (Kingdom of Swaziland 1997).

When the king launched the NDS in 1999, the government had been pressured to doctor the original document by removing all references to the political question. The explanation given was that the CRC was working on those matters. The legal ramifications were perhaps exaggerated, for no national strategy or development plan carries any force of law.

A series of blunders that have compromised the judiciary since the late 1990s have resulted in yet another formation: the Swaziland Coalition of Concerned Civic Organisations (SCCCO). Launched on 2 January 2003, the SCCCO comprises the Federation of Swaziland Employers, the Swaziland Chamber of Commerce and Industry, the Association of Swaziland Business Community, the SFTU, the Swaziland Federation of Labour, the various churches, the Law Society, the Co-ordinating Assembly of NGOs, and the Swaziland National Association of Teachers.

Repeating the sentiments of earlier formations and calls made over the past two decades, the SCCCO is

> concerned with the disastrous state of affairs prevailing in the country, breakdown in the rule of law, deepening bad governance, deteriorating economic environment and growing threat to the country's trade privileges i.e. GSP and AGOA and absence of convincing political direction, attendant fear and uncertainty to the social and business environment (*Swazi Observer* 2003).

It is increasingly becoming clear that the ideology of traditionalism is under severe threat. Unless adjustments are made in both the traditional and modern political structures, the winds of change might shake the foundations of kingship and compromise the (false) peace and stability that Swaziland has been known for since independence. The trend is that basic tenets of modern governance should supersede the traditional notions that have only succeeded in silencing dissenting voices and providing fertile ground for corruption and political failure. To the traditionalists, Sobhuza II's understanding of the dual role of the kings of Africa who ruled and reigned needs to be preserved and entrenched. The competing view is that such a combined role is dangerous for the continued existence of the monarchy itself, hence it is imperative to respond to modern democratic processes.

As the tensions rage between the old and the new, matters of national security cannot be ignored. The preservation of the old, as indicated above, affected the military in Swaziland in 1973. What has been emerging ever since is an amorphous re-creation that pretends to respond, reluctantly, to modern democratic ideals that could be easily subsumed into a skewed cultural colouring. The major players in the process of selecting and adaptating what can be subsumed are the ruling elite who, as has been argued above, use their individuated understanding of tradition as a yardstick both in the selection process and the adaptation agenda. When attempts are made to establish national consensus on fundamental issues, the dominant group uses its power to edit the final product so that it confirms and conforms to its own values and aspirations. In Swaziland, one is not overstating the case to say that the people were colonised at two levels: the external, by a foreign power that lasted effectively until 1968; and then the internal, by the colonising forces that predated European colonialism and aimed to perpetuate the Dlamini aristocracy beyond independence from Britain. The intention may be to work for the common good and stability of the nation, but the lack of honest openness perpetuates allegations of dictatorship.

Conceptions of security: the apartheid challenge

Two regional liberation struggles affected Swaziland in historical terms: that led by the ANC against apartheid South Africa, and that of SWAPO in Namibia. The context of these struggles was the express intention of Southern African countries to devise ways of isolating South Africa by minimising economic dependence on that country. Swaziland's position geographically is vulnerable indeed: land-locked, bordering on South Africa, and with close economic ties to that country. For that reason, the Swazi state could not sever quasi-diplomatic ties with apartheid South Africa, mutually masquerading as trade missions. Whereas it remained a historical fact that the Swazi royalty had supported the formation of the ANC in 1912, and the incumbent king had maintained his membership of the ANC, by nature royal politics was conservative. Thus, in one sense, any gain of momentum by the ANC was seen as a potential threat to Swazi royal politics and hegemony.

This led the Swazi state to refuse to give open support to the regional liberation struggles, especially where South Africa was involved or had a direct interest. Lack of support meant practically preventing such movements from operating within the borders of Swaziland. Cordial relations also existed between the Swazi regime and the Portuguese colonial government in Mozambique. While over 90 per cent of Swaziland's imports came from South Africa and most exports had to be sent outside the region, the SADCC and the Commonwealth, as well the UN, approved of aid only on the Lomé Convention principle that any bilateral links with Pretoria would disqualify the country concerned from receiving such aid. Meanwhile, South Africa created a lucrative deal that would tempt its immediate neighbours: the establishment of the South African Customs Union. Commenting on the predicament Swaziland found itself in during that period, Davies *et al.* (1985: 72–73) remarks:

> The Swazi regime further appears aware of the inevitable domestic political risks of being seen by its own population to be closely identified with the apartheid regime. At the regional level, the actions of the SADCC countries and Frontline States have some restraining impact on the Swazi regime's stance in the region. Finally, there have been intangible ideological factors whose effect is difficult either to assess or predict. The most important here was the express reluctance of King Sobhuza to act openly against the ANC, for the apparent reason that the Swazi monarchy was involved in its formation in 1912 and retained some sentimental attachment to the organisation.

However one looks at these factors, they suggest a confused policy on crucial regional issues that Swaziland had to grapple with. This confusion was evidenced by especially the following positions. In 1969, one year after independence, Swaziland signed the Lusaka Manifesto binding all African states to ostracise South Africa, save only when the issue of power transfer to the majority in South Africa was on the table. In 1970, Swaziland abstained from voting for an OAU resolution condemning the 'dialogue offensive' tactics of the apartheid regime. But Swaziland supported all the UN resolutions that sought to nullify South Africa's occupation of Namibia. Meanwhile, and with meticulous care and diplomacy, Swaziland accepted South African refugees. The latter was to become the most irritating practice for the apartheid regime, hence pressure was put on the Swazi state to restrict its generosity in this area or face the wrath of Pretoria. At this time, the apartheid regime was hell-bent on fostering a willingness among its neighbours to be 'police agents' against any possible guerrilla attack on South Africa (see Geldenhuys 1981).

To enforce the creation of the South African-proposed Constellation of Southern African States, South Africa offered bribes that ranged from cash to capital projects. Meanwhile the ANC guerrilla agents desperately wanted to make Swaziland a 'second front', something that Pretoria caught on to, and it embarked on offensive campaigns against ANC operatives in the country. The most lucrative offers Pretoria dangled were the construction of the Komatipoort–Richards Bay railway line via Swaziland, which would ensure access to the sea; and the offer to return the KaNgwane Bantustan and the Ngwavuma area near KwaZulu to Swaziland, as both were initially part of Swazi territory. Sobhuza II could not resist these offers, and in February 1982, in the twilight months of his long reign, he signed a secret non-aggression pact with Pretoria. The pact bound Swaziland and South Africa to combat terrorism, insurgency, and subversion within the two territories, and also provided that joint forces would be detailed to deal with such threats.

The result of this pact was the selling out of ANC activists to the South African forces. A number of ANC guerrillas were murdered within the boundaries of Swaziland, following police co-operation at the highest level. Most of the atrocities committed in Swaziland were revealed for the first time during the South African Truth and Reconciliation Commission's hearings, headed by Archbishop Desmond Tutu. Evidence led pointed at one apartheid operative, Eugene de Kock, as having been especially commissioned to deal with possible insurgents in Swaziland. It was the open signing of the Nkomati Accord between Mozambique and South Africa that cemented Swaziland's relationship with Pretoria. In May 1984 the prime minister of Swaziland led a huge government delegation on a state visit to South Africa, ostensibly to formalise the establishment of diplomatic relations. Sobhuza had died in 1982, and domestic instabilities were mounting and threatening the Swazi interim regime. Perhaps that was the reason for the paradigm shift from being secretive with Pretoria to being open, creating further hostilities between the Swazi regime and the ANC.

The liberation of South Africa in 1994 meant that there had to be shifts once again on the part of the Southern African states to include South Africa as a major economic role player. Matters of defence and security also had to take on a fresh dimension. Swaziland has been keenly involved in the creation of the SADC ISDSC and has prepared its soldiers for regional commitments by training them in peacekeeping, which has been undertaken with great enthusiasm. Peacekeeping is now part of the training curriculum for every soldier, while senior personnel have been sent for additional training at the Regional Peacekeeping Training Centre in Harare.

A sterling contribution to the resolution of a simmering dispute between

Angola and Zambia was made by Swaziland's former minister of foreign affairs and trade, Albert Shabangu. Swaziland was chairing the ISDSC when Angola accused Zambia of harbouring rebels for diamonds as payment in kind. Shabangu successfully mediated between the two countries. This showed that Swaziland had the potential of contributing positively to regional peace and stability, despite its tainted past.

National security revisited

Nevertheless, as indicated in this study, civil discontent indicates that national security is strongly contested. The powers that be, depending on the pressures of the moment, do try to make concessions, however inadequate and clumsy, for the sake of maintaining the (false) peace and the make-believe view that change in Swaziland is by national consensus. This study has indicated that in practice, national dialogue is more idealistic, and therefore ideological, than empirical. National policy on matters of security thus hinges on the ideology of domination first coined by Sobhuza II, who philosophised that he had no enemies because he believed in dialogue. This has become Swaziland's quasi-national policy in matters of conflict resolution. Yet in reality, as an anonymous interviewee indicated, 'this is seldom the intention in Swaziland. Dialogue to us means monologue ... for when issues are of a political nature, the monarchy resorts to heavy-handed tactics in order to deter dissenting opinion and deflate militant malcontents'.

Another anonymous interviewee reasoned thus:

> [T]he national conception of security in Swaziland centres around the conservative ruling elite whose philosophy is to safeguard the king's authority and the attendant rituals like the Incwala, king's birthdays, and independence celebrations. All these and other ceremonies are for the ritualisation of kingship, which is the centre and axis of Swazi socio-political and religious life. Active security measures are taken to protect these ceremonies that extol the head of state as custodian of Swazi ethos.

Swaziland does not have a written security policy. It is assumed that every soldier will know what it is he must protect the minute a gun is thrust into his hands. Internal security policy is determined on a case-by-case basis, largely influenced by personal considerations.

An informant from the intelligence department of the UDF explained this point thus:

> The head of state determines the approach to be taken whenever there is an internal security issue. The antagonising forces are identified in terms of leadership and then appropriately targeted. As such, it not the issues these leaders raise that matter, but themselves as frontline players. Therefore, policy directives are engaged based on personalities rather than the issues at hand.

The processes followed in deciding security policy are as follows: firstly, the commissioner of police identifies a problem and gathers intelligence information to support his case. He then takes the matter to the king with all the facts he has obtained. The king then summons the heads of the army and prisons, who naturally cannot hold opinions contrary to that of the commissioner of police. The king then takes the matter to his various advisory bodies, most, if not all, of which have no expertise on matters of security. The resultant action is taken based on the advice given by these advisory bodies. But it must be underscored that as commander-in-chief, the king takes charge of all operations where the army is involved. The Defence Council exists only in name, according to most of the key people interviewed for this study. The rules of procedure for the council are neither here nor there. An anonymous senior Swazi soldier responded to the question on intelligence as follows:

> Most national security-related actions taken in this country are more reactive than proactive. This has largely been influenced by members' fears of being the harbinger of bad news. The system has an in-built tendency to shoot the messenger rather than address the issue. Therefore people [are] loathe to offer proactive advice. In addition to this, such offer[s] may show a relatively advanced knowledge of security matters, which in turn may be interpreted as a threat by the powers that be.

The study could not establish if Swaziland actually has an external security policy. However, the country has participated actively in the ISDSC and in drafting the SADC Mutual Defence Pact, and in other regional initiatives. Regarding Swaziland's external policy, the case of the actions of the former foreign minister, Albert Shabangu, in his mediation of the Zambian–Angolan crisis is enthusiastically quoted as an example of a success story. Apart from that, the UDF has participated in peacekeeping exercises and continues to send its officers on advanced training in peacekeeping in defence colleges in the region.

Conclusion

Swaziland's uniqueness in the SADC region, and indeed in Africa, is that it is a kingdom that has vested all executive authority in the monarchy. This clearly is an imposition by the monarchy itself, playing on the notion that tradition does not recognise power contests. In the Swazi context, this has occurred while there are growing voices calling for the redefinition and reconceptualisation of kingship and traditional authority. If kingship elects to remain in the mainstream body politic, how far can it accommodate dissenting voices?

Swaziland needs to solve the fundamental issues raised in this study, namely, the functional role of tradition, from being an ideology of domination to a shared value system in a transitory situation dictated by modern imperatives of the ideal society. Khumalo (1996) argues that a meaningful strategy in the goal of creating a constitutional dispensation is to determine the nature of the interconnections in a single unit between traditional and modern structures. Once the interlinkages have been carefully identified, the tensions caused by the competing elements between modernity and traditionalism might be minimised. Khumalo's suggestions have been raised by several other commentators, although agreement on the way forward has not been found. But voices calling for meaningful democratic change are growing louder, and the attention and role of the international community cannot be ignored. Swaziland might be in danger of being isolated internationally. The diplomatic interventions by some SADC heads of state, in addition to the demands expected from states that participate in trade initiatives such as NEPAD, are indicators that if Swaziland continues to be intransigent and deceptive in the project of democratisation, it might itself become a security risk in the region sooner rather than later.

Chapter 12

Tanzania

Mohammed Omar Maundi

Tanzania has experienced substantial political transformation since independence in 1961. The country adopted a new constitution in 1962, which emphasised consolidating its independence. In 1964 Tanganyika and Zanzibar formed the United Republic of Tanzania, which soon moved from a multi-party to a one-party political system. In 1967, the country proclaimed the Arusha Declaration, which aimed at *ujamaa,* or socialism and self-reliance. Socialism focused on turning Tanzania into an egalitarian society, while self-reliance aimed at reducing the country's dependence on foreign resources for its social and economic development.

The 1964 union produced complex political structures. Zanzibar maintained its autonomy and all the important institutions of state – executive, legislature, and judiciary. Its government, headed by an executive president, consists of all ministries except those of foreign affairs, home affairs, and defence, which are shared between the two entities that make up the union. The former Tanganyika, however, surrendered its autonomy to the union. Therefore, instead of having three governments, there are only two: one for Zanzibar and the other for the union.

The 1964 merger was not extended to the ruling parties: the Tanzania (formerly Tanganyika) African National Union (TANU) for the mainland, and the Afro-Shirazi Party (ASP) for Zanzibar. Thus by 1965 Tanzania became a peculiar 'one-party' state with one 'sovereignty', two governments and two political parties. This unconventional structure made it difficult to determine whether Tanzania was a unitary state, a federation, or a confederation, and whether the country was a one-party or multi-party state. This was changed in 1977, when the two political parties merged to form Chama cha Mapinduzi (Party of the Revolution – CCM). In the same year a permanent constitution replaced the 1965 interim constitution.

The mid-1980s witnessed more political changes. The 1977 constitution was amended in 1984, leading to the separation of the presidential post from the chairmanship of the ruling party and limiting presidential terms to two of five years each. In 1985 the presidency changed hands from Julius Nyerere to Ali Hassan Mwinyi, following Nyerere's voluntary retirement. President Mwinyi served the last ten years of the one-party political system. He was replaced by President Benjamin William Mkapa, who was elected in 1995 through a re-introduced multi-party political system. President Mkapa was re-elected in 2000 to serve his last term. The 2005 general elections produced a new president, Jakaya Mrisho Kikwete.

Democratic transition

Tanzania's democratic transition began in 1992, when legislation was introduced for a multi-party democratic system (Maundi 2002c: 42–47). The drivers of the process were civil society and the ruling party, the CCM. The last two years of the 1980s witnessed a robust civil society lobby pressing for democratic reforms. The lobby drew its inspiration from neighbouring Zambia, Kenya, and Burundi, and also capitalised on the favourable regional and international political environment, which encouraged political reforms.

Amid this pressure from civic organisations, former President Nyerere encouraged a national dialogue on political transformation. Nyerere's initiative demonstrated his foresightedness in interpreting correctly the changing domestic, regional, and international situations. Domestically, there was economic liberalisation that needed to be complemented with political transformation. Regionally, many African regimes were losing their legitimacy due to political and economic mismanagement. At the international level, the donor community was applying pressure to African governments to liberalise. Also, the collapse of the Soviet Union encouraged the democratisation of Eastern Europe and Africa. With the demise of socialist solidarity, Tanzania had to come up with its own formula for a democratic transition.

Conditions for the democratic transition in Tanzania were set by the ruling party, the CCM, and its governments. A presidential commission was established in March 1991 – the Nyalali Commission – which recommended a transition to a multi-party political system. In January 1992 the National Executive Committee of the CCM endorsed the commission's recommendations, and in May the National Assembly enacted a multi-party law, which became effective in July 1992. By 2005 there were 18 registered political parties.

In 1995 Tanzania held its first multi-party elections both on the mainland and in Zanzibar. Some 13 political parties presented 1,338 candidates for the 232 parliamentary seats. Only four political parties put up candidates for the presidency. The elections were monitored by local and foreign observers.

While the elections were declared free and fair for the mainland, the situation was different in Zanzibar, where the process was not only considered not free and fair, but its outcome was contested by the major opposition party.

The holding of the second multi-party elections in the year 2000 was a demonstration that Tanzania's democratic process was maturing. This time only 701 candidates competed for the same number of seats as in the 1995 elections. The decrease could have been the result of streamlining within the political parties. As in 1995, only four parties put up candidates for the presidency.

These elections were considered free and fair, but again, only for the mainland. In Zanzibar the major opposition party, the Civic United Front (CUF), refused to accept the results and to recognise the government, just as in 1995. This created a political impasse, which reached a climax on 27 January 2001 when the CUF decided to demonstrate in order to press for a repeat of the elections, the rewriting of the union and Zanzibar constitutions, and the reconstitution of the mainland's and Zanzibar's electoral commissions. The demonstrations resulted in more than 20 deaths and the first crop of Tanzanian political refugees.

The controversies of the 1995 and 2000 elections in Zanzibar had their genesis in the islands' historical, racial, political, and regional divide. Controversies date back to the pre-independence elections of 1957, 1961, and 1963, which paved the way for independence in 1963 (Maliyamkono 2000). Pre-independence elections demonstrated that the islands were deeply divided along ethnic lines. While the ASP largely represented the interests of the Zanzibari Africans, the Zanzibar Nationalist Party catered for the Arabs' interests. The Zanzibar and Pemba People's Party, which broke away from the ASP after the 1957 elections, demonstrated the regional dimensions of Zanzibari politics (Kaiser 2003: 104). The dominance of the CCM in Unguja and the CUF in Pemba is a replay of the old political legacy. Unlike in Zanzibar, the character of politics on the mainland has never been predominantly ethnic.

Resolving conflicts

Tanzania has demonstrated the ability to deal with conflicts arising from its democratic process. The political impasse resulting from the 2000 elections and the subsequent events of January 2001 obviously tarnished the country's pride and image.

The leaders of the major political parties, the CCM and CUF, acknowledged that the impasse was a threat to political stability. They also recognised that durable political stability could only be guaranteed by sustained efforts to resolve their political differences through dialogue and reconciliation rather than through confrontation, by giving priority to national and not sectarian interests. It was through this conciliatory thinking that the CCM and CUF initiated direct talks in February 2001 to find a solution to the political crisis. The talks culminated in a reconciliation agreement, Mwafaka, which was signed in October 2001.

Much ground has been covered in the implementation of Mwafaka. Many of the instruments for its implementation have been established, including the Joint Presidential Supervisory Commission and an independent commission of inquiry to investigate the events of 27 January 2001. Other steps taken are the release of CUF members accused of treason and the nullification of court cases against individuals arising from the 27 January 2001 events. The Zanzibar constitution and the Electoral Law of 1984 have been reviewed in order to meet multi-party requirements.

One of the most important steps taken so far is the establishment of the independent Zanzibar Electoral Commission (ZEC). Its first test was during the by-elections in 17 constituencies in Pemba that took place in May 2003. Sixteen of the constituencies fell vacant following the expulsion of CUF parliamentarians from the National Assembly for contravening the house regulations, including absenting themselves from its sessions. Apart from a few technical shortcomings, the by-elections were well organised and the participating political parties and local and international observers characterised them as free and fair. They also expressed the view that the new ZEC had performed better than its predecessor (Commonwealth Expert Team 2003; TEMCO 2003).

Prospects for democratic consolidation

It can generally be concluded that Tanzania's democratic transition has been relatively smooth and positive. However, much needs to be done to consolidate these gains. The first issues that need addressing are the strengthening of political parties, the electoral process, and the electoral institutions. With the exception of the CCM, many of the political parties are weak and plagued by infighting.

Another challenge is to build internal democracy within the political parties, whose absence has been a source of infighting. There has been a discouraging trend towards political apathy in general and regarding popular participation in the democratic process. This is a result of the weakness of the opposition parties and the limited scope of civic education.

A democratic process cannot be sustained without an appropriate body of democratic knowledge, which guarantees effective popular participation. For the majority of the people, democratic knowledge is acquired through civic education and through taking part in the actual political process. The little civic education that has been provided has always been in the urban areas. The country needs to address these shortcomings in order to be able to consolidate its democracy.

Participation of women

Mainstreaming gender has been part of Tanzania's political tradition. Women have been politically active since the time of independence struggles. After independence there was a deliberate policy to bring women into the political and socio-economic mainstream. This was based on a conviction that gender equality is a developmental imperative.

In order to attain gender equality, the empowerment of women was necessary. Tanzania has been striving to achieve this through advocacy and affirmative action. During the one-party system, special seats were reserved for women in all the decision-making bodies of the party and in parliament. This was maintained when the country reverted to a multi-party system. Prior to the first multi-party elections in 1995, constitutional provision was made for at least 15 per cent of MPs to be women. At least 25 per cent of the local government seats were also reserved for women. The 1995 elections brought 45 women into the parliament, constituting 16.4 per cent of the total seats. The number included eight who were directly elected, with the remainder coming through affirmative action. The affirmative action seats are allocated proportionally to the number of seats parties held in parliament (Kassim 2003: 167).

The 1997 SADC Declaration on Gender and Development set a minimum target of 30 per cent women's representation in politics and decision-making positions by the year 2005. In Tanzania, the 15 per cent minimal female representation in parliament was, therefore, increased to 20 per cent for the 2000 elections. It is not clear why the figure was set below the regional target. This decision, however, increased the number of women MPs to 63, constituting 21.4 per cent of the total seats. Had it not been for affirmative action, women's representation in parliament would have been marginal. The Tanzanian constitution gives the president the power to nominate ten MPs, but by 2003, out of the nine President Mkapa had nominated during his second term, only one was a woman.

Key positions in parliament continue to be occupied by men, including those of speaker, deputy speaker, clerk of the National Assembly, and chairs of the parliamentary standing committees. Other areas dominated by men included the cabinet, which by June 2003 had only four women out of 27 ministers and four women deputy ministers out of 17. The situation is no different in the leadership of all the political parties, where men dominate key decision-making positions (*Guardian* 30 June 2003).

Despite affirmative action, women are not sensitised enough to take the challenge to stand for elections. While a total of 67 women contested seats in the 1995 elections, the figure for the 2000 elections was 70. In the Pemba by-elections of May 2003, only three out of 56 contestants for 17 seats were women. It seems that popular political participation in Tanzania is still inhibited by socio-cultural norms, particularly the patriarchal political system. Affirmative action therefore needs to be complemented by vigorous advocacy.

However, compared to other SADC countries, Tanzania is not doing badly. By 2003, among the 14 SADC member states, Tanzania ranked third, with a 22.5 per cent proportion of women in parliament (*Guardian* 25 August 2003). Given the socio-cultural inhibitions that prevent women from standing for election, it is obvious that Tanzania may not reach the regional target of 30 per cent of women's representation in parliament unless this target is provided for in the constitution or the electoral law.

Democratic governance and security

Before analysing the extent to which the democratic process and practice have influenced Tanzania's perception of national and regional security, it is important to see how national and regional security were perceived previously. Tanzania's perceptions of national and regional security have been evolving, and can be categorised into three periods. The first is from 1961, when the country became independent under the Westminster constitutional model, to 1965, when it became a one-party state. The second is from 1965 to 1992, when the country was under the one-party political system. The last is from 1992, when the country reverted to a multi-party system, to the present.

The multi-party system of 1961–65 needs explaining. Following independence in December 1961, Tanzania's experiment with the Westminster model was brief. It was actually a colonial legacy. The country moved to independence with two nationalist parties, the popular TANU and the African National Congress,[1] and an inherited colonial legislature.

Although there were two political parties, all the members of the legislature, except one independent candidate, were from TANU. Therefore, the situation was uncharacteristic of a true Westminster model. While formally there was a political opposition, it was not so in the legislature. This is why some analysts argue that in Tanzania political opposition died a natural death, and that the country was a *de facto* one-party state even before 1965 (Omari 2001).

Security perceptions, 1961–65

In the first two years of its independence, Tanzania did not formulate any clear foreign, defence, or national security policies (Baregu 1993: 45). With the emergence from colonialism, matters of consolidating independence and the provision of basic needs needed immediate attention rather than foreign policy, defence, and national security.

However, the focus on the consolidation of statehood did not mean national security was ignored. There was a national conception of security at this stage, although it was not consensual. There were two opposing views on security: internalist and externalist (Bienen 1978: 140). The two differed in their perception of threats to independence. The 'internalists' perceived threats to security purely in domestic terms. In consonance with what is now the human security approach, the proponents of this view identified three enemies that threatened independence and national security: poverty, ignorance, and disease (Nyerere 1966: 115). In order to guarantee security, efforts were to be directed towards the eradication of these three enemies. The 'externalists' perceived threat to national security in more conventional terms, as something emanating from outside the country. The internalist group was constituted by government leaders, especially President Nyerere, while the externalist group was formed mainly by MPs (Baregu 1993: 97).

The opposing views impacted on how the government addressed the question of national defence. The issue that pitted the two groups against each other was the necessity of having a national army – its objectives, size, and the mode of its organisation (Baregu 1993: 48). Although they did not oppose the idea of having a national army, the internalists preferred a modest one, trained and deployed to fight the three national enemies that they had identified. In a view informed by the events in the Congo, the army was perceived as potentially subversive, particularly in newly independent countries. The externalists preferred a large and strong army that could secure the country's borders.

The lack of clear foreign and defence policies within the first two years of Tanzania's independence had an impact on the country's perception of regional security. Guided by the internalist perspective, the leadership did not have a wider vision of security beyond the country's borders. Even the country's early commitment to eradicating colonialism was not seen as one in which its national interests were directly threatened (Baregu 1993: 42). Lacking regional threats, Tanzania had no perception of regional collective defence or common security at this stage.

However, at the beginning of 1963, the externalist perspective gained ground. The shift in perception was triggered by a number of factors, including the events in the Congo and the assassination of Patrice Lumumba; a coup in Togo; support for the liberation struggles in Southern Africa; growing Tanzanian opposition to international injustice and international racist exploitation; and the country's pursuance of a policy of non-alignment. The events in the Congo and the coup in Togo influenced the internalist group to change its perception, because both were thought to be externally instigated and serve foreign interests; while support for liberation struggles brought Tanzania on to a collision course with the racist regimes in Mozambique, what was then Southern Rhodesia, and South Africa.

Nyerere was uncompromising with the racist regimes. He expressed this to TANU's national conference, saying, among other things, that with those countries Africa can never negotiate until they abandon their rejection of the basic principle of human intercourse – the equality of humans (Nyerere 1967: 4). Linking Tanzania's freedom to that of Mozambique, Southern Rhodesia, and South Africa and stressing the threat of white supremacy to peace, Nyerere was emphatic regarding the country's support for armed liberation struggles (Nyerere, 1967: 9–10). This uncompromising stance catalysed antagonism from the racist regimes.

Tanzania's staunch position created enemies beyond the region. There were also serious political and economic disagreements at the international level, as Tanzania challenged the world economic order and the international politics of the Cold War.

The new perception of security was both reactive and proactive. It was reactive because it responded to domestic, regional, and international realities. Likewise, it was proactive because the country took bold practical measures. This is what Nyerere termed 'the second scramble for Africa' (Nyerere 1966: 37). The practical measures began with the creation of the Ministry of Foreign Affairs and Defence in March 1963, bringing the two under one ministry, on the understanding that diplomacy is the first line of defence. The new ministry catered for the country's national security, because foreign policy and defence policy fall under the ambit of the security sector. Thus the new ministry was responsible for the country's activist foreign policy.

The principles of the new foreign policy included safeguarding national sovereignty and security, pursuing non-alignment, respecting the UN Charter, working for African unity, and supporting the liberation struggles (Nyerere 1966: 3). Defence policy focused on building a force capable of defending these principles and participating in efforts towards national development.

The creation of the Ministry of Foreign Affairs and Defence was followed by a threat to re-consider Commonwealth membership if Britain failed to grant majority rule in Southern Rhodesia. Following the Rhodesian unilateral declaration of independence in 1965, Tanzania broke off diplomatic relations with Britain in line with an OAU resolution (Nyerere 1967: 11). Other practical measures included the provision of diplomatic, moral, and material support, and sanctuary to the Southern African liberation movements. From 1964, Tanzania hosted the OAU's liberation committee in Dar es Salaam, and it continued to do so for the next 30 years.

Security perceptions: 1965–92

Less than a year after new foreign and security policies were put in place, the inherited colonial army, the Tanganyika Rifles, mutinied in January 1964. The government asked for British assistance in putting down the mutiny. The army was disbanded and a new one, composed of members of the TANU youth wing, was created. From then until 1992, all members of the armed forces were required to be members of the party. The mutiny and the new army were part of the process that hastened the movement towards a one-party system in 1965 (Omari 2001). From 1965, the armed forces were politicised and the party was central in guiding policy on defence and security. From 1971, the army had a parallel party structure, its officers were appointed to the party and other bureaucracies, and the Tanzanian administration system increasingly came to look like a civilian–military coalition (Omari 2001).

Tanzania started developing a view of regional security from 1963. Its early thinking started within the East African sub-region. This was a result more of geographical proximity, colonial history, the policy of good neighbourliness, and the imperatives of regional co-operation than of actual threats within the sub-region. Policies of good neighbourliness and regional co-operation were emphasised (Nyerere 1966: 16–17). In April 1963 Tanzania negotiated with Uganda the possibility of co-ordinating future defence policy in the context of an East African federation. Given a lack of a common enemy or a common security threat, the negotiations were never sustained. Ironically, Tanzania's relationship with Uganda deteriorated following the coup that brought Idi Amin Dada to power. The climax of the strained relationship was the

1978–79 war between the two neighbouring countries. The war undermined the possibility of Tanzania's immediate participation in common security initiatives within the East African region.

Tanzania's real desire for common security lay in Southern Africa, however. As many of the Southern African countries were still under colonialism, the main actors Tanzania could co-operate with in collective defence against a common enemy were the liberation movements. The first expression of common security was in the form of a 'defence alliance' (Breytenbach 1995), i.e. the FLS, initially formed by Tanzania, Zambia, and Botswana. The liberation of Mozambique and Angola in 1975 and that of Zimbabwe in 1980 were triumphs not only for the liberation movements, but also for Tanzania, which supported them. Their victories were a sign that the scales were tipping in favour of the liberation alliance (Breytenbach 1995). Having contributed to the liberation of some of the members of the FLS, Tanzania felt proud to continue co-operating with them in a defence alliance against colonialism and apartheid.

Following destabilisation, which was part of South Africa's 'Total Strategy', the FLS were forced to change their tactics. Instead of continuing with confrontation, they allowed Mozambique to sign a non-aggression pact with South Africa in 1984 (the Nkomati Accord), and then Angola did so too in 1988 (the New York Accord). The New York Accord paved the way for Namibia's independence in 1990. After that, the liberation struggle had only apartheid South Africa to deal with.

Security perceptions after 1992

Since 1992 Tanzania has been in a changed security environment domestically, regionally, and internationally. Domestically, the country had reverted to a multi-party system after 28 years. While its democratic transition has been relatively smooth, the country has experienced real and potential domestic conflicts and insecurity. The Zanzibar political impasse, for example, has threatened Tanzania's political stability and peace.

The country has experienced isolated and low-intensity conflicts. These are disputes over land between farmers and pastoralists, and over natural resources, mainly in the mining areas; and clan rivalries. There have also been religious disputes between Roman Catholics and the Lutheran church, and among various Muslim groups. Although low-scale and isolated, if steps are not taken to address them, they have the potential to intensify.

At the regional level, Tanzania's major security concerns are within Southern Africa and the Great Lakes Region. With the end of colonialism and apartheid, and the advent of democracy in Southern Africa, Tanzania no longer feels threatened from this region. Since 1992, however, it has been made insecure by conflicts in Rwanda, Burundi, and the DRC, especially through the resulting refugee influxes. By 2002 Tanzania was hosting 800,000 refugees, constituting 5 per cent of the world total and 20 per cent of Africa's total refugee population.

At the international level, Tanzania has been a victim of international terrorism. The US embassy in Dar es Salaam was bombed in August 1998, causing the deaths of innocent Tanzanians. There have also been scares of terrorist attacks on Zanzibar, prompting the United States to issue travel alerts discouraging its citizens from visiting the island (*Guardian,* 13 May 2003). While the country has domestically taken steps to support international anti-terrorism efforts, this has had some negative effects. The passing of an anti-terrorism law in 2003 raised hackles in the Muslim community, as some members argued that the law targeted them as a group. Other Tanzanians felt that the law served US interests more than national interests. The war against terrorism has also affected Tanzania's economy, negatively impacting on tourism and foreign investment flows (*Guardian* 24 June 2003).

The democratic process has influenced changes in foreign, defence, and security policies and in their implementation. There thus seems to be a causal relationship between democratisation and perceptions of national security, although current perceptions of national security have been partly influenced by real and potential local conflicts, conflicts in the Great Lakes Region, and international terrorism.

A new foreign policy was prepared in 2001 in the context of changed domestic, regional, and international circumstances. While the achievements of the old foreign policy in the political and diplomatic spheres were appreciated, the focus shifted towards economic diplomacy, which is aimed at building a strong economy. Defence and foreign policies are an integral component of the greater national security and economic development strategy. Thus foreign, defence, and security policies are seen as complementary.

In practice, the formulation and implementation of foreign, defence, and security policies have been influenced by the democratic process. The most significant change is that, given the new multi-party environment, the ruling party is no longer the major actor in setting the agenda and formulating security policy. These roles are now played by many stakeholders, although largely co-ordinated by the National Security Council.

One is tempted at this juncture to pose a hypothetical question: What would happen, in terms of political stability and security posture, if the CCM were to lose a general election? Would the defence and security institutions accept such an outcome?

As the question is hypothetical, its response must also be so. Tanzania is one of the very few countries in Africa that has enjoyed political stability since independence. While the CCM and its predecessor, TANU, as well as its leadership, have been instrumental in inculcating a culture of peace and political stability, the people themselves have contributed a lot to this culture. They are also the greatest beneficiaries. Whether the CCM continues to govern or not, one would venture to predict that Tanzanians would continue to maintain a culture of peace and political stability. With the added component of democratic governance, one hopes that the defence and security agencies will respect the will of the people.

Common security in Southern Africa

Collective security regimes are relevant so long as they can operate beyond their two inherent weaknesses. The first of these is that, both in theory and practice, they are based on the old model of security thinking, their preoccupation being the preservation of the state's sovereignty against external threats. This thinking is statist and anachronistic. The second is their perception of the use of force as the rational and logical solution to the security threats. Thus their major focus becomes militaristic. Given the local and national nature of current insecurity, it is doubtful whether the emphasis on power-based mechanisms (military power) will be an appropriate instrument to address the situations of both national and regional insecurity.

From the cultural, historical, and political standpoint, Tanzania is organically linked to the Southern African region. That is why the country played a leading role in the creation of appropriate mechanisms to deal with threats during the era of colonialism and apartheid. This was done through the OAU's Liberation Committee at the continental level and through the FLS at the regional level.

Following the end of colonialism and apartheid, Tanzania has been part of the shift from the traditional to the wider security concept that incorporates human and other dimensions. The country does not feel externally threatened in the traditional sense. It feels a sense of a common bond and destiny with the other regional partners rather than a sense of fear and enmity. Beyond the historical factors, this perception has been influenced by internal and regional democratic processes and practices. Tanzania has been part of the emerging common democratic culture in the region.

The country's involvement in regional security co-operation is demonstrated through the ratification of both the SADC Treaty and the Protocol on Politics, Defence, and Security Co-operation, and its participation in all the functional and technical committees. This has included the ISDSC, the SARPCCO, cross-border crime prevention, joint planning for peace missions, military training exchanges, and the operationalisation of the Protocol on Politics, Defence, and Security Co-operation. The Southern African Defence and Security Management Network is another means of regional co-operation.

Conclusion

This chapter has explored how Tanzania's democratic processes and practice have influenced the country's perceptions of national and regional security. Adopting a historical perspective, the analysis has been carried out through three major phases: from 1961 to 1965, from 1965 to 1992, and from 1992 to the present.

The survey has established that during the first phase the country had conflicting internalist and externalist perceptions of national security. The two views differed on their perception of threat. Whereas the internalists perceived threats to national security in domestic terms, the externalist view perceived such threats as emanating from outside. Regarding regional security, Tanzania had no perception of regional collective defence or common security during this period.

During the second phase there was a growing consensus on an externalist perception of national security. This shift was attributed to a number of factors, including the country's commitment to the liberation struggles in the region where collective defence arrangements were made with the liberation movements and independent Southern African countries under the umbrella of the FLS.

During the last phase, Tanzania has been operating within changed domestic, regional, and international environments. At the domestic level, the country has a multi-party political system through which its democratic process and practice have gained mixed results. That process has to some degree influenced the country's national and regional security perceptions.

At a time when the country is seriously committed to collaborative security as an important framework for addressing its security interests, Tanzania is faced by a number of challenges. The main challenge is how to balance its economic and security interests in the regional groupings of which it is a member. Tanzania is currently a member not only of SADC, but also of the East African Community (EAC) and Indian Ocean Rim Association for Regional Co-operation .

One of the difficult decisions it had to make on regional groupings was to withdraw from COMESA, but it still has a 'straddling dilemma' through its membership of the EAC, which has provisions for security co-operation. While both regions (Southern Africa and East Africa) and their organisations are crucial to Tanzania, the challenge is how the country is going to balance its participation in both without negatively affecting either organisation in its efforts towards regional co-operation and integration.

ENDNOTES

1 This should not be confused with the better-known African National Congress of South Africa.

Chapter 13

Zambia

Bizeck Jube Phiri

Zambia, a landlocked country, is bordered by Angola, the DRC, Tanzania, Malawi, Mozambique, Zimbabwe, Botswana, and Namibia. This situation has shaped the character and practices of Zambia's overall politics over time.

Zambia's post-colonial political history is divided into three periods: the First Republic, 1964–72; the Second Republic, 1973–90; and the Third Republic, which began in 1990. The country became independent on 24 October 1964 as a unitary state with a multi-party system, headed by Kenneth Kaunda. In 1973 the country became a one-party participatory democracy, with the United National Independence Party (UNIP) as the sole political party permitted by the constitution (Republic of Zambia 1973: art. 4[1]).

After 17 years of one-party rule, in December 1990 Zambia reverted to multi-party politics, thereby ending the Second Republic. In October 1991 the first general elections were held after the ending of one-party rule. The elections were celebrated as a return to democracy and a victory for the people of Zambia, who generally perceived it as a step towards good or democratic governance. Despite regular elections during the one-party-state era, there was a feeling that the Second Republic had increasingly become dictatorial and was no longer observing human rights and the rule of law.

From one-party rule to democracy

It is important to go back to the time of independence and examine how Zambia's geopolitical situation impacted upon its national security concerns. In 1964, four of the country's neighbours – Angola, Namibia, Zimbabwe, and Mozambique – were still under colonial rule, while South Africa was under apartheid. Immediately after independence, the Zambian leadership decided to assist its neighbours in their fight for freedom.

Zambia openly supported the people from countries under racist and colonial rule, and hosted thousands of refugees and freedom fighters under the umbrella of the OAU. This decision shaped the country's national and regional security concerns: the government argued that as long as its neighbours remained under colonialism, Zambia would never feel safe. There is a sense in which Zambia's national security concerns were directly linked to regional security. This, indeed, was the main argument for the introduction of one-party rule: the administration headed by President Kenneth Kaunda believed that multi-party politics would greatly compromise both national and regional security. In 1973 Zambia was declared a one-party state under UNIP, and all other political parties, such as the African National Congress (ANC),[1] went into voluntary liquidation. Article 4 of the constitution made UNIP supreme over all other institutions (including parliament).

The changing political situation in the region, coupled with the fatigue of one-party rule, compelled Zambians to demand a return to multi-party politics. Angola, Mozambique, Zimbabwe, and Namibia were independent (though the first two were both undergoing civil wars). The situation in South Africa was changing fast. Clearly, there was little justification left for UNIP to perpetuate a one-party regime under the banner of national and regional security concerns.

Before the 1990s, Zambia's economy was performing poorly. The parastatals created during the 1965 economic reforms were no longer doing well, and there was no serious intention by the UNIP government to review the economic situation. Instead, the government blamed the IFIs for the failure of the economy – it was 'conditionality' and the structural adjustment programmes that were to blame. In response, Zambia tried to cut ties with the IFIs, which only made the situation worse.

From the mid-1980s, deteriorating economic conditions created a fertile atmosphere for Zambians to press for liberalisation in both the political and economic spheres. Food riots in the Copper Belt, generally believed to be the hub of Zambian politics, soon engulfed the whole country. Some members of the army saw this as an opportunity to overthrow the Kaunda regime. Thus at the height of demands for political change, Lieutenant Mwamba Luchembe tried to take over the government (Chisala 1991). The attempt failed, but it galvanised the entire nation into a frenzy of multi-party politics.

International developments also helped to push democratisation to the fore. The collapse of the Soviet Union, the main ally of the one-party state in Africa, signified the ideological triumph of the neo-liberal capitalist paradigm over the Marxist model. After the Cold War, the IFIs adopted what they considered to be 'a new conception of democracy and good governance, in a bid to foster the relationship between economic growth and democracy' (Salih 2001: 12). For the first time, the World Bank report linked aid flows to 'governance', which it defined as the 'exercise of political power to manage a nation's affairs' (World Bank 1989: 60–61). Initially, good governance was not directly connected with multi-party systems. Yet the implications of the pronouncements indicated the desirability of freedom of speech, transparency, and open political debate. The West argued that good governance involved more than just elections. More importantly, democratic governance was recognised to be an integral part of peace building and conflict resolution (Mulikita 1999: 3).

Arguably, therefore, Zambia's reintroduction of multi-party politics in 1990 was an endorsement of the global view that democratic governance entailed plural politics in which opposition parties played a key role. That a coalition of NGOs under the rubric of civil society rose against Kaunda's one-party regime reaffirmed the belief that multi-partyism was a means towards peace building and conflict resolution.

Interestingly, the first ten years of the Third Republic produced a character of democratic practice that was not dissimilar to that of the Second Republic. The 1991 elections secured the removal of Kaunda, but produced a National Assembly that was overwhelmingly dominated by the Movement for Multi-party Democracy (MMD). In effect, by voting in the MMD so overwhelmingly, Zambians contributed to producing *de facto* one-party rule. Within three years of taking power, some leading members of the MMD felt that the party was no longer adhering to the ideals of good governance, transparency, and the creation of an enabling economic and political environment. Thus, in early 1993, some key ministers resigned and founded a new political party, the National Party, with a view to removing the Frederick Chiluba-led MMD government (Mulikita 2002).

Meanwhile, civil society organisations joined those seeking a return to the original mandate and vision of democratic governance that saw the birth of the MMD in 1990. The most outspoken of these were the Zambian Independent Monitoring Team, the Forum for Democratic Process, and the Inter-African Network for Human Rights and Development. Another civil society organisation born during the Third Republic concerned with issues of security and good governance was the Southern African Centre for Constructive Resolution of Disputes. These civic organisations continued to play a significant role in the democratisation process and also in challenging the government to adhere to good governance.

Ongoing conflicts in Angola and the DRC created insecurity on Zambia's borders, which threatened the country's democratisation process. The Zambian government was concerned about these developments, prompting it to issue a statement in 2000 that both Angolan government soldiers and UNITA rebels were involved in military incursions into the North-Western and Western Provinces of Zambia (*Times of Zambia* 2000). These events shaped, to some degree, the nature and character of Zambia's regional and national security perceptions in the post-1990 period.

The role of defence and security forces in the transition to democracy also became a major issue in Zambian politics, although a consensus and normative framework emerged as to the most important issues, which are summarised below. Prior to 1990, Zambia experienced several failed coup attempts in a geopolitical environment characterised by armed liberation struggles in neighbouring countries. Arguably, therefore, because of the changing political environment in the country and the region, the political leadership believed that in the new political dispensation it was important to reorient the role of the armed forces regarding their obligations in a democracy. It was in this respect that emphasis was squarely placed on the need to depoliticise the Zambia Defence Forces and create a professional defence force.

Defence and security forces in a democracy

The armed forces are part of the executive power of the democratic state. They must acknowledge the primacy of democratic and legitimate politics. The loyalty of the armed forces lies with the government of the day, parliament, the constitution, and the law, of which they should have a detailed and comprehensive knowledge. As is the case with all other institutions of the executive power, the mission, role, and performance of the armed forces should be strictly defined and controlled by the constitution and relevant parliamentary institutions.

Security policy and its military implications demand the consensus and co-operation of the majority of the citizens. However, the very nature of military forces makes this a complicated subject. Additionally, some form of tension exists in a democratic state, and has to be reconciled in one way or another. Among the areas of tension are the following:

- the power concentration that the military asserts and that makes a defence force efficient, versus the restriction of power required by democratic control; and
- the freedom of the individual based on the human and democratic rights of the citizen, versus the requirements of authoritarian military discipline and order.

This tension is better reconciled by integrating the armed forces into society: there should be no attempt to separate the defenders of the state from democracy. Clearly, therefore, the armed forces in a democracy require a far more precise legitimacy than those organisations in other political and social systems. A balance, however, is required between the interest of the security of the state and the rights of the public. It is imperative to balance rights and duties in such a way that freedom can exist without threatening the very structure that has to defend these democratic rights. The principle of mutual loyalty between the state and its military servants is the cornerstone of this principle.

In the execution of national duties and tasks after the re-establishment of democratic rule, both the political leadership and the armed forces must bear in mind the following:

- *Survival*: The re-established democracy must survive and military discipline is essential.
- *Growth*: The re-established democracy and good governance must grow and the country must develop politically, economically, socially, technologically, and militarily.

The goals of governance must be achieved with minimum interference from external or internal enemies. The military must occupy a position of political neutrality above the play of partisan politics. The military must be a national institution, recruited on a national basis and without biases. Recruitment procedures should be seen to be public, equitable, and transparent, and both civilian and military leaders should make a public commitment to the goal of national representation in the armed forces.

In a democratic political order, the military should be brought under the control of the civil authority. The armed forces must enjoy professional autonomy to ensure greater effectiveness and conformity with the constitution. At the same time, political authorities and civil society have obligations towards the armed forces. These include not asking the armed forces to take on inappropriate or impossible tasks contrary to the constitution.

Defence forces in democratic transitions

The transition from authoritarian to democratic rule poses complex problems for armed forces. It involves three distinct stages:

- *Disengagement from the existing authoritarian system:* This is helped by good governance and nation building, in which the armed forces share the same understanding with civilians. Disengagement in Zambia was symbolised by the discontinuation of politicisation 'in the barracks' six months before the November 1991 multi-party elections.
- *Encouraging neutrality in the transition process:* This can cause greater strains in the armed forces, especially if the new leaders threaten the existence of

these establishments in the new government. The reaction of the defence and security forces to such developments can range from the case of Mali, where the army played the principal role in setting up and supervising the elections, to the Zambian experience, where the civil service took charge and limited the defence and security forces to the role of transporting ballot boxes to and from the remote districts.

- *Establishment of new relationships among the armed forces, political authorities, and civil society:* The general feeling of the armed forces is that politicians should not underestimate the nervousness with which military officers may approach relations with the new authorities. This apprehension may arise out of concern for what the civil authorities may do to the military as an institution, and also fears of personal retribution, particularly if elections bring to power a political party that had denounced the defence and security forces' complicity with the previous regime.

Relations with civil society should not be left entirely to chance. Active sensitisation programmes should be undertaken within both the armed forces and civil society. Civil authorities should educate the civilians about the military's rights and their own responsibilities towards the military, just as the military should be instructed about its responsibilities towards civil society.

It is necessary for the new government to ensure that the military functions within the constitutional and legal framework. The state must be committed to care for its soldiers and not to abuse their willingness to serve. The soldier should also be protected from command abuse by well-defined legal parameters. Such obligations and protection should also prevent soldiers from acting beyond the law. If soldiers' rights are violated, for instance by wrongful deployment or intolerable conditions of service, they cannot be counted on to respect the rights of others. Clearly, therefore, the defence and security forces continue to play a crucial role in the democratisation process in Zambia, as they did especially during the brief transition period.

Parliamentary oversight of defence and military expenditure

During the Second Republic, as a result of Zambia's support for the liberation struggles, there was apprehension in the government that if defence and intelligence budgetary allocations were exposed through debates in parliament, the country's enemies would assess and undermine the country's defence capabilities, thus compromising the government's ability to preserve and defend the sovereignty of Zambia. The executive then argued that it was not in a position to define clear limits to transparency in relation to defence and intelligence functions. Through the president, it maintained the colonial policy of government directly allocating money for defence and intelligence services secretly, without subjecting it to parliamentary oversight. The government justified this by arguing that security organs were forged by the exigencies of war – both hot and cold.

After 1993, all MPs belonged to one party, UNIP, and this made it difficult for parliament to debate defence expenditure. At the same time, despite the fact that parliament passed several laws related to defence, intelligence, and emergency powers, the lack of a parliamentary committee responsible for national security or defence made the house ineffective in scrutinising the increased governmental defence responsibilities. The complexity of laws related to defence did not allow every member to examine these bills satisfactorily within the tight parliamentary timetable.

One result of the lack of parliamentary surveillance of the operations of defence personnel was that most Zambian national service camps operated with inadequate facilities due to insufficient funding. For example, this culminated in the outbreak of typhoid at the women's Luamfumu Camp in Mansa in 1980–81. The investigation carried out on the causes of the outbreak found that drinking water in the camp was not treated, and that it was important to quarantine the recruits for 21 days. The investigating team then recommended that the camp be closed. Consequently, the government was forced to suspend and later completely stop the compulsory national service programme. The abandonment of the programme demonstrated the need for parliamentary oversight.

Internationally, the late 1980s marked the end of the Cold War, and of apartheid and the one-party state system in Zambia. The Zambian parliament repealed article 4 of the constitution, thereby facilitating the reintroduction of the multi-party system. Since the country's sovereignty was no longer externally and internally threatened, it became unnecessary for the executive to keep defence and intelligence budgets secret.

In addition, with the lifting of the state of emergency in Zambia in February 1992, it was no longer necessary to maintain a large army. A programme was introduced for early retirement and retrenchment in both the defence and intelligence services. While these processes were being implemented, parliament also regained its control functions over defence expenditure, and was now allowed to debate and approve defence allocations in the annual budget. Furthermore, since 1992, the Public Accounts Committee (PAC) of the parliament has been considering reports through the auditor-general on defence expenditure.

The first report of the PAC on defence expenditure was based on a special report of the auditor-general on the procurement of goods and services in the army and air force from 1992 to 1998. The committee's report revealed some irregularities in the way the MoD expended approved funds. The report also exposed the procurement of a presidential aircraft, and other irregularities in the supply of aircraft refurbishment and training services for the defence forces.

The PAC deplored the practice by which the army command considered itself to be above the law and therefore not obliged to adhere to financial regulations. The committee called for the cessation of malpractices and directed that service commands should comply with all established procedures and regulations. It also directed the defence forces to strengthen the ministerial tender committee through which all purchases should be channelled for appropriate scrutiny and advice. The committee observed that the above parliamentary directives were necessary to avoid the negligence and loss of public resources that were documented in the auditor-general's report. It further directed that all funds paid to suppliers should be recovered, especially where goods or services had not been received.

The committee recommended disciplinary action against officers from the Ministry of Finance and National Planning who connived with defence personnel in making irregular payments of public funds. It concluded by recommending control over the financial operations of the services. It also recommended that the Defence Act be amended to provide for a clear chain of authority in the handling of public funds in the services.

The PAC has effectively taken on the responsibility of scrutinising how money it approves is expended by the MoD. That this is being carried out is a clear indication that the democratic process initiated in 1990 has reshaped Zambia's perception of national security. The process was further informed by the changing regional security situation.

To complement the role of the PAC in providing checks and balances to the executive in general, and the MoD in particular, parliament also empowered the Committee on Foreign Affairs to institute oversight on policy matters in 1999. This committee changed its name to the Committee on National Security and Foreign Affairs (CNSFA).

The speaker of parliament annually appoints members of the CNSFA for one session. The duties of the committee are determined by the speaker or any other orders of the house to oversee the Ministries of Defence, Home Affairs, and Foreign Affairs, and include the following:

- to study, report on, and make recommendations to the government on the mandate, management, and operations of the relevant ministries;
- to scrutinise activities being undertaken by these ministries;
- to make recommendations to the government on the need to review certain policies or laws;
- to consider bills; and
- to undertake tours of selected projects and security institutions to examine their operations.

Not every MP is eligible to be appointed to the committee. Appointment takes into consideration the constitutional obligation to ensure the representation of all parties; gender sensitivity in terms of balance and representation; and members' adequate qualifications, experiences, and preferences.

As stated earlier, the CNSFA provides checks and balances on policy matters through oversight. When it comes across financial irregularities in the MoD, it refers them to the PAC for further scrutiny. Its mandate is to examine the accounts showing the appropriation of sums granted by the National Assembly to meet public expenditure. It also scrutinises the report of the auditor-general on the national accounts, and exercises the powers conferred on it under article 103(5) of the constitution. Among the topics considered by the CNSFA have been the status of Zambia's international boundaries with its neighbours, Zambian troops serving on UN peacekeeping operations, Zambia's security concerns and their impact on the country's foreign policy, and the welfare of defence personnel.

However, despite the CNSFA and PAC providing checks and balances on defence policy and expenditure, the two have never been involved in defence pre-budget consultations, which is an important component in budget formulation. Even when the defence budget is presented to parliament for scrutiny and approval, it is never referred to the two committees for comments and input.

The two committees have no powers to scrutinise the operations of the defence service, as such scrutiny is considered a threat to national security. They have also had no mandate to scrutinise the operation of the intelligence services since independence, and this has led to a popular perception that the services abuse their mandate. There is, therefore, a need for these services to be kept in check by the two committees in order to restore the trust of the citizenry. It is in this light that parliament welcomed the government's announcement of January 2003 that directed the director of public prosecutions to proceed with the prosecution of all those named in the 16 PAC reports approved by parliament for misappropriation of public funds (*Saturday Post* 2003).

Evidently, Zambia's conception of national security in the post-1990 period has been informed and shaped by the democratisation process, which was also enhanced by the changing regional geopolitical environment, as well as by globalisation.

Zambia's approach to national security

Zambia's conception of national security is defined by the constitution, which established the legality of the Zambian Defence Forces. The 1964 independence constitution's article 100 provided for the establishment of an armed force. This was to be non-partisan, national in character, patriotic, professional, disciplined, productive, and subordinate to civil authority. The 1964 Defence Act provided for the creation and maintenance of a defence force. This constitutional provision was reaffirmed in the Constitution of Zambia (Amendment) Act of 1996 (part VII, sec. 100).

Since Zambia became independent at a time when most countries around it were still under colonialism, the conception of national security was largely informed by this fact. Between 1964 and 1973 the Zambian parliament passed laws that assisted the executive in fulfilling its responsibility of ensuring the maintenance of peace and security (Haantobolo 2002).

Although Zambia was a multi-party democracy between 1964 and 1972, there is little evidence that the national conception of security was contested. Both the ruling UNIP and the opposition ANC were products of the struggle against colonial rule. Both shared the view that the major threat to newly won independence was the colonial and white minority regimes in the region. Both UNIP and ANC viewed national security concerns from the point of view of the liberation struggles in Southern Africa.

The transformation from multi-party democracy to one-party rule in 1973 was easily achieved, because it was perceived as a way in which Zambia would guard against insecurity. In 1972 the UNIP government had begun to feel uncomfortable with opposition parties, especially the ANC, which was gaining political ground. Opposition parties were suspected of working with the white regimes in the region and thus of undermining the country's security. That UNIP easily used the question of national security as one of the main reasons for abandoning multi-party politics in 1972 suggests that the question of national security in Zambia was consensual. Arguably, therefore, the establishment of one-party rule can be seen as a process designed to manage national security concerns and conflict in a volatile political environment for a recently independent nation.

During the Second Republic, Zambia witnessed a systematic process of politicisation of the defence force along socialist lines. This was a clear departure from the practice of the First Republic. The UNIP government formed party branches in army barracks and facilitated the training of members of the defence force in political education both in the country and in other socialist countries. This was because during the Second Republic, Zambia's conception of national security was also inward-looking.

However, with the inception of the Third Republic in 1990, there was a change in the conception of national security in Zambia. The reintroduction of multi-party politics meant that the management of, and conception of, national security became a matter for all political parties, especially those that were represented in parliament. This was reflected by the composition of the membership of the CNSFA, which was drawn from all political parties represented in parliament. In fact, in the 1992 and 1994 sessions, the committee was chaired by members of opposition political parties. Thus it can be safely argued that the depoliticisation of the defence forces was achieved through this process. Arguably, therefore, the conception of national security in the Third Republic is considered to be a matter for all citizens in the country. It is in this context that citizens and civil society organisations are invited to give evidence at sittings of the CNSFA. This is possible because since 1990 the government has conceptualised national security as not being a preserve of members of the ruling party or of citizens in uniform.

As discussed above, the end of colonialism and white minority rule, coupled with the end of the Cold War, led to a much less threatening security context, and Zambia felt able to restore multi-party democracy and adopt a much more open approach to the conception of both national and regional security.

Who makes security policy in Zambia?

To answer this question, it is important to understand the nature, character, and role of civil control of the Zambian Defence Forces. The role of civil control is enshrined in the constitution, in the first instance in the powers conferred upon the president, who is the commander-in-chief. These include the power to determine the operational use of the armed forces, to appoint members of the armed forces, to make appointments or promotion to any office in the armed forces, and to dismiss any member of the armed forces (Republic of Zambia 1964: chap. 1, sec. 54(2)).

Civil control is ensured by parliament, which regulates the exercise of the powers conferred upon the president. The roles of parliament are policy formulation and monitoring on matters of defence and security through the

CNSFA. Members of the committee are all civilians, because, according to the constitution, no serving member of the defence forces is permitted to stand for election for a parliamentary seat until he/she has retired.

The president plays a dual role, that of chief executive of the elected civilian government and commander-in-chief of the armed forces. Civil control of the defence forces is meant to guard against military subversion, while ensuring that military strategy remains a tool of national political goals under the civil authority. The executive plays a significant role in maintaining civil control of the defence forces, while the legislature maintains a strong influence in military affairs under the parliamentary committee that deals with defence and security. Simultaneously, the defence forces are expected to protect and defend the democracy as it evolves, and the democratic institutions associated with it. All this is achieved through the principle of separation of powers – an essential element in democratic governance.

Policy formation

The responsibility of making policy on national security is the responsibility of the Defence Council, composed of the ministers of defence (chairperson), home affairs, legal affairs, and finance; the attorney-general; and the commanders of the army, air force, and national service. Other members are the inspector-general of police and the director of intelligence services (secretary of the council). Although political parties are not members, depending on the issues at hand, a representative of the ruling MMD attends some meetings. Permanent secretaries of the Ministries of Defence, Home Affairs, and Foreign Affairs are also in attendance.

As stated, the minister of defence ordinarily chairs meetings. However, when it is believed that matters to be discussed require the attention of the president in his capacity as commander-in-chief, he/she will chair the council. These occasions include deployment of troops in war areas along the borders, and declaration of war. Clearly, the composition of the council signifies civil control of the defence forces. This aspect also demonstrates the major role played by civil authority in making policy on security and foreign affairs in Zambia. However, matters of military operations are the preserve of the military command and are, therefore, outside the jurisdiction of civil control. There is a clear line between policy formulation and policy execution.

During 2002 the Defence Council embarked on a process of reviewing policy on security. The exercise involved a reformation of both policy and practice. In the past, the document dealing with the defence policy was generally classified. However, in 2002 the president instructed the council that once the defence policy document was finalised and adopted, it was to be circulated widely within the MoD and other ministries to ensure its proper implementation.[2] This decision followed observations that in the past it was difficult to execute the defence policy because civilians working in the Ministries of Defence, Home Affairs, and Foreign Affairs, who were expected to implement the policy, were not given access to the document, which placed unnecessary hurdles in the way of implementation.

Approach to regional security

Zambia's perception of regional (i.e. SADC) security is historically determined. From the time of independence in 1964, the country's security concerns were shaped by the liberation wars in Southern Africa. Although Zambia openly supported the liberation movements, it avoided direct involvement in the fighting despite numerous violations by the white regimes in the name of 'hot pursuit' of the guerrilla fighters who were based in Zambia. After 1994, following South Africa's democratisation, Zambia's security perception was informed by the desire firstly to strengthen the democratic dispensation within and outside Zambia, and secondly to urge other countries in the region to democratise. In this respect, Zambia strongly supported SADC's decision not to support undemocratic changes of government.

To this effect, Zambia's second president, Frederick T. J. Chiluba, was emphatic in his address to the OAU in 1996, requesting other leaders not to support undemocratic changes of government in Africa. The message was the same for the SADC region. Zambia believes that democratisation and the strengthening of democratic institutions are the main guarantees for both national and regional security. Zambia is therefore a strong believer in the idea that regional security integration can only be achieved once SADC member states democratise their political institutions.

Pitso (1999) observes that 'the first efforts to establish interstate security co-operation in Southern Africa dates back to 1974, when Tanzania and Zambia formed the Front Line States ... to co-ordinate their efforts for the liberation of Namibia, South Africa and Zimbabwe'. The FLS generally functioned on an informal basis. Their policies were implemented by the ISDSC. As a founder member, Zambia's involvement in the region's security co-operation practices has been stable and firm.

Zambia is also a founding member of SADC and its Parliamentary Forum. Zambia co-operates fully with the AU in all its efforts aimed at resolving conflicts in the sub-region. Since 1992, the country has pursued a policy of peacemaking with respect to continued conflict in Angola. This led to the signing of the Lusaka Peace Accord, which aimed at ending hostilities between UNITA and the Angolan government, although the accord collapsed because of continued fighting by UNITA. Peace only came when UNITA leader, Jonas Savimbi, was killed in February 2001.

Another effort by Zambia in the process of peace-building in the region was through the 1998 Lusaka Peace Accord over the civil war in the DRC. Although the accord did not initially sustain peace, it provided opportunities for some cease-fire agreements between the warring parties. Zambia is an active member of the SADC Organ on Politics, Defence, and Security Co-operation and supports the objectives of the SADC Parliamentary Forum and its attempts to manage conflicts in the region.

Zambia has not been drawn into battle with forces fighting in the neighbouring countries. It did not send troops to the DRC when Namibia, Angola, and Zimbabwe sent their forces to protect the Kabila regime in 1998. Zambia did not want to import the conflict, which would have had serious implications for the democratic process. Instead, it opted to play a mediation role and hosted several meetings to try and end the conflict.

Nevertheless, Zambia attracted some mistrust from both Angola and the DRC. This was because certain key individuals in government were accused of supplying arms to UNITA in Angola and some rebel groups in the DRC. A UN report implicated the director-general of Zambia's Intelligence and Security Services, Xavier Chungu, in dealings with the UNITA leader, Jonas Savimbi. The report further suggested that in August 1999 Zambian authorities were forced to impound a Ukrainian plane at Lusaka International Airport after receiving consistent reports that Angola would attack Zambia in pursuit of UNITA rebels. Zambia evidently was in a difficult position regarding UNITA (*Monitor* 2000), because for ten years, during Chiluba's rule, the Zambian government had tolerated trade between UNITA and Zambian business people in arms and fuel supplies.

Regarding dealings with the DRC, Zambia started off as a neutral country, whose interest was to see peace and the rule of law return to the troubled country. However, the DRC began to question Zambia's sincerity and commitment, and accused it of supporting some rebel movements. In particular, the Chiluba administration's dealings with Raphael Soriano, alias Katebe Katoto, raised suspicions (Mwanawasa 2002). There is no doubt, therefore, that Zambia's national and regional security concerns were compromised by these dealings during the Chiluba administration.

Peacekeeping

Apart from its involvement in regional security arrangements, Zambia has been involved in international peacekeeping missions. The Zambia Police Service, for example, has been actively involved in missions abroad, notably in Kosovo. A total of 25 officers returned from Kosovo in April 2003, ending their one-and-a-half years of peacekeeping. The remaining group of seven completed their tour of duty at the end of 2003. Another group of 37 left to replace the 25 before the end of April 2003. Furthermore, another six officers were sent for peacekeeping duties to East Timor in 2003, giving a total of 57 officers in the UN peacekeeping missions by mid-2003, including some who were involved in peacekeeping missions in several African countries.

Conclusion

The chapter has examined the extent to which the process of democratisation and democracy in Zambia has influenced the state's perception and practice of national security in the context of regional security threats and arrangements. It has been shown that Zambia's approaches to both national and regional security were influenced by its history and the geopolitical situation. It is also important to note that Zambia's security relations with its neighbours, particularly Angola and the DRC, have been fragile because of clandestine activities of some top-ranking officials during the Chiluba administration. The democratic dispensation seems to have checked such dealings during President Mwanawasa's administration.

ENDNOTES

1 Throughout this chapter, this party should not be confused with the more widely known South African party of the same name.

2 Author's interview with E. Katukula of the Zambian MoD, November 2002.

Chapter 14

Zimbabwe

Ken D. Manungo

Issues of democracy, good governance, human rights, and security management are topical among social analysts, and the international community is currently embroiled in debates over such issues. As Swartz (1998: 26) puts it so succinctly, 'the notion of governance has only quite recently, perhaps no more than a few years ago, entered the lexicon of public debates'. The world has changed since the fall of the socialist bloc in the closing years of the 1980s. The question of human rights and democratic governance has never been more relevant and urgent than in our times. All over the world, every country's human rights record is under the microscope.

Zimbabwe is no exception. It may be the only country in Southern Africa that is presently receiving the attention of the whole international community on issues of good governance, human rights, and democracy. There are reasons behind this unusual attention.

The historical setting

Zimbabwe, like its Southern African neighbours Angola, Mozambique, Namibia, and South Africa, traces its independence to the armed struggles of the 1960s and 1970s. These struggles liberated most of the Southern African countries that were under white minority colonial rule. Previously, the African majorities in these countries were denied the most basic human rights, such as the right to participate in the selection of a government of their choice. They also had no say over many other issues that affected their daily lives. The wars of liberation were therefore fought in order to give Africans the franchise and a meaningful input into decisions and laws that affected their daily lives. The question, therefore, is: Has the post-liberation government of Zimbabwe been able to deliver on the issues the Zimbabwe liberation movement went to war for? There are certain broad parameters and stages in the history of post-colonial Zimbabwe that should be looked at in order to come up with a meaningful analysis of the situation as it exists at present in the country. The conduct of the war of liberation, as with most wars of liberation, demanded the suspension of normal day-to-day human rights.

The individual's rights and democracy were normally suspended. This is what Krige (1995: 5–8) has referred to as 'guerrilla coercion'. Manungo (1991) has argued that in order to win the war against the colonisers, individual interests had to give way to what was perceived as the will of the majority. The leaders of the struggle had to mobilise all available resources for the cause. Did these leaders evolve into new political leaders after independence who knew that their new roles required periodic mandates from the people if they were to continue in power? The Zimbabwean experience shows that there was a gradual change over the years regarding the interpretation of legitimacy and the right to rule the country.

Political evolution: 1980–90

The liberation war in Zimbabwe ended with the Lancaster House talks in London, which produced the Lancaster House Agreement in November 1979. That agreement called for general elections based on adult suffrage: the African majority could at last participate in the selection of a government of their choice. Nine parties contested the 1980 parliamentary elections. The constitution guaranteed whites 20 seats, which were contested by the Rhodesian Front (RF) of Ian Smith and other white minority parties. The RF won all 20 entrenched seats. The Zimbabwe African National Union (Patriotic Front) (ZANU [PF]), led by Robert Gabriel Mugabe, won a majority of the seats (64 per cent) in the National Assembly and formed the first African majority government. Even though ZANU (PF) had a parliamentary majority, it invited its wartime partner, the Zimbabwe African People's Union (ZAPU), led by Joshua Nkomo, to take up some cabinet positions in the new government. The alliance was, however, short-lived, as it was rocked by the 1981–82 rift between the former Zimbabwe African Peoples' Revolutionary Army (ZIPRA), which was the ZAPU armed wing in the liberation war, and the Zimbabwe African National Liberation Army, the armed wing of ZANU (PF).

But even if the incoming government had been more genuinely committed to transforming colonial power relations – e.g. through a democratic land redistribution process and economic development strategy based on the needs of the majority of the people – it had inherited several kinds of debts. Among the most serious was the legacy of colonial development funded by foreign loans, and the capacity of the World Bank and IMF to set the agenda for post-colonial development (Bond and Manyanya 2002: 9).

The February 1981 clashes were soon followed by a more serious war in Matebeleland and the Midlands from 1982 to 1987 (Alao 1995: 111–15). The Catholic Commission for Justice and Peace produced a report on that war (CCJP 1997) cataloguing the attempts by the Zimbabwe National Army (ZNA) to suppress ZIPRA dissidents and stating that atrocities were committed by the various arms of the security forces in the course of their duties. But it went on to state that atrocities were committed not only by the security forces, but also by the dissidents (CCJP 1997: xi).

The war in Matebeleland has left a dark shadow on the history of post-colonial Zimbabwe. There are those who feel that the government has not been sufficiently open on the atrocities allegedly committed by the security forces in suppressing the dissidents in that region and the Midlands. The government set up a commission to investigate reports coming from Matebeleland civilians in the early 1990s. The findings have not yet been made public. There are those on the government side who have argued that the country would be better off if it put what happened in Matebeleland behind it and concentrated on the new challenges. They argue that reopening the 'wounds' from that experience would divide the country rather than unite it. Others have suggested that the experience of South Africa's Truth and Reconciliation Commission could be used as an example to introduce such a process in Zimbabwe. And some believe that if there were a change of government in Zimbabwe, many witnesses might come forward to tell what happened during those turbulent years of the dissident era. The activities of the ZNA Fifth Brigade, which were central to winning the war against the dissidents, were largely the source of civilian complaints (CCJP 1997). A truth and reconciliation commission would give both sides an opportunity to be heard and perhaps that would start the process of healing.

The ZNA was also waging another war between 1982 and 1992, in Mozambique against RENAMO (also called the MNR, the Mozambique National Resistance). This movement had been set up by the Rhodesians and apartheid South Africa to destabilise the new governments of Mozambique and Zimbabwe. Zimbabwe needed the port of Beira in Mozambique for its exports and imports, and decided to attack RENAMO. The wars in Matebeleland and Mozambique strained the economic development programmes planned in this period. Many people were displaced in Matebeleland and north-eastern Zimbabwe, while many ended up as refugees in Botswana and South Africa. This period can therefore be characterised as one that presented security problems for Zimbabwe, both internally and regionally. It is believed that some former Rhodesian whites took advantage of these refugees, training them and sending them back to fight the ZNA in Matebeleland and the Midlands. These same former Rhodesian agents assisted RENAMO in fighting against the Mozambican and Zimbabwean armies. While this period seems to have been plagued by turmoil and insecurity, the crisis in Matebeleland was resolved when ZAPU and ZANU recommitted themselves to a second alliance by signing the Unity Accord in December 1987 (CCJP 1997: xi), and the intervention in Mozambique came to an end in 1992, when RENAMO and FRELIMO signed the Rome Peace Accord. The Zimbabwean alliance was strongly criticised by some in Matebeleland, who accused Joshua Nkomo of selling out the Ndebele people by agreeing to merge ZAPU with ZANU (PF) in terms of the Unity Accord. The Zimbabwean government, on the other hand, accused apartheid South Africa of sponsoring both the dissidents in Matebeleland and RENAMO in Mozambique. Through all this, the question of good governance seemed not to be an issue, although some NGOs were already criticising the Zimbabwean government for the way it was conducting the war, especially the issue of civilian victims who were reported to be suffering at the hands of the security forces.

Regional security and shared resources

Zimbabwe's past has been tied to those of Zambia, Malawi, and South Africa. Zimbabwe and Zambia share a common border, and historically these two countries had been intertwined in the British imperial plans that Cecil John Rhodes tried to implement in Central Africa in the nineteenth century, which still affected the region in the twentieth century. The Federation of Rhodesia and Nyasaland shared resources, albeit unequally, for ten years, from 1953 to 1963. Zambia (known as Northern Rhodesia at the time) was on the losing end in the resource sharing during the federation period. The Kariba hydropower scheme, for instance, was supposed to be a shared resource, but the infrastructure was designed to favour Zimbabwe (Rhodesia at the time), as all the turbines and controls were placed on the Zimbabwean side. Zambia was also adversely affected by the Zimbabwean war of liberation because of its support for Zimbabwean guerrillas. Rhodesian soldiers attacked Zambian infrastructure as a way of punishing the Zambian government. Many Zambian civilians were killed when the Rhodesian security forces claimed they were in hot pursuit of guerrillas who were using Zambia as a base to attack Rhodesia. The situation changed after 1980 when Zimbabwe achieved independence. The two countries worked together as members of the FLS, helping the South African liberation movements in their fight against apartheid South Africa.

Difficulties, however, continue to exist. The Victoria Falls, on the Zambezi River that forms the border between Zambia and Zimbabwe, and one of the 'seven wonders of the world', has not brought co-operation between the two countries, but has of late become a source of competition for tourists between the two countries. The Zambezi River has also been a site of conflict as poachers cross from Zambia into Zimbabwe in search of ivory and rhino horn. Zimbabwean National Parks security agents have actually declared war on Zambian poachers over the years. The situation has improved recently as the new Zambian government of President Mwanawasa is co-operating with the Zimbabwean government in combating poaching in the Zambezi valley.

Another Zimbabwean neighbour, Malawi, has had to cope with problems arising out of the return of its citizens following the closure of many mines in Zimbabwe where the Malawians had been employed. Malawi has supplied South Africa and Zimbabwe with migrant labour for many years. Similarly the plight of former farm workers in Zimbabwe, who were largely of Malawian descent, has caused tensions between the countries. The land reform process in Zimbabwe has not fully addressed the plight of these former migrant workers (Manungo 1997).

Relations between Zimbabwe and its southern neighbours, South Africa and Botswana, have not been smooth either, as a result of an influx of Zimbabwean economic refugees. There is no consensus on the causes of the Zimbabwean economic decline that have led to this situation. Some critics point to land redistribution in Zimbabwe, whereby land that once was used by a minority of white farmers has been repossessed by government and redistributed to black small-scale farmers and new black commercial farmers. The distribution process has been criticised, as the government is accused of taking land from former white farmers and then giving it to senior ZANU (PF) people. This criticism has not been without foundation. In an attempt to respond to its critics, the government has recently instituted a department, led by a senior cabinet minister, to take stock of the distribution process and take farms away from those who are found to have been allocated more than one.

The political tensions between the opposition Movement for Democratic Change (MDC) and the ruling ZANU (PF) have also contributed significantly to the economic decline that has led many people to flee into Botswana and South Africa in search of a better life. This is perhaps the one major conflict that has contributed to the declining economic fortunes in Zimbabwe, particularly as the political contestation between the two parties was accompanied by mutual violence and the limitation of rights and freedoms. Some critics of the government have blamed this on the media laws passed during Jonathan Moyo's tenure as information minister which, they argue, directly contributed to a lack of democratic space in the country. Most Western countries have imposed sanctions on Zimbabwe because of the political impasse between the MDC and ZANU (PF). The AU and SADC have tried to mediate in the conflict, but so far there have been no meaningful results. The Zimbabwean government accuses the MDC of being a front for the British government, the former colonial power.

The 1991 Framework for Economic Reform, better known as the Economic Structural Adjustment Programme (ESAP), was introduced by Finance Minister Bernard Chidzero and a small number of technocrats. The key documents were prepared by the World Bank and then revised to secure the support of cabinet. In retrospect, ESAP did not deliver on many of its strategic targets by 1995. For example, GDP growth reached 5 per cent only in one year, 1994, and averaged just 1.2 per cent from 1991 to 1995. Inflation averaged more than 30 per cent during the same period, and never dropped to anywhere near the 10 per cent target. The budget deficit was more than 10 per cent of GDP during the ESAP era, double the 5 per cent target, and reached a high of 13 per cent in 1994–95 as a consequence of a crippling drought (Bond and Manyanya 2002: 32).

Elections and democracy

The parliamentary elections of 1985, 1990, and 1995 were won by ZANU (PF) by very wide margins. It must be pointed out that voter turnout decreased with each election, and some pundits say that this was as a result of voter apathy. Those sympathetic to the government say voters stayed home because they were satisfied with the way the government was running the affairs of the state. It does seem as though there is a third dimension or interpretation of this decreased voter turnout, however. The voters may have been staying away from the polls (and they still do) because they realised they could not make any meaningful changes to the political arena, especially as the candidates presented had to be endorsed by the party hierarchy, not by the people at the grass-roots level. In addition, there were no real opposition parties to speak of before the emergence of the MDC. Table 1 shows that voter turnout decreased significantly over the years.

Table 1: Voter turnout in parliamentary elections, 1980–2000

Year	Vote for	Turnout
1979	Parliament	59.9%
1980	Parliament	84.1%
1985	Parliament	75.5%
1990	President	56.4%
1995	Parliament	26.8%
1996	President	26.7%
2000 (February)	Referendum	33%
2000 (June)	Parliament	48.3%

Source: Zimbabwe Election Support Network, http://www.zesn.org.zw

If the 49.3% voter turnout for the presidential elections of March 2002 is included, the same trend is observed. This time the opposition performed much better than other opposition parties had done in the past. There must be reasons why this should have been so for the first time in the history of elections in Zimbabwe, and those reasons cannot be ignored or brushed aside by the ruling party. The ruling party, however, performed much better in the 2005 parliamentary elections, ceding only 41 of the 120 contested seats to the opposition. The opposition challenged the results of some of the constituencies in the courts, without success.

Economic issues and democracy, 1993–98

The early part of the period 1993–98 has been described by Innocent Matshe of the Department of Economics at the University of Zimbabwe as one of quasi-democracy.[1] He argues that most government institutions, such as the parastatals, the civil service, and security agencies, were run on professional lines, albeit with some government intervention here and there. However, in the latter part of this period some of the institutions began to be headed by former military personnel, becoming as a result very undemocratic. Critics would argue that the appointments were based on political patronage and not on professional grounds. The operations and decisions of such institutions as the Reserve Bank of Zimbabwe, the National Oil Company of Zimbabwe (NOCZIM), and others had a tremendous impact on the daily lives of the people. The foreign exchange control measures introduced impacted negatively on society, although the government would argue otherwise – there are issues of the effects of uncontrolled foreign exchange on the prices of commodities, especially on basic goods. NOCZIM's monopoly on the acquisition and distribution of fuel plunged the country into an economic crisis that persists to this day. The government did, however, liberalise the acquisition of fuel even to the extent of allowing consumers to purchase it with hard currency. Khapoya (1994: 213) states that 'centralised economies and one-party states failed to deliver [the] prosperity and democracy which African people fought for and their leaders promised them'.

The intervention of the IMF and the World Bank with its ESAP did not turn the economy around. The introduction of price controls on basic commodities and a lack of foreign currency worsened the economic situation. Human security was and is further eroded by HIV/AIDS. The pandemic has not spared Zimbabwe, and has compounded the problems of an already declining economy. The most affected groups are women, children, and men in their prime, a situation that deprives the country of the very people who should be the leaders of tomorrow. The resources that should go into developmental projects are being diverted to assisting the victims of HIV/AIDS. Zimbabwe is one of the few countries in the world to have levied a tax on the working population in order to raise funds for victims of the pandemic, but the distribution of these funds has been criticised for lacking transparency.

National security perception and its impact on regional security

Zimbabwe has a National Security Council (NSC) that is composed of the president, all cabinet ministers, the secretary to the president and cabinet, the commander of the defence forces, the director-general of the Central Intelligence Organisation, the commissioner of police, and the commissioner of prisons. The president chairs the council. Under it is the Defence Council (DC). The president also chairs this, as it is a committee of the NSC. The other members of the DC are the ministers of foreign affairs, defence, state and national security, finance, home affairs, information and publicity, justice, and parliamentary affairs; the commanders of the defence forces, the ZNA, and the air force; the secretary of defence; and the secretary to the president and cabinet. Then there is a Defence Committee, made up of the minister of defence (in the chair), the commanders of the defence forces, the commissioners of police and prisons, the secretary for defence, and the deputy secretary for policy in the MoD.[2] The NSC and the DC drive security policy in Zimbabwe; there is no input from civil society as such. Parliament would have been the representative of civil society, but where the ruling party has a dominant majority in parliament, it leaves very little room for other parties to provide input into national security policies. It is against this background of the composition of the national security councils and committees that one has to examine some of the decisions affecting the region and internal politics.

The intervention in the DRC in 1998 is a case in point. The ZNA and the air force went into the DRC amid controversy, as some argued that the intervention had not been authorised by the regional organs. The Zimbabwean government has argued otherwise. It is obvious that the Zimbabwean security councils had taken the decision to go to the assistance of the DRC, which they perceived as being threatened by external forces. That decision and the intervention that followed did not entirely enhance regional security. Instead, tensions arose, particularly between South Africa and Zimbabwe. The intervention was viewed as a selfish move by the political leadership and army brass, who were said to be personally benefitting from the troops' intervention. The leaders of the intervention were described as 'modern day carpet-baggers' (*EDC News* 2002) – a reference to the American business people from the northern states who profited from the American South after the Civil War of 1861–65.

The major criticism was about the amount of money the government was spending in the DRC when the country's economy could not meet other needs, such as assistance to AIDS victims. The *Financial Gazette* (1999) reported that Zimbabwe was spending close to USD 1 million a month on the war in the DRC. The government argued otherwise, and defended the intervention as a response to a sister country's call for help after it had been invaded by its neighbours, Rwanda and Uganda. What cannot be denied is that the intervention used up huge amounts of resources that could have been used at home. The relations that emerged between DRC and Zimbabwe have been criticised, as it is alleged that the links benefitted individuals, and not the country. The UN and some Western countries have accused the Zimbabwean army top brass of exploiting the DRC's resources.

The emergence of the MDC as a strong opposition party has presented problems for the government internally. There had been no strong opposition party since 1980; most parties had not presented a serious challenge to the government. When the MDC was formed in September 1999 and began to prepare for the parliamentary elections of June 2000, the political arena changed. The ZANU (PF) government was not used to facing a challenge such as that presented by the new opposition party. There was a lot of violence during the campaign period leading up to the elections. Internal security was threatened as both parties exchanged accusations as to who was initiating the violence. Regional security was also affected, as refugees left Zimbabwe for Botswana and South Africa, stating that they were fleeing from the violence between ZANU (PF) and MDC supporters. There was no red-carpet reception for the refugees from either the governments or the ordinary people of Botswana and South Africa. The governments accused the new arrivals of criminal activities; the people accused them of taking jobs meant for the countries' nationals. The same tensions spilled over into 2002, when the Zimbabwean presidential elections were conducted. Both sides continued to hurl accusations at one another. There was more violence between ZANU (PF) and the opposition during the 2000 and 2002 elections than there had been in all the previous post-independence elections combined. The discrepancy in the urban and rural support for the two sides puzzled some observers. The explanation is found in the fact that the rural areas were where most of the war of liberation was fought, and therefore the majority of the rural people have remained firm supporters of ZANU (PF). Some rural people have even said that the urban dwellers have no idea what the war was all about and that is why they are engaging in 'battles' with ZANU (PF).[3] There are those who also point out that the drought relief food distribution programme in rural areas has been used as a weapon to garner support for the ruling party. The ruling party has denied these accusations.

The referendum on the proposed new draft constitution once again proved to the ruling party that the new opposition party had considerable support. There was a 55 per cent 'no' vote and 44 per cent 'yes'. Did this rejection of the constitution, however, mean a vote for the opposition? It does not necessarily seem that way if one realises that only 1,313,038 voters, or 22 per cent of the electorate, voted (Helen Suzman Foundation 2000: 1). Nevertheless, this was the first time the ruling party had been challenged by the electorate.

Greg Linnington, a lawyer and lecturer in the Department of Politics and Administration at the University of Zimbabwe, stated that one did not have to be an MDC supporter to see the problems with the present constitution of Zimbabwe. The issue of the executive presidency was being questioned, especially the president's power to nominate 20 non-constituent MPs in a parliament of 150 members. In addition to the 20 nominated members, ten traditional chiefs become MPs after being selected by the council of chiefs. These ten are also indirectly appointees of the president as, according to the constitution, the president appoints chiefs.[4] Linnington went on to state that clearly there was no democracy unless all the National Assembly members were elected by the electorate. The powers of the executive president have been criticised by many who see the presidential powers as having no check. This is a weakness of the constitution that needs addressing. In addition, the independence of the judiciary has been questioned by many observers. The pre-independence judges, for example, were viewed by the government after independence as sympathetic to the former white settlers and their interests. In a bid to 'correct' that colonial legacy, the post-independence government tried to appoint judges who had the 'correct' orientation.[5] This induced criticism, as the executive was viewed as interfering in the one arm of government that should normally be left to do its duties independently. The 2003 arrest of a judge for what the executive saw as interference in the course of justice attracted wide condemnation.

The present government views Zimbabwe as a nation under siege. This has affected its formulation and implementation of national security policy. The government has presented the opposition as the enemy of the state and the people of Zimbabwe. The criticism is not entirely without foundation, as the opposition has not done enough to distance itself from the former colonial masters.

For its part, the opposition has accused the government of human rights violations and documented them. Pictures of tortured people have appeared in the private press. The government of Zimbabwe has denied these charges, but has to accept that the security forces sometimes go beyond legal bounds in trying to deal with the opposition. Individuals seeking asylum in the United

Kingdom have alleged torture, and some have told graphic stories of torture. It is even alleged that asylum seekers sell each other pictures of the alleged tortures in order to persuade British officials to allow them to stay in the United Kingdom. Some would argue that the true picture of human rights violations might become clearer if a truth and reconciliation commission were to be set up, as it was in South Africa.

Conclusion

Zimbabwe went through a liberation war in order to bring democracy to the majority of Zimbabweans. The party that led the liberation war and most of the leaders of the revolution have been in power since independence. This has contributed to the way the country's problems are perceived. The lack of meaningful opposition parties for most of the period since independence has meant that the ruling party has only been challenged recently. This development has earned the opposition the label of 'the enemy of the people' from the government. Mistakes have been made by the Government of Zimbabwe, but one of the points of interest is that the world has suddenly woken up and discovered violations of civil rights in Zimbabwe. It would seem as if that world, especially the West, hardly knew that problems in Zimbabwe existed until the land invasions of 2000. George Shire, a Zimbabwe government sympathiser, said:

> According to the British government and the mainstream press, you would be forgiven for thinking that Zimbabwe's [post-]independence history consists of only two periods: before the 'land-grab' and after the 'land-grab'. Before the 'land-grab' Zimbabwe was a model African state with a progressive leader, after the 'land-grab' it has become a disaster zone with a 'madman' in charge! (Shire 2003).

This view sums up the government side. Dr Stan Mudenge, the minister of foreign affairs, has pointed out that an IMF report of 1996 labelled Zimbabwe one of the best African economies.[6]

There is no doubt that the international community has suddenly awakened to the cry of good governance and democracy, and that regional security has been severely affected by what is going on in Zimbabwe. The economic refugees from Zimbabwe have brought problems to South Africa and Botswana, thereby creating tensions among SADC partners. Have civil society organisations been helpful in working with the government in mapping out the problems facing the country? Not at all, and government has seen most such organisations as plotting against it and working for its downfall.

There is no national perception of security in Zimbabwe. The government sets the agenda for the country's security. The intervention by Zimbabwe in the DRC, though now over, did not go down well with the opposition in Zimbabwe and with some SADC countries. It is anyone's guess, however, who will finally take credit for the peace that is now apparent in the DRC.

There is a need for SADC to go back to the drawing board, to determine what needs to be included in its OPDSC. At present, countries such as Zimbabwe and South Africa will always act in the best interests of their nations. It is important that the declaration in the treaty that 'provides for strengthening regional solidarity, peace and security, in order for the people of the region to live and work together in peace and harmony' be adhered to (Malan and Cilliers 1997: 1). There is no doubt that the situation in Zimbabwe today needs to be turned around. The economy is collapsing, and one hopes that moves by the governor of the Reserve Bank will achieve the turnaround. Recently, very high-ranking party officials have been arrested on fraud charges, and certain prominent business executives have fled the country after realising that the law was closing in on them – although it puzzles many people that these executives have sought asylum in the United Kingdom and the United States, countries that are the most critical of Zimbabwe. One hopes the government will keep the pressure on so that any other culprits may be held accountable.

Council elections and parliamentary by-elections have shown that the ordinary Zimbabwean, urban or rural, is becoming less and less interested in politics and more focused on surviving economic hardship. Statistics show that with each election fewer people are turning out to vote. It has been suggested that the country needs more voter education so that the people can participate fully in the election processes. Voter education and the appointment of an independent electoral commission would go a long way in assisting the processes of democracy in Zimbabwe. There is also a need to revisit the Lancaster House constitution so as to come up with a nationally accepted new constitution. Many areas in the present constitution need to be addressed. Zimbabwe as a country within SADC is a vital cog in the wheel of economic success for the region.

ENDNOTES

1 Author's interview with Innocent Matshe, economics lecturer, University of Zimbabwe, February 2003.

2 Author's interview with Brigadier-General T. Mugoba, Zimbabwe MoD, March 2004.

3 Personal interviews with rural people in Shurugwi, Midlands Province, Zimbabwe.

4 Author's interview with Greg Linnington, political science lecturer, University of Zimbabwe, February 2003.

5 *Ibid*.

6 Author's interview with Dr Stan Mudenge, April 2003.

Chapter 15

Conclusion

Gavin Cawthra, Khabele Matlosa, and Anthoni van Nieuwkerk

At the heart of this study is the investigation of the interface between security at both the national and regional levels, on the one hand, and democracy and democratisation on the other. The assumption that security and democratic governance are inextricably intertwined and mutually reinforcing underpins all the country studies. This approach is neither novel nor new, given that various previous studies have pointed to this important linkage. For instance, Chris Landsberg (2003: 1) aptly observes that 'in the conventional view, peace-building has largely been accomplished once the formal peace agreements have been signed. However, building sustainable peace is, in fact, a long-term and multi-dimensional process, which ultimately requires accountable and democratic governance'. For Robin Luckham (2003: 3), 'national security and public order depend upon a democratic (and thus legitimate) framework of public authority'.

What is not always clear, however, is exactly *how* democratic governance impacts on national security perceptions and practices, and how, in turn, this translates into national approaches to the collaborative security project in Southern Africa. In some cases – in some of the country studies – it has been possible to answer this question in this book. In others, the relationship appears to be less clear, while at the multinational level, this issue has been addressed only at a fairly high level of generality.

Understanding democracy, democratisation, and security

Some broad observations can be made. This study has demonstrated that, much as progress has been registered in respect of the democratisation process in the region, critical policy and capacity challenges still remain for democracy to be firmly entrenched as a value, a process, and a political practice.

Democratisation has been uneven and partial, and in some states has barely begun, while in others there are signs of democratic reversals. Furthermore, the process of democratisation itself has been accompanied in some cases by violent conflict, most notably in the DRC. This supports the more general findings of Cawthra and Luckham (2003) and others: that transitions to democracy are seldom linear, often fail, and are accompanied by new insecurities. There is some evidence in the region, in the form of Botswana, Mauritius, and Seychelles, and perhaps also post-apartheid South Africa, to support the 'democratic peace' thesis – that democracies do not go to war with other democracies, and by extension that they are less prone to internal conflict (although the context of this needs to be closely interrogated). However, the process of democratisation itself appears to be associated at least in some cases with conflict and insecurity. This would support the findings of, for example, Mansfield and Snyder (1995).

If one accepts Larry Diamond's typology of democracies (see Du Pisani in this volume) – i.e. electoral democracies, liberal democracies, and pseudo-democracies – and add, as Du Pisani suggests, social or developmental democracies, then how can one characterise the countries in this study? With the possible exception of Seychelles, none can be considered to be social democracies. Some, such as Swaziland, can hardly be considered to be democracies at all. Others, perhaps the majority of countries in the region, would qualify as liberal democracies, but there are clearly some cases where democratic political systems and processes are so stressed or weak that they would best be described as pseudo-democracies or shell democracies. In other words, there is a mixed bag, and this could put limits on the evolution of common security (of which more later). The situation is compounded by the fact that it is not clear in what direction some of the countries in the region are heading: is Zimbabwe, for example, transiting from what was effectively a one-party state to a multi-party democracy (a process accompanied by conflict and insecurity), or is it on a trajectory that will lead to greater authoritarianism? Southall (2003) is not alone in arguing that 'there are deeply worrying indications that the democratic wave which broke upon the region's shores in the 1990s is now moving into reverse'. This would be too bold a statement in our view, but nevertheless, there have definitely been stalls and reverses in the processes, and democracy remains fragile in many countries.

The debate on the security architecture in the SADC region is as robust as the democracy and governance discourse (see Cawthra and Luckham 2003; Vale 2003). Some of this debate revolves around different conceptions of security: In particular, a distinction is made between 'narrow' security (the concerns of the 'security sector', i.e. the police, defence force, and intelligence agencies), and 'widened' security in which issues such as economics, the environment, and society are regarded as having security dimensions. In general in this study the authors have adopted a wider definition of security, although without losing a focus on the traditional security sector itself, which remains at the core of our concerns. The debate between the 'wideners' and the 'traditionalists' has in turn spawned the concept of human security, which is often seen in opposition to state security. This is really the application of 'widened' security to the referent level of the individual, or society, or social formations, depending on who is using the term.

While the concept of human security is useful (and it is embedded in the policy discourse on security in many SADC countries, especially South Africa), it remains contested (see, for example, the discussion by several scholars referred to in Burgess and Owen 2004). On the whole, when this study talks about security, it has tended to focus on the state in the first instance, in the belief that the traditional security task of the maintenance of sovereignty and territorial integrity, and of law and order, cannot simply be taken for granted in Southern Africa; but within that sovereignty, human security issues should be paramount. However, this debate tends to impact on security architecture by dividing analysts and practitioners alike into two camps: those who want to concentrate on state security, and those who argue that human beings or collectivities are more important. Perhaps quite naturally, government officials tend to favour the former and civil society the latter. Later in this chapter, a way in which this matter can be approached will be suggested by determining the roles and functions of different structures within SADC.

In virtually all the country studies (although the Indian Ocean island members of SADC are an exception), security interdependence was identified as being a key issue driving the collaborative security project. Political instability and violent conflicts in one SADC member is as much a matter for concern for the larger collective of member states as it is for that member state. This reality helps in part to explain why states have entered into security collaboration. But Southern Africa is not completely a 'security complex' in Buzan's (1991) sense, where the security (or insecurity) of one state is dependent on that of the others. The link between (in)security in say, Namibia, and that in Mozambique, for example, is now fairly tenuous.

Nevertheless, even where they might not be directly threatened by spillovers of insecurity, the countries of the region share a history of struggle against colonialism and apartheid that is an important ideological gel: solidarity is a key value, and ranks are often closed, for example in support of the Zimbabwean government, which has faced international disapproval and sanctions.

This solidarity is driven primarily by the political elite and, to a considerable degree, so are security perceptions and practices. Furthermore, it is also evident that many of the concerns regarding security are propelled by state or regime, rather than human security, imperatives. This returns us to the debate on the character of democracy in the region. As Du Pisani argues, human security is a necessary condition for human development, which can arguably best be achieved by social as opposed to liberal democracy. But as Cawthra (in this volume) concludes, regional security co-operation in the developing countries in general 'is clearly aimed at stability and regime security' rather than human security. In this scheme of things, the state tends to be the only agent of security, to the exclusion of other critical actors in society. Zacharias (1999: 153) reminds us that

> the state is not and it should not be the only agent of security. It has limited initiative and resources. It does not constitute the totality of social life. There are other agents equally important for security that complement the activities of the state, and it is their empowerment that is likely to make a difference in security. These include societal organisations such as civic, charity and various other interests, groups normally referred to as 'civil society'.

It must be noted, however, and this is borne out in some of the studies in this book, that civil society in itself is not a vehicle for democratisation: it is also in many cases elite-driven.

The history of regional integration or co-operation in Southern Africa suggests that, as in many other parts of the globe, SADC states initially came together in 1980 in the form of the then SADCC, and some of them even before that in the FLS alliance, mainly because of a perceived common external threat, basically in the form of apartheid South Africa (see Omari and Macaringue in this volume). Although the co-operation arrangement was first and foremost a political response to South Africa's regional destabilisation strategy, and thus linked strongly to the FLS arrangement, SADC concentrated on economic co-operation, focusing on reducing the economic dependence of member states upon South Africa. The situation changed dramatically following the political transformation in South Africa in 1994. When South Africa was subsequently admitted into the newly reformulated SADC, economic integration and political and security co-operation were pursued in tandem, and this remains the reality today.

However, how to combine the political/security agenda with the economic one was a strongly contested issue, as Omari and Macaringue have highlighted in this book. Following a protracted conflict and tension over the exact role and position of the OPDSC within the SADC structures, some consensus has emerged that the best way to proceed is to integrate this security co-operation mechanism into the SADC summit rather than have it as an autonomous entity, as was the case with the FLS (Van Nieuwkerk 1999; Matlosa 2001). This dilemma – the relationship between security and economic co-operation, and which takes precedence – is common to many regional and sub-regional organisations, as Cawthra has argued earlier. There is some evidence to support the thesis that although economic co-operation may be the formal expression of the project, it is driven by shared security threat perceptions – but as time goes on, interactions develop their own logic, and economic, political, and security co-operation become intertwined and synergetic.

Global dynamics influencing national security perceptions

Regional integration is in part both a response to and a localised expression of accelerated globalisation. Efforts towards regional integration in different parts of the globe have been motivated in part by an aim to minimise the adverse effects of globalisation, such as marginalisation, fragmentation, and disintegration (Nabudere 2000; Cheru 2002; Zeleza 2003).

A plausible argument can be canvassed, too, that the new wave of globalisation has provided impetus for regional organisations to move beyond the economic realm of inter-state co-operation towards political and security co-operation. However, as recent studies suggest (SAPES/UNDP/SADC 2000; Mandaza and Nabudere 2002), more progress has been registered in the economic than the political field in Southern Africa. SADC has agreed to more than ten protocols aimed at deepening regional economic integration, yet member states have been sharply divided on strategies for security co-operation through the OPDSC, and have only recently agreed on key protocols and structures. This distinction is reflected also in the SADC Secretariat, where the vast majority of staff are engaged on economic issues rather than political and security ones.

Globalisation has been made even more profound and urgent by the terrorist attacks of 11 September 2001 (Ellis and Killingray 2002), which have thrown into sharp relief questions about what the major internal and external threats to security are, and how states should best protect and ensure their security in the new world order. It should be noted, however, that in few of the countries studied in this volume is terrorism seen as a major security issue (Tanzania being a major exception), although many states feel obliged to realign their policies and practices with the exigencies of the United States-driven 'war on terror'. It is too early to determine exactly what effect this might have on common security in the region. On the one hand, US unilateralism may propel SADC and other regional bodies to adopt even more multilateralist strategies and to seek to develop some balance in the international system by cementing global alliances; on the other, states may opportunistically seek to ally themselves with the United States and its agenda, thus potentially undermining regional solidarity.

As shown in many of the country studies, globalisation is thus an important driver of regional integration. But at the same time it tends to weaken already weak states, which in turn might undermine regional integration. This is because weak states might cling to what little sovereignty they retain, particularly in the security field. It is understandable that states such as Malawi or Zambia, which have lost virtually all control over their national finances due to chronic indebtedness and the interventions of IFIs, cling to sovereignty in the political and security domain. It must also be remembered that most of the countries in Southern Africa are fairly new states, and that many of them engaged in protracted liberation struggles to assert their sovereignty; they are thus naturally reticent to cede it, particularly if this is seen as surrendering to global agendas driven by former colonial powers.

It is debatable how fast SADC's integration has been, and the results have been mixed: intra-regional trade has increased significantly, but on an asymmetric basis in favour of South Africa; barriers to intra-regional trade in the form of bureaucracy, tariffs, and transport deficiencies remain high; and SADC has certainly not yet turned the corner in breaking dependence on primary export products, donor assistance, and debt.

However, security perceptions and practices in the region are not only shaped by external or exogenous dynamics: internal or endogenous dynamics are also at play. The next section interrogates possible implications for security of the democratisation process in the SADC region.

Democratisation in SADC

It is now common cause that the Southern African region has undergone a profound political transition from authoritarian governance towards a multi-party political dispensation.[1] The transition has been marked in the main by a wholesale embrace of party-competitive political systems and the jettisoning of one-party regimes. But questions must be asked – as this volume has done – about the nature and depth of democratisation within this political liberalisation. Put somewhat differently, does this political change amount to simply formal rather than substantive democracy, or to pseudo-democracy? Researchers are divided on this subject. While some argue that the process that has taken place is simply tantamount to political liberalisation devoid of democratic content, others argue that the recent political changes, although limited, amount to a democratic transition (Baker 1999).

And how does democratisation impact upon security perceptions? How does democratisation influence internal security policy and external (specifically regional) security policy? Has the process of democratisation since the early 1990s had a clear-cut or indirect bearing on regional security co-operation in the SADC region?

Andreas Schedler (2001: 91) reminds us that 'sustaining democracy is often a task as difficult as establishing it. In the immediate aftermath of ... democratic transitions, pressing concerns have quickly arisen about how to strengthen and stabilize these new regimes'. Critical challenges still remain for the SADC region to experience sustainable democratic consolidation. In his chapter in this volume, Du Pisani cites Linz and Stepan, who propose five key prerequisites for democratic consolidation, namely a vibrant and robust civil society, an active and autonomous political society, observance of the rule of law, an effective and efficient state bureaucracy, and an institutionalised economic society.

According to Lodge (1999: 1)

> starting democracy is easier than keeping it. This contention is especially relevant to the early history of post-colonial Africa. Between 1960 and 1970, about fifty states acquired independence as well as various kinds of liberal constitutional arrangements; by the end of the decade all but a fraction were either governed by military dictatorships or one party systems with at best limited democratic pretensions.

Can this scenario repeat itself?

The country studies in this volume show that the democratic transition in the SADC region is still an unfinished business beset with complex endogenous and exogenous challenges. They also demonstrate that democratisation has had little positive impact on socio-economic development. Indeed, most countries of the region have slipped down on the UNDP HDI since the onset of democratisation in the 1990s. Although a significant factor in the decline in human development must be HIV/AIDS (which can hardly be blamed on democracy), it is nevertheless abundantly evident that there is little or no correlation between democratisation and human development, at least in the short to medium term. The cases of Botswana and Mauritius, which are the richest countries per capita in SADC, however, might suggest that over a longer term a 'virtuous circle' is possible where democracy reinforces economic growth and that same growth sustains democracy, but this is not yet evident in the states undergoing democratisation.

It can indeed be argued that a majority of the SADC states, in adopting liberal democracy, often of a fairly superficial nature, may have foregone the possibility of socio-economic redistributional change through social or developmental democracy. The kind of governance evolving in the SADC region is described by some scholars as 'exclusionary democracy' (Mhone and Edigheji 2003; Edigheji 2004) wherein the political, especially the ruling, elite dominate the political space to the exclusion of other key actors such as civil society. According to this argument, political ruling elites have been able to stamp their hegemony over the whole democracy agenda and the crafting of both national and regional security projects. Our studies support this only partially: politics seems to remain an elite process in many states, but in other countries there is, for example, a high level of involvement in national elections and an active civil society (although, of course, civil society itself can be elitist). Southern Africa seems to be no worse off in this respect than the majority of developing countries, and in many respects democracy seems to be considerably deeper than in other parts of the world where post-Cold War democratic transitions have taken place, for example Eastern and Central Europe or South-East and Central Asia.

Democracy–security interface

In most of the country studies, it has not been possible to determine precisely and comprehensively how democratisation has impacted on national security and on security co-operation, although in some cases the changes in approach are explicit (South Africa, for example). Even greater difficulty was experienced in forming an aggregate picture. However, it can be observed that the nature of the interface between democracy and security perceptions and practices of states seems to differ from one SADC country to the other depending on the stability of each country, the nature of its democratic transition (or lack of it), and the degree of institutionalisation of its democratic governance. With regard to countries very recently emerging from war (i.e. Angola and the DRC), the conceptual approach the studies adopted has proved inappropriate and they were therefore not included in this analysis.

The table below attempts to classify the countries studied in terms of their democratic transitions and the implications thereof for security. Of course, many of the countries underwent earlier transitions, mostly in the form of liberation struggles against colonialism, apartheid, and settler minority rule.

This study has, however, focused on the transitions that have taken place since the end of the Cold War.

Table 1: Classification of states studied in terms of democratic transitions since 1989

Authoritarian	Established liberal democracies	Transitions from apartheid	Transitions from military rule	Transitions from one-party rule
Swaziland	Botswana	Namibia	Lesotho	Tanzania
	Mauritius	South Africa		Zambia
				Zimbabwe (*previously* de facto *one-party rule, not* de jure)
				Malawi
				Seychelles
				Mozambique (*also from civil war*)

Swaziland has not yet undergone a democratic transition and continues to be ruled in an authoritarian manner, although with some checks and balances and some signs of change (Mzizi in this volume). In such situations, the security perceptions and calculations of the ruling elite are not only driven by regime security concerns, but even simple political opposition or criticism of policy postures of the government may be considered a security threat. This lends some support to the argument of Regan and Henderson (2002: 119–36) that the level of threat faced by a regime is strongly associated with political repression, especially in semi-democracies – Zimbabwe is a case in kind.

Botswana and Mauritius are the longest-enduring liberal democracies in the SADC region, although the character of their democracies is very different, and Botswana has yet to experience a change of governing party (Molomo *et al.*, and Cawthra in this volume). These countries have experienced relatively stable democratic governance since the 1960s. In both countries, the key drivers for democracy and security policy formulation are the ruling elites, with minimal involvement of civil society organisations. However, given their strong economies, both these countries potentially have the capacity to complement state security with human security, given the right policy mix, and have arguably done so to some extent. It is notable that these two democracies are not only just about the richest countries in the region in per capita terms, but have also been the most stable and peaceful, giving some support to the 'democratic peace' thesis.

Namibia (Lindeke, Kaapama, and Blaauw in this volume) and South Africa (Schoeman) exhibit some common features, given that both experienced extreme forms of racial segregation and domination from which they managed to extricate themselves in the early 1990s, following armed liberation struggles. In both, the liberation struggles did not result in outright military victory by the liberation movements, but led to a negotiated settlement leading to democratic governance. Both countries have made tremendous strides towards institutionalising democracy. However, in both cases, the former liberation movement holds sway in the political process and has entrenched its hegemony to the extent that opposition parties exhibit little political wherewithal to become an alternative government. The dominant party syndrome seems destined to endure under conditions of fragmented and enfeebled opposition parties, and there is not much the dominant party can (or arguably should) do about this. While there are positive aspects to a dominant-party system, most notably in terms of nation building, reconciliation, and stability, both case studies have identified emerging problems in terms of the governance and management of national security.

The political culture of military rule has not generally been a feature of the political systems of Southern Africa, compared to the rest of Africa. The reasons for this have not been fully explored in this study, except for the legacy of the liberation struggles, which is probably an important element in this regard. During often-protracted armed struggles the military dimension was generally suborned to politics, while most revolutionaries regarded themselves to greater or lesser extents as both soldiers and civilians, thus cementing a form of revolutionary civil–military relations that was carried through into the new states. In this regard, it is interesting to note that the Southern African countries that have experienced the greatest degree of military threat to governance through attempted coups (Lesotho, Zambia, and Tanzania) were those in which armed liberation struggles did not take place. It was only in Lesotho, however, that the military came to power, as Matlosa has documented in this study. The military relinquished state power and retired to the barracks in the early 1990s. This process ushered in the new era of a fragile democracy in Lesotho – fragile because various forms of conflicts between and among key institutions have generated considerable instability.

The final, and largest, category is that of states that have experienced a transition from one-party to multi-party systems of governance. These include Tanzania (Maundi in this volume), Zambia (Phiri), Zimbabwe (Manungo), Malawi (Phiri), Seychelles (Van Nieuwkerk and Bell), and Mozambique (Lalá). Within this category there are a wide range of differences, but also some similarities. A majority of states in this category adopted some form of African socialism and one-partyism[2] shortly after independence, including Tanzania, Zambia,

Mozambique, Zimbabwe, and Seychelles. Socialism had more content in some cases (Mozambique, Tanzania, and Seychelles) than in others, where it was an ideological shell within which capitalist systems operated on the basis of neo-patrimonialism (Zambia and Zimbabwe). Whatever the case, the ideology of socialism in part propelled the institutionalisation of one-party regimes, although in the case of Zimbabwe this was never formalised.

Since the end of the Cold War, most of these countries have basically abandoned socialist ideology and have formally embraced liberal democracy, holding regular multi-party elections. This feature of the liberal democratic model has not only ensured that the political marketplace is relatively open for competition among various parties, but in many cases has shaken the hegemonic hold of the ruling parties. Although mostly still dominant, the ruling parties in these countries now have to contend with opposition forces that continuously threaten their hold on power (and indeed, the historic ruling parties in Zambia and Malawi have lost office).

Zimbabwe is more complex. It is fairly clear that before the monumental changes that marked the end of the Cold War and of apartheid, Zimbabwe was becoming a *de facto* one-party state. It began on the trajectory of economic liberalisation and multi-partyism at the same time as many other states in the region, but the ruling ZANU(PF) party has fiercely resisted political opposition and has reversed many of the economic liberalisms, which, coupled with a land reform programme and human rights violations, has resulted in an economic and political crisis. It is uncertain whether the Zimbabwe that emerges from this crisis will be a more authoritarian state or a more genuine multi-party democracy: yet again, this is an example of the unpredictable and uneven processes associated with economic and political liberalisation.

There are, of course, many other differences among the countries in this category. Malawi, for example, did not go the route of African socialism, but that of one-person autocracy under Kamudzu Banda. But the winds of change swept the authoritarian Banda regime to the wayside, opening up the system to multi-party competition. Seychelles, on the other hand, was a stable one-party welfare state, and it was elite and external pressure rather than mass disaffection that led to the introduction of multi-partyism.

The state and character of security co-operation

As elsewhere in the world, the Southern African region has embraced regional integration since the end of the Cold War in a much more forceful and purposive manner than had hitherto been the case. Since 1992 when the Windhoek Treaty established SADC, the region's states have committed themselves to deeper integration than mere economic co-ordination, which was the *raison d'etre* of SADCC. SADC has taken up a triple mantle of economic, political, and security co-operation. On all the three fronts, especially the economic plane, considerable progress has been made, signified by the signing of a number of protocols.

Would this have been possible without democratisation? Countries of the region co-operated quite closely through the FLS during the 1970s and 1980s, and none of the FLS member states, at least until 1980, was a multi-party democracy. However, the nature of this was secretive, informal (there was no treaty), and carried out almost entirely at executive level. It is unlikely that SADC as it is currently constituted, including the OPDSC, would have been possible without democratisation.

In terms of institutional co-operation, one could argue that regional co-operation on security issues has evolved from an intergovernmental forum where defence, security, and foreign policy issues were discussed, to a more institutionalised arrangement. As the 'new institutionalism' literature suggests (Smith 2004), such an evolution went through various phases, and in the case of the SADCC and SADC, it experienced intensified goal-oriented communication, which led to the demand for greater structure. The establishment of a permanent organisation to administer this policy domain represents an additional degree of institutionalisation.

The theoretical literature suggests that such formal organisations can change the nature of co-operation. At the very least, organisations can provide some institutional memory concerning previous decisions. At most, the organisation itself can become an autonomous actor with policy influence. But what is the impact of SADC and the OPDSC on security co-operation? At the very least, it allows the states of the region to pursue their security and defence interests in an organised fashion. As Table 2 indicates, the organisation plays a significant policy co-ordination role.

Table 2: Institutionalisation of defence and security co-operation in Southern Africa

Level of institutionalisation	Southern African structures
Informal intergovernmental forum for dialogue on defence and security issues	FLS, 1977 (ISDSC)
Information sharing: mainly policy co-ordination; sometimes specific co-operative policy actions	SADCC, 1980–92

Norm creation and codification: establishing norms, rules, laws	SADCC, and SADC since 1992
The establishment of a permanent organisation to administer policy	SADC, especially after restructuring in 2001, including the OPDSC and its ISDSC and ISPDC
Governance: the authority to make, implement, and enforce rules in a specific domain	?

As discussed previously, early regional co-operation, mainly via the FLS and later the SADCC, was motivated largely by a shared regime-threat perception, prompted by the violent policies of regional destabilisation of the apartheid regime. SADC's current key objectives and its vision, as a whole, resonate both with state and human security agendas. In the analysis of the UN Commission on Human Security (2003), key areas requiring policy intervention for human security include violent conflict, the movement of people, post-conflict peace building, poverty, health, and education.

In short, there has been a move towards a human, rather than a state or regime, security approach, at least on the official policy level. Numerous references are made throughout SADC documents to what is in effect human security, even if the term itself is not actually used. At the same time, the mandate of the OPDSC is restricted largely to state security, and the focus is on the traditional security sector – the military, police, and intelligence. This need not be a problem, as the mandate of SADC as a whole is both state and human security. As the UN Security Council, for example, deals with narrowly defined security issues ('threats to and breaches of the peace'), while other UN institutions, such as UNDP, deal with wider human security issues, so too can a division of labour with regard to security be established within SADC structures. The real test, however, comes when SADC – through the OPDSC, the summit, or whatever other structure – is obliged to make hard choices between state and human security, for example, when confronting human rights abuses in a member state. The track record in this regard is not promising, as SADC institutions have seldom, if ever, criticised member states, even when human rights abuses have been manifest.

We noted earlier that SADC has been mostly a state-centric exercise. Nevertheless, SADC increasingly appears to follow the trends of 'new regionalism' (see Cawthra in this volume) in which multidimensional co-operation involves the state, market-oriented actors, and civil society actors, and covers economic, cultural, political, security, and environmental aspects, and regionalism grows organically or spontaneously, emerging in part 'from below' through popular movements and from within the regions themselves.

The growing tendency of NGOs in the region to place the term 'Southern African' before their names is just one indication of this.

The reformed SADC therefore seems to be pursuing multiple security objectives: in the first place through various forms and levels of co-operation, including economic and trade integration, and secondly via the Protocol on Politics, Defence, and Security Co-operation. This protocol makes provision for the promotion of state security, but also includes the promotion of common political values (article 2 of the protocol). Although too early to judge, SADC has a mixed intervention record. At the time when its security structures were under debate, various SADC member states intervened militarily in other member states, although at the invitation of the governments concerned: Lesotho hosted the armies of South Africa and Botswana; and the DRC those of Angola, Namibia, and Zimbabwe. Earlier, in the mid-1990s, Lesotho and Mozambique benefited from SADC leaders' mediation efforts, as the DRC later did. However, there is no firm record by SADC as a whole of successful conflict resolution of crises in member states (Angola, the DRC, Tanzania with regard to Zanzibar, Zimbabwe, Swaziland), between member states (Angola–Zambia, Namibia–Botswana), or on its periphery (the Great Lakes Region, Central African Republic and Republic of Congo, Sudan, Uganda, Madagascar, or the Comores). Instead, SADC has tended to establish task groups of two, three, or more countries to deal with crises, and some successes have been notched up, notably in the DRC and Lesotho.

Does SADC therefore represent a common security, collective security, or collective defence regime? Historically, security co-operation was driven by regime survival. The post-apartheid SADC chose to focus on economic integration and mask or downplay disagreements over security co-operation. The restructured SADC seems committed to pursuing collective (or collaborative) security via the Protocol on Politics, Defence, and Security Co-operation, and has signed the Mutual Defence Pact. If by common security is meant a high level of institutionalisation (see Table 1) – i.e. that multidimensional arrangements are put in place to mediate relations among members states and govern their internal security processes[3] – then SADC appears not to have gained the critical mass of shared values to cross into the common security terrain. In fact, some observers see a contest in the region over the future direction SADC ought to take: the first vision is a militaristic and traditional one; the second is a wider, human security-based vision based on the governance goals of the AU and its developmental programme, NEPAD; including democracy, human rights, justice, negotiation, and other forms of peaceful dispute settlement.

Regional integration in all the three planes, namely economic co-operation, political co-operation, and security co-operation, has been hampered by the individual regional states tenaciously clinging to rather than 'pooling' sovereignty. As was pointed out earlier, it is to be expected that weak states, and states that are relatively newly independent, will hang onto what remains of their sovereignty in this globalised world, and that political and especially security functions (and within security, probably intelligence) will be the last to be ceded. However, as Cawthra has argued earlier, without some pooling of sovereignty, further substantive progress towards a common security regime will be impossible. How this is managed – e.g. through confidence- and security-building measures, by restraining the hegemon, by constructing win-win scenarios, by ensuring that benefits outweigh costs, and by respecting national sensitivities – will be critical to the success of the common security project.

Controversy still surrounds the desirability of a regional hegemon for the achievement of stated goals and objectives of regional integration, and the question is whether or not it is desirable for South Africa to play this role. The country studies in this project have not demonstrated any strong resistance to South African hegemony. In reality, with its overwhelming economic strength (even if this is not always translated into military and political preponderance), South Africa can make or break SADC. By building confidence and common values and sharing sovereignty, the hegemon can be 'checked' or locked into policy processes, as has happened in other regions, but its dominance cannot be wished away. In any case, true hegemonism, at least in its original Gramscian sense, involves not the use of brutal force but of 'soft power', and is most successful when it is built on consensus rather than coercion.

The way forward

Progressively institutionalised co-operation in the area of defence and security is needed if SADC is to move beyond low levels of co-operation, and to graduate from organisational and normative co-operation to common security. To do this, resources are key: without appropriate contributions from member states (not just donors), sub-regional organisations cannot evolve beyond limited functional co-operation. On the downside, a continued narrow focus on regime security constrains the promotion of human security. Evolutionary progress towards common security will boost the human security agenda and provide more evidence for the thesis that democratic governance will assist peace and stability, which in turn will enable economic growth and development – a thesis upon which the continent's hopes are currently pinned through NEPAD.

Throughout the SADC region, the trend is that the political elite and the state are the main agents driving the actual process of democratisation and the formulation of security policy, thereby emphasising the state-centric nature of these projects. Some of the exclusionary tendencies of liberal democracy in the region are traceable, in part, from the tradition of one-party rule of yesteryear. Some may be directly attributed to the proliferation of neo-liberal economics that has accompanied democratisation. And the political culture of several SADC states is marked by the dominant-party syndrome. This further explains, in part, why the dominant interest and concerns around security policy focus mainly on state/regime security rather than human security. The challenge that this situation clearly poses is that the SADC region still has to entrench democratic practice and culture that embraces broad participation of various actors. This is why it is so important that civil society organisations are allowed space to make meaningful contributions to both democracy and security projects in the region.

However, this study does not seek to counterpose state security and human security, as is so common, especially and unsurprisingly in the analysis emerging from civil society organisations. It is normally weak, not strong, states that revert to repression and human rights abuses – or at least states that are weak in the sense that they lack coherence and legitimacy and thus feel profoundly threatened. Human security and human development clearly requires state action: in developing contexts such as Southern Africa it is, after all, the state that is primarily responsible for providing education, clean water, health, and so on. There are certainly many cases where states can become instruments of insecurity rather than security for their citizens, or at least for significant sections of the citizenry. There are also trade-offs that have to be made, e.g. in making decisions about budget allocations ('guns or butter'). But, in general, policymakers should seek to enhance the legitimate democratic functions of states, including the governance and management of security, in order to promote human security and human development.

The states of the region, with some exceptions, are weak and have been further weakened by globalisation, and in some cases (although this will hopefully be temporary) by democratisation. Their ability to manage security, both nationally and multilaterally, needs to be strengthened in ways that reinforce rather than undermine the rather fragile democratic values, processes, and practices that have taken root in the region. Security co-operation, and beyond this, a common security regime, should be seen in terms of ways of underpinning the state system, although it will require a pooling of sovereignty, thus gradually transferring key executive (and eventually judicial and legislative) functions to the collective from individual states. At the same time, civil society co-operation within the region also needs to be strengthened, so that an emerging SADC security community can be constructed on the basis of shared democratic values (this project itself is a very small example of the way individuals and institutions in the region can collaborate). The challenge – at both national and multilateral levels – is to deepen and consolidate democracy, prevent democratic reversals, and address the social and economic dimensions of democracy, without which it will not be sustainable in Southern Africa.

ENDNOTES

1 Multi-partyism does not, of course, necessarily mean democracy: it is quite possible, albeit unusual, for authoritarian systems to accommodate other political parties (e.g. the former German Democratic Republic), and proponents of one-party systems have often held that they can be democratic (e.g. President Museveni's claims for the Ugandan system), but in the current Southern African context, and in this book, multi-partyism is regarded as indispensable for democracy.

2 While there is no necessary relationship between socialism and one-partyism, there is certainly a contingent one.

3 In its original sense, e.g. the Palme Commission, institutionalisation was not necessary for common security, but it has come to take this form, e.g. the Organisation for Security and Co-operation in Europe.

Appendix 1

Research Briefing: Democratic Governance and Common Security in Southern Africa

Multi-party democracy, once an exception in Southern Africa, is now the official practice of virtually all countries of the Southern African Development Community (SADC). At the same time, SADC has embarked on an ambitious economic, political and security co-operation project. But this has been slow to develop and there have been many crises, not least over responses to conflict in the Democratic Republic of the Congo.

To assist in understanding the challenges that have accompanied the regional security co-operation project, the Centre for Defence and Security Management at the Graduate School of Public Development Management, University of the Witwatersrand, commissioned a research project to examine the relationship between national security, the regional security project, and the nature of democratic transitions and the practice of democracy in Southern Africa.

The findings of the study can be summarised in two parts: findings related to the state and character of democratisation and democracy in the region; and findings related to regional security co-operation and its links with democratisation.

Democratisation and democracy

The study concludes that democratisation has been uneven and partial in Southern Africa. With the possible exception of Seychelles (which has now withdrawn from SADC) none of the 14 countries studied can be considered to be social democracies. One (Swaziland) has yet to embark on a democratic transition, while two others (Angola and DRC) have only recently emerged from protracted and widespread civil conflict, with all the negative effects such conflict tends to have on democratic governance. Namibia and South Africa are still dealing with the legacies of decades of apartheid and white minority rule. The majority of states, however, are essentially in transition from one-party or authoritarian rule (although in some cases one-party rule was a consequence of a dominant party rather than a constitutional provision).

These transitions are still in progress and beset with many problems. Some analysts have dismissed democracy in Southern Africa as exclusionary or elitist in nature, but this study only partly supports this, pointing out that in many countries there are high levels of popular participation in electoral politics and active civil societies.

A major concern for the consolidation and sustainability of democracy in this region is that it appears not to have met expectations of socio-economic progress. Indeed, most countries have slipped down the UN Human Development Index, although HIV/Aids has played a significant part in this.

Botswana and Mauritius, the two longest-established democracies in Southern Africa, demonstrate through their sustained economic growth and social development that in the long term there may be a virtuous relationship between democracy and socio-economic progress.

Nevertheless, democratic transitions are risky and at least some of the insecurity and violent conflict in the region may be associated with such transitions: the DRC is the most obvious case. Nor is the result of transition predictable. Authoritarian rule remains a possibility.

It is notable that only one country in Southern Africa, Lesotho, is transiting from military rule. Civil-military relations in the region remain fairly stable, and the study attributes this in part to the legacy of liberation struggles where 'politics ruled the gun'.

Regional security co-operation

In most cases, the study was unable to determine exactly how democratic transitions have impacted on regional security co-operation, as they appear to have many contradictory effects. It concludes that regional political and security co-operation is driven by:

- Globalisation, which tends to weaken marginalized states, obliging them to club together, and engenders transnational security threats requiring multinational responses, as well as economic imperatives to co-operate.
- Solidarity forged in the liberation struggles, which remains an important ideological gel.

- Security interdependence where conflicts in one country are seen as impacting on the others.

But these powerful motives also have opposite effects. Globalisation has undermined state sovereignty in the economic sphere so that states understandably cling to what freedom of action remains in the political and security terrains. Solidarity may be a virtue but it tends to restrict critical engagement on issues such as citizen rights. And security interdependence can also lead to interference in the internal affairs of neighbouring states, on the principle that 'the enemy of my enemy is my friend'.

The study concludes that security co-operation in SADC remains fairly rudimentary, and has yet to significantly affect domestic policy formation. One reason for this is that there are strong counter-impulses, mostly springing from the insecurity of states. Security co-operation is primarily a state-centric process, driven by political elites, although there are signs of growing co-operation between civil societies and business interests. SADC is nevertheless pursuing an ambitious agenda, including developing a collective defence capability and UN-type principles of collective security.

At the same time, SADC is also aiming at 'wider' security: economic, social and environmental security. Like many of its member states, it often describes this as 'human security', although properly speaking human security is not merely wider, it is directed at the citizen rather than the state.

Somewhat surprisingly, the study did not reveal much concern about the role of South Africa as a potential hegemon in the region. Rather, it was expected that it should exercise greater leadership.

Policy recommendations

The study did not focus on strategic or tactical issues, but a series of broad policy proposals arose from the workshops which considered the findings, drawing on the expertise of both academics and practitioners. These can be summarised as follows:

- It is fashionable to argue that 'human security' should take precedence over 'state security'. While states can become instruments of insecurity for citizens, usually when they adopt repressive actions, one of the key problems with the consolidation of democracy in the region is the weakness of states. The security of states is an essential condition for human security, and policy-makers should seek policy options that simultaneously enhance both state and human security.

- At the same time, efforts should be made to involve civil society more widely in order to deepen political and security co-operation.

- Consolidation of democratic governance will tend to promote peace and stability, which in turn should enable economic growth and development. This will require broadening the involvement of a wide range of organisations, as well as implementation of SADC protocols providing for the development of democratic institutions and the entrenchment of human rights. It is essential that the social and economic dimensions of democracy, not just the formal criteria, are taken forward.

- Building a common security regime in Southern Africa will require moving beyond solidarity between states and regimes in power. SADC protocols now make it the duty of other states to intervene in 'internal affairs' in cases of gross human rights abuses, violent conflict and other extreme conditions, yet on the whole SADC has been very reluctant to criticise states on human rights and governance grounds. Practices for dealing with such issues need to be developed.

- SADC states have already 'pooled' some functions that were previously strictly the preserve of individual states. Further pooling of formerly sovereign functions will be necessary for the benefits of shared security to be felt, eventually transferring some executive, judicial and legislative functions from the individual state to the collective, but without weakening state capacities.

- In particular, progress will mean building the multinational institutions of SADC and integrating the Southern African project with that of the African Union.

Appendix 2

The Southern African Defence and Security Management network

The SADSEM network seeks to contribute to peace and security in Southern Africa by strengthening the democratic management of its defence forces and other security organs. It does so primarily by offering specialised training programmes to police and military officers and others involved in managing security in the region.

It also undertakes research on security issues, and helps governments in the region to develop defence policy.

The SADSEM network comprises ten tertiary partner institutions, which implement the programme in the 14 member countries of the Southern African Development Community (SADC).

It is managed by the Centre for Defence and Security Management (CDSM) in the Graduate School of Public and Development Management of the University of the Witwatersrand in Johannesburg, South Africa.

The SADSEM network is primarily funded by the Danish government. It is also attracting growing support from other institutions as well as governments in the region.

Overview of activities

The SADSEM network offers a range of services and activities, including:

- Training courses offered in all SADC countries, based on common curricula, but utilising teaching methods that are responsive to local requirements.
- Research and policy analysis, largely undertaken by network partners for SADC governments.
- An internship programme for students from SADC member states who wish to gain experience at institutions active in the fields of defence and security.

- Higher degree scholarships for all staff members of SADSEM network partners.

Aims and objectives

The vision of the SADSEM network is to contribute to the effective democratic management of defence and security functions in southern Africa, and to strengthen peace and common security in the region. It seeks to do this by:

- providing training and education for defence and security management and planning, civil-military relations, peace-building, and the management of peace missions;
- building scholarly capacity and developing a regional network of institutions to provide education, training, policy, and technical support and research output in these areas.

Background

Following the end of apartheid rule, South Africa's defence and security sector underwent a transformation process in which civil-military relations were normalised and the role of defence in a democracy was re-established. The Graduate School for Public and Development Management of the University of the Witwatersrand set up a defence management programme to assist with these challenging tasks. It assisted with transformation and helped to enhance the management skills of senior military officers and defence officials.

Countries in southern Africa simultaneously faced the challenge of managing complex security problems, and what started as a purely South African project was quickly widened to cover the whole SADC region.

At the end of 1999 the defence management programme was upgraded to include a Centre for Defence and Security Management (based at P&DM), as well as a regional network of programmes and centres for defence management. The network also maintains links with the Danish Institute for International Studies (DIIS).

Since then, the SADSEM network has played an important role in promoting peace and security in southern Africa, and developing a basis for common security in the region. It has done so by developing the capacity of governments in the region to:

- manage their defence forces and other security organs in a democratic manner;
- participate in regional security initiatives; and
- co-operate with multinational conflict resolution and peace missions.

Its targeted training programmes have benefited some 3 000 senior government officials, military officers and civil society leaders in all 14 SADC member states.

It has also made an important contribution to building sustainable local research and policy capacity, and promoted the involvement of civil society in these activities.

Management

The SADSEM network is co-ordinated the Centre for Defence and Security Management (CDSM) at the Graduate School of Public and Development Management of the University of the Witwatersrand. CDSM provides the network with management and administrative support.

Network activities are overseen by a steering committee comprising representatives of all network partners, which meets four times a year. Oversight is provided by an advisory board comprising representatives of all SADC governments, which meets annually.

SADSEM Network partners

The SADSEM network comprises ten tertiary partner institutions which implement the programme in the 14 SADC member states. These network partners are described below.

Angola

Centro de Estudos Estratégicos de Angola
CEEA is an independent, non-profit research institute based in Luanda. Established in 2001, it studies issues surrounding peace and security, social development and human rights, particularly in Southern and Central Africa.

It has developed a good working relationship with government institutions as well as non-state actors in Angola, particularly in respect of consultancy work on the electoral process. Among other things, CEEA is providing the state with a new system for voter registration.

Botswana

Centre for Strategic Studies, Department of Political and Administrative Studies, University of Botswana

The Centre for Strategic Studies was established in 2001 to participate in the SADSEM network and to present appropriate courses. It is attached to the Department of Political and Administrative Studies at the University of Botswana, which has a long track record of dealing with security and related issues. The centre has delivered a number of executive courses in defence and security management as well as the management of peace missions.

Democratic Republic of Congo (DRC)

Southern African Defence and Security Management Project, Chaire UNESCO, University of Kinshasa

UNESCO established the *Chaire UNESCO pour la culture de la paix, le reglement des conflicts, les droits humains, la democratie et la bonne gouvernance* (UNESCO Chair in Peace, Security and Good Governance) at the University of Kinshasa in November 2000 with the aim of improving the participation of Congolese academics and policy-makers in peace processes in SADC and Central Africa. It has involved several academics in the DRC in research, policy analysis, and teaching related to peace and security, and has hosted and facilitated numerous workshops and conferences on these topics as well as SADSEM executive sourses. The staff of the Chair have an extensive network of contacts in Central and Southern Africa. The Chair also has a subcentre at the University of Bukavu in eastern DRC.

Malawi

Defence and Security Management Project, Centre for Security Studies, Mzuzu University, Malawi

The Centre was established in response to the need for well-educated and informed personnel in the Malawi Defence Force as well as other security organs in the country. It seeks to contribute to peace and security in the country by building the capacity of policy-makers, security personnel, and civil society leaders. In particular, it seeks to produce excellent officers for the defence force. Mzuzu University currently offers short courses in security management, but intends to develop longer academic programmes as well. Its membership of the SADSEM network is helping it to achieve this goal, and the university has presented a number of SADSEM courses.

Mozambique

Defence and Security Management Project, Centre for African Studies, Eduardo Mondlane University, Mozambique

The Project has developed and delivered several executive courses, including one on managing peace missions; researched a number of key security issues in Mozambique; produced several publications, including a thematic issue of CEA's journal *Estudos Moçambicanos* on the Mozambican peace process; and helped to develop the Mozambique white paper on defence and other key policy documents.

Namibia

Defence and Security Management Project, Department of Political and Administrative Studies, University of Namibia

The Department of Political and Administrative Studies has developed capacity for research and training in defence issues especially through its participation in the SADSEM network, for which purpose it has established a Defence and Security Management Project. It has sought to integrate its work on defence and security with its wider public management programmes, and has developed a programme of research on these issues.

The university has good technical facilities for organising and hosting training courses. The department also has good relations with key domestic actors in defence and security. The project has delivered several executive courses on defence and security management, including ones specifically tailored for parliamentarians and NGO personnel.

South Africa

Centre for Defence and Security Management (CDSM), University of the Witwatersrand

CDSM co-ordinates the SADSEM network, and provides it with management and administrative support. Headed by the Chair of Defence and Security Management of the Graduate School of Public and Development Management (P&DM) of the University of the Witwatersrand, the Centre has more than ten years of experience in training for defence and security governance and management, and is a leader in its field.

CDSM has provided the South African government with extensive policy support, notably by helping to develop its White Paper on Defence, the Defence Review, the White Paper on Peace Missions, and the White Paper on Defence-Related Industries. It has also contributed to broader policy analysis via papers delivered at SADC and international conferences. Given its relatively small staff, it has an impressive research and publications record.

Tanzania

Defence and Security Management Subcentre, Centre for Foreign Relations, Tanzania

The Centre for Foreign Relations (CFR) has made a sustained contribution to peace and security studies in southern Africa. It was established in 1978 by the governments of Tanzania and Mozambique to provide training and research in international relations and diplomacy. It is still nominally owned by both countries, but for all practical purposes it is a Tanzanian institute. Its main activity is still the training of Tanzania's foreign affairs officials, but it has expanded its training programme, and offers courses to the public as well.

The CFR is very well-connected, and has strong links with key ministries and other stakeholders in the country. It has run several SADSEM executive courses, including some specifically tailored for the National Parks security environment, and has developed a programme of research as well as providing other training and policy support. The defence and security activities are run by a subcentre that has high-level representation from the defence and security services.

Zambia

Defence and Security Project, Department of History, University of Zambia

Since 2000, the Project has presented several executive SADSEM courses, some in association with the Centre for Foreign Relations in Tanzania. The University of Zambia became a full member of the SADSEM network in December 2003.

The Project enjoys the support of the university administration as well as the Ministry of Defence. The latter are the key stakeholders, since the executive courses presented thus far have been aimed at equipping officials in the ministries of Defence, Home Affairs, and Foreign Affairs with skills and knowledge in the area of defence and security. The Project now has enough resources to manage executive courses with a minimum of regional support.

Zimbabwe

Centre for Defence Studies, Department of History, University of Zimbabwe

The University of Zimbabwe has achieved a high level of expertise in the academic teaching of security studies, and has links with the national defence force as well as other government departments, which provide many of its students. The Centre's War and Strategic Studies Unit provides education in this field at four levels: a diploma, a batchelor's degree, a master's degree, and a doctorate. More than 200 people have obtained one of these qualifications.

Courses

The SADSEM network offers two types of courses in four subjects, organised in partnership with SADC governments. The four subjects are:

- Defence and Security Management
- Management of Multinational Peace Missions
- Security Sector Governance
- Parliamentary Oversight of Defence and Security

The two types of courses are:

Certificate courses, leading to a certificate of competence. These run for three to five weeks. These courses are presented in Johannesburg, and participants are drawn from all over the region. Participants are assessed on the basis of group presentations, individual assignments, and written examinations.

Executive courses of two to ten days, presented in all SADC member states. Participants are not assessed.

The network is also developing a series of masters degrees in security sector management, to be offered by network partners.

An interactive and participatory approach to teaching and learning is followed. Extensive use is made of case studies and simulations. Participants work in groups, which enable them to share experiences and deal with real management problems. The learning process is structured to enable participants to become more confident about expressing and exploring their own ideas, and draw upon their own experiences.

Lecturers include academics from network partners, African and international experts, and practitioners of defence and security governance and management.

Research and policy support

SADSEM network partners are involved in a number of multinational research projects, focusing on democratic governance and the management of security in the SADC region. Current and previous research partners include the Canadian International Development Research Centre (IDRC), the German Friedrich Ebert Foundation (FES), the British Department for International Development (DFID), the Botswana Institute for Development Policy Analysis (BIDPA), the Norwegian C Michelsen Institute (CMI), the Swiss-based Centre for the Democratic Control of the Armed Forces, and various other institutions.

SADSEM has a twinning arrangement with the Danish Institute of International Affairs, which involves collaborative research, exchanges, and other forms of co-operation.

Network partners are also involved in other individual research projects

Bibliography

Chapter 1: Democratic Governance and Security: A Conceptual Exploration

Ake, Claude. 1994. *Democratisation of Disempowerment in Africa.* Lagos: Malthouse.

——. 1996. *Democracy and Development in Africa.* Washington, DC: Brookings Institution Press.

——. 2000. *The Feasibility of Democracy in Africa.* Dakar: Council for the Development of Social Science Research in Africa.

Ayoob, M. 1986. *Regional Security in the Third World.* London: Croom Helm.

Baregu, Mwesiga and Christopher Landsberg (eds). 2003. *From Cape to Cairo: Southern Africa's Evolving Security Challenges.* Boulder: Lynne Rienner.

Bobbio, Norberto. 1990. *Liberalism and Democracy.* London: Verso.

——. 1996. *The Age of Rights.* London: Polity Press.

Bond. P. 2000. *Unsustainable South Africa.* Johannesburg: Wits University Press.

——. 2001. *Against Global Apartheid: South Africa Meets the World Bank, IMF and International Finance.* Cape Town: UCT Press.

Bratton, Michael and Nicolas van de Walle (eds). 1997. *Democratic Experiments in Africa: Regime Transitions in Comparative Perspective.* Cambridge: Cambridge University Press.

Brown, M., S. Lynn-Jones, and S. Miller (eds). 1996. *Debating the Democratic Peace.* Cambridge, Mass.: MIT Press.

Buzan, B. 1991. *People, States and Fear: An Agenda for International Security Studies in the Post-Cold War Era,* 2nd ed. London: Harvester Wheatsheaf.

——, O. Waever, and J. de Wilde. 1998. *Security: A New Framework for Analysis.* Boulder: Lynne Rienner.

Cawthra, Gavin and Robin Luckham (eds). 2003. *Governing Insecurity: Democratic Control of Military and Security Establishments in Transitional Democracies.* London: Zed Books.

Chazan, Naomi, Robert Mortimer, John Ravenhill, and Donald Rothchild. 1988. *Politics and Society in Contemporary Africa.* Boulder: Lynne Rienner.

Cheru, Fantu. 2002. *African Renaissance: Roadmaps to the Challenge of Globalisation.* London: Zed Books.

Cilliers, Jakkie. 2002. *NEPAD's Peer Review Mechanism.* ISS Paper No. 64. Pretoria: Institute for Security Studies. November.

Clapham, Christopher (ed). 1982. *Private Patronage and Public Power: Political Clientilism in the Modern State.* London: Pinter.

Comte-Sponville, Andre. 2001. *A Short Treatise on the Great Virtues: The Uses of Philosophy in Everyday Life.* London: William Heinemann.

Dahl, Robert. 1971. *Polyarchy: Participation and Opposition.* New Haven: Yale University Press.

——. 1989. *Democracy and Its Critics.* New Haven: Yale University Press.

——. 1991. *On Democracy.* New Haven: Yale University Press.

Diamond, Larry. 1999. *Developing Democracy: Towards Consolidation.* London: Johns Hopkins University Press.

Elman, M. 1997. *Paths to Peace: Is Democracy the Answer?* Cambridge, Mass.: MIT Press.

Falk, Richard. 1995. *On Humane Governance: Toward a New Global Politics.* Cambridge: Polity Press.

Galtung, Johan. 1975. 'Violence, peace and peace research.' In Johan Galtung, *Ideals, Peace, Research, Education, Action: Essays in Peace Research*, vol. 1. Copenhagen: Christian Eljers Forlag.

——. 1985. 'Twenty years of peace research: Ten challenges and some responses.' *Journal of Peace Research*, 22(1).

——. 2000. 'Alternative models for global democracy.' In B. Holden (ed), *Global Democracy: Key Debates.* London: Routledge.

Gowa, J. 1999. *Ballots and Bullets: The Elusive Democratic Peace.* Princeton: Princeton University Press.

Harbeson, J. W. 1999. *Rethinking Democratic Transitions: Lessons from Eastern and Southern Africa.* Boulder: Lynne Rienner.

Held, D. 1992. 'Democracy: From city-states to a cosmopolitan order?' *Political Studies*, 40, special issue.

——. 2000. 'The changing contours of political community: Rethinking democracy in the context of globalisation.' In B. Holden (ed), *Global Democracy: Key Debates.* London: Routledge.

Horowitz, Donald L. 1991. *A Democratic South Africa?: Constitutional Engineering in a Divided Society.* Cape Town: Oxford University Press.

——. 2003. 'Constitutional design: Proposals versus process.' In Andrew Reynolds (ed), *The Architecture of Democracy: Constitutional Design, Conflict Management, and Democracy.* Oxford: Oxford University Press.

Huntington, S. 1991. *The Third Wave: Democratization in the Late Twentieth Century.* Norman: University of Oklahoma Press.

Hyslop, Jonathan (ed). 1999. *African Democracy in the Era of Globalisation.* Johannesburg: Witwatersrand University Press.

Jackson, Robert H. 1982. *Personal Rule in Black Africa: Prince, Autocrat, Prophet, Tyrant.* Berkeley: University of California Press.

Joseph, Richard. 1989. *Beyond Autocracy in Africa.* Emory University African Governance Program, Carter Center, Working Paper Series. Atlanta: Carter Center.

——. 1991. 'Africa: The rebirth of political freedom.' *Journal of Democracy*, 2(4), Fall.

Linz, Juan J. and Alfred Stepan. 1996. 'Toward consolidated democracies.' *Journal of Democracy*, 7(2).

Luckham, Robin. 2003. 'Democratic strategies for security in transition and conflict.' In Gavin Cawthra and Robin Luckham (eds), *Governing Insecurity: Democratic Control of Military and Security Establishments in Transitional Democracies.* London: Zed Books.

——, A. M. Goetz, and M. Kaldor. 2000. *Democratic Institutions and Politics in Contexts of Inequality, Poverty and Conflict.* IDS Working Paper No. 104. Brighton: Institute of Development Studies.

Marais, H. 1998. *South Africa: Limits to Change. The Political Economy of Transformation.* Cape Town: UCT Press.

Matlosa, K. 2000. 'Aid, development and democracy in Lesotho, 1966–1996.' In L. Thompson (ed), *Development, Democracy and Aid in Southern Africa*. Centre for Southern African Studies Monograph Series. Cape Town: University of the Western Cape.

Nyong'o, Anyang. 1991. 'Democratisation process in Africa.' *CODESRIA Bulletin*, 2.

Nzongola-Ntalaja, Georges. 1997. 'The state and democracy in Africa.' In Georges Nzongola-Ntalaja and Margaret C. Lee, *The State and Democracy in Africa.* Harare: AAPS Books.

—— and Margaret C. Lee. 1997. *The State and Democracy in Africa.* Harare: AAPS Books.

OAU/AU (Organisation of African Unity/African Union). 2002. Protocol Relating to the Establishment of the Peace and Security Council of the African Union. Addis Ababa.

Owusu, M. 1994. 'The domesticisation of democracy: Culture, civil society and constitutionalism in Africa.' *Comparative Studies in Society and History*, 39.

Pateman, Carole. 1970. *Participation and Democratic Theory*. Cambridge: Cambridge University Press.

Picard, Louis A. 1987. *The Politics of Development in Botswana: A Model for Success.* Boulder: Lynne Rienner.

Ray, J. 1995. *Democracy and International Conflict: An Evaluation of the Democratic Peace Proposition.* Columbia: University of South Carolina Press.

Reynolds, A. and B. Reilly. 2002. *International IDEA Handbook of Electoral System Design.* Stockholm: IDEA.

Russett, B. 1993. *Grasping the Democratic Peace: Principles for a Post-Cold War World.* Princeton: Princeton University Press.

SADC (Southern African Development Community). 2001. Protocol on Politics, Defence, and Security Co-operation. Gaborone: SADC Secretariat.

Sandbrook, Richard. 2000. *Closing the Circle: Democratization and Development in Africa.* London: Zed Books.

Selebi, J. 1999. 'Building collaborative security in southern Africa.' *African Security Review*, 8(5).

Shivji, Issa G. 1991. 'Contradictory class perspectives in the debate on democracy.' In Issa G. Shiva, *State and Constitutionalism: An African Debate on Democracy.* Harare: SAPES Trust.

Sorenson, Georg. 1993. *Democracy and Democratization: Dilemmas in World Politics.* Boulder: Westview Press.

Tickner, J. Ann. 1995. 'Re-visioning security.' In K. Booth and S. Smith (eds), *International Relations Theory Today.* London: Polity Press.

UN (United Nations). 2002. *Study on Women, Peace and Security.* Draft report. New York: UN.

——. Commission on Human Security. 2003. *Human Security Now.* New York: UN.

UNDP (UN Development Programme). 1994. *Human Development Report 1994: New Dimensions of Human Security.* <http://www.hdr.undp.org/reports/global/1994/en/

——. 2002. *Human Development Report 2002: Deepening Democracy in a Fragmented World.* New York: Oxford University Press.

Waever, O. 1995. 'Securitization and desecuritization.' In E. Lipschutz (ed), *On Security.* New York: Columbia University Press.

Young, Crawford. 1999. 'The third wave of democratization in Africa: Ambiguities and contradictions.' In Richard Joseph (ed), *State, Conflict, and Democracy in Africa.* Boulder: Lynne Rienner.

Chapter 2: Comparative Perspectives on Regional Security Co-operation among Developing Countries

Aarts, P. 1999. 'The Middle East: Eternally out of step with history?' In K. P. Thomas and M. A. Tetreault (eds), *Racing to Regionalise: Democracy, Capitalism and Regional Political Economy.* Boulder: Lynne Rienner.

Adler, E. and M. Barnett. 1998. *Security Communities.* Cambridge: Cambridge University Press.

Alagappa, M. 1998. *Asian Security Practice: Material and Ideational Influences.* Stanford: Stanford University Press.

Al-Bab. n.d. Web site. http://www.al-bab.com/arab, accessed 4 February 2005.

Baregu, M. 2003. 'Economic and military security.' In M. Baregu and C. Landsberg (eds), *From Cape to Congo: Southern Africa's Evolving Security Challenges*. Boulder: Lynne Rienner.

Berman, E. G. 2002. 'African regional organisations' peace operations: Developments and challenges.' *African Security Review*, 11(4).

—— and K. E. Sams. 2000. *Peacekeeping in Africa: Capabilities and Culpabilities.* Geneva: UN Institute for Disarmament Research, and Pretoria: Institute for Security Studies.

Bessho, K. 1999. *Identities and Security in East Asia.* Adelphi Paper No. 325. London: International Institute for Strategic Studies.

Buzan, B. 1991. *People, States and Fear.* Hemel Hempstead: Harvester Wheatsheaf.

Cawthra, G. 1997. 'Sub-regional security co-operation: The Southern African Development Community in comparative perspective.' *Southern African Perspectives*, 63. Cape Town: Centre for Southern African Studies.

Cleary, S. 2001. 'Variable geometry and varying speed: An operational paradigm for SADC.' In C. Clapham, G. Mills, A. Morner, and E. Sidiropoulos (eds), *Regional Integration: Comparative International Perspectives.* Johannesburg: South African Institute of International Affairs.

Deutsch, K. 1957. *Political Community and the North Atlantic Area.* Princeton: Princeton University Press.

Elman, M. F. 1998. *Paths to Peace: Is Democracy the Answer?* Cambridge, Mass.: MIT Press.

Farer, T. J. 1993. 'The role of regional collective security arrangements.' In T. G. Weiss (ed), *Collective Security in a Changing World.* Boulder: Lynne Rienner.

Fawcett, L. and A. Hurrell. *Regionalism in World Politics: Regional Organization and International Order.* Oxford: Oxford University Press.

Furley, O. and R. May. 2001. *African Interventionist States.* Aldershot: Ashgate.

Grugel, J. and M. de A. Medeiros. 1999. 'Brazil and MERCOSUR.' In J. Grugel and W. Hout (eds), *Regionalism across the North–South Divide: State Strategies and Globalisation.* London: Routledge.

Henderson, J. 1999. *Reassessing ASEAN.* Adelphi Paper No. 328. London: International Institute for Strategic Studies.

Hettne, B., A. Inotai, and O. Sunkel. 2000. *National Perspectives on the New Regionalism in the South.* Houndmills: Macmillan.

IPA (International Peace Academy). 2002. *The Infrastructure of Peace in Africa: Assessing the Peacebuilding Capacity of African Institutions.* Report submitted by the Africa Programme of the IPA to the Ford Foundation. New York: IPA.

Lawson, F. H. 1999. 'Theories of integration in a new context: The Gulf Cooperation Council.' In K. P. Thomas and M. A. Tetreault (eds), *Racing to Regionalise: Democracy, Capitalism and Regional Political Economy.* Boulder: Lynne Rienner.

Macmillan, J. 1998. *On Liberal Peace: Democracy, War and the International Order.* London: Tauris.

Mansfield, E. D. 1994. *Power, Trade and War.* Princeton: Princeton University Press.

—— and J. Snyder. 1995. 'Democratization and war.' *Foreign Affairs,* May–June.

Mills, G., G. Shelton, and L. White. 2003. 'Comparative security arrangements in the Americas, Asia and the Gulf.' Unpublished paper. Johannesburg: Institute for Global Dialogue.

Mortimer, R. A. 1996. 'Ecomog, Liberia and regional security in West Africa.' In J. Keller and D. Rothchild (eds), *Africa in the New International Order: Rethinking State Sovereignty and Regional Security.* Boulder: Lynne Rienner.

Narine, S. 2002. *Explaining Asean: Regionalism in Southeast Asia.* Boulder: Lynne Rienner.

Oneal, J. R., B. Russett, and M. L. Berbaum. 2003. 'Causes of peace: Democracy, interdependence, and international organisations, 1885–1992.' *International Studies Quarterly,* 47.

Pereira, L. V. 1999. 'Toward the Common Market of the South: MERCOSUR's origins, evolutions and challenges.' In R. Roett (ed), *MERCOSUR: Regional Integration, World Markets.* Boulder: Lynne Rienner.

Regan, P. M. and E. A. Henderson. 2002. 'Democracy, threats and political repression in developing countries: Are democracies internally less violent?' *Third World Quarterly*, 23(1).

Russett, B. 1993. *Grasping the Democratic Peace: Principles for a Post-Cold War World.* Princeton: Princeton University Press.

Than, M. and D. Singh. 2001. 'Regional integration: The case of Asean.' In C. Clapham, G. Mills, A. Morner, and E. Sidiropoulos (eds), *Regional Integration: Comparative International Perspectives.* Johannesburg: South African Institute of International Affairs.

Tow, W. T. 1990. *Subregional Security Cooperation in the Third World.* Boulder: Lynne Rienner.

Tripp, C. 1995. 'Regional organisations in the Arab Middle East.' In A. Hurrell and L. Fawcett, *Regionalism in World Politics: Regional Organization and International Order.* Oxford: Oxford University Press.

Vale, P. 2003. *Security and Politics in South Africa: The Regional Dimension.* Boulder: Lynne Rienner.

Vogt, M. A. 1996. 'The involvement of Ecowas in Liberia's Peacekeeping.' In J. Keller and D. Rothchild (eds), *Africa in the New International Order: Rethinking State Sovereignty and Regional Security.* Boulder: Lynne Rienner.

Weart, S. R. 1998. *Never at War: Why Democracies Will not Fight One Another.* New Haven: Yale University Press.

Chapter 3: Southern African Security in Historial Perspective

Africa Research Bulletin. 1966. Political, Social, and Cultural Series. Oxford: Blackwell. March.

——. 1986. Political Series. Oxford: Blackwell. September.

Baregu, Mwesiga and Christopher Landsberg (eds). 2003. *From Cape to Cairo: Southern Africa's Evolving Security Challenges.* Boulder: Lynne Rienner.

Cilliers, Jakkie. 1999. *Building Security in Southern Africa: An Update on the Evolving Architecture.* ISS Monograph Series No. 43. Pretoria: Institute for Security Studies. November.

Cox, Richard. 1964. *Pan Africanism in Practice: An East African Study, PAFMECSA 1958–1964.* London: Oxford University Press.

De Klerk, Frederik W. 1991. 'Address at the opening of the third session of the ninth parliament of the Republic of South Africa', Cape Town, 1 February. Pretoria: Bureau for Information.

Deng, Francis M. 1995. *War of Visions: Conflict of Identities in the Sudan.* Washington, DC: Brookings Institution Press.

Gibson, Richard. 1972. *African Liberation Movements: Contemporary Struggles against White Minority Rule.* London: Oxford University Press.

Isaacman, Allen. 1988. 'Regional security in Southern Africa: Mozambique.' *Survival,* XXX(1), February–March.

Khadiagala, Gilbert M. 1994. *Allies in Adversity: The Frontline States in Southern African Security 1975–1993.* Athens, Ohio: Ohio University Press.

King, Preston. 1986. *An African Winter.* Harmondsworth: Penguin.

Macaringue, Paulino. 2004. 'Operationalisation of the SADC Organ on Politics, Defence and Security Co-operation.' *African Regional Peace Exchange,* 1(2), October.

Omari, Abillah H. 1991a. 'Angola and Namibia: Beyond the capability of the Front Line States.' In Larry A. Swatuk and Timothy M. Shaw (eds), *Prospects for Peace and Development in Southern Africa in the 1990s: Canadian and Comparative Perspectives.* Lanham: University Press of America.

——. 1991b. *The Rise and Decline of the Front Line States (FLS) Alliance in Southern Africa: 1975–1991.* PhD thesis, Dalhousie University, Halifax, Nova Scotia, Canada.

——. 1995a. *Regional Security: One View from the Front Line States.* The Arusha Papers No. 5. Dar es

Salaam: Centre for Foreign Relations, and Bellville: Centre for Southern African Studies, University of the Western Cape. July.

——. 1995b. *Development and Security in Southern Africa: Non-traditional Considerations*. Working Paper No. 2. Dar es Salaam: Centre for Foreign Relations. July.

——. 1995c. *Causes and Prevention of Coups in Southern Africa*. Southern African Perspectives Working Paper No. 45. Bellville: Centre for Southern Africa Studies, University of the Western Cape. June.

—— with Larry A. Swatuk. 1995. 'Regional security: Southern Africa's mobile frontline.' In Larry A. Swatuk and David R. Black (eds), *Bridging the Rift: The New South Africa in Africa*. Boulder: Westview.

—— with Peter Vale. 1995. *The Southern African Institute (SAI): A Forum for Security and Development Concerns*. The Arusha Papers No. 4. Dar es Salaam: Centre for Foreign Relations, and Bellville: Centre for Southern African Studies, University of the Western Cape. June.

SADC (Southern African Development Community). 2001. Protocol on Politics, Defence, and Security Co-operation. Gaborone: SADC Secretariat.

Chapter 4: Botswana

Balise, J. 2003. 'Gaolatlhe defends BDF budget.' *Botswana Guardian*, 21 February.

Baraedi, Chenjelani. 2002. 'Botswana Snubs Zimbabwe Investigators.' *Botswana Guardian*, 29 November.

Dale, R. 1995. *Botswana's Search for Autonomy in Southern Africa*. Westport: Greenwood Press.

Danevad, A. 1993. *Development Planning and the Importance of Democratic Institutions in Botswana*. Bergen: Christian Michelsen Institute.

Gastow, P. 2002. *The SADC Region, a Common Market for Criminals?* Cape Town: Organised Crime and Corruption Programme. 29 November. http://www.iss.co.za.

Harvey, C. and S. Lewis. 1990. *Policy Choice and Development Performance in Botswana*. London: Macmillan.

Holm, J. and P. Molutsi (eds). 1989. *Democracy in Botswana*. Gaborone: Macmillan.

Holm, J., P. Molutsi, and G. Somolekae. 1996. 'The development of civil society in a democratic state: The Botswana model.' *African Studies Review*, 39(2).

Leepile, M. 1996. *Botswana's Media and Democracy*. Gaborone: Mmegi.

Letsididi, Bashi. 2002. 'Zim Torture Claims Probed – Merafhe.' *Botswana Guardian*, 29 November.

Malan, M. 1998. *Regional Power Politics under Cover of SADC: Running Amok with a Mythical Organ*. ISS Occasional Paper No. 35. http://www.iss.co.za.

Maundeni, Z. 2004. *Civil Society, Politics and the State in Botswana*. Gaborone: Medi.

Mbabazi, A. 2002. 'Foreword.' In Uganda Ministry of Defence, *Uganda Defence Review*. Kampala: Intersoft Business Services.

Media Institute of Southern Africa. n.d. *Botswana*. http://www.misanet.org/samd/BOTSWANA.html.

Merafhe, M. 2000. 'Statement by the minister of foreign affairs of the republic of Botswana, honourable lt. general Mompati S. Merafhe, on the occasion of the official opening of the International Peace Academy Seminar on Southern Africa's evolving security architecture prospects and problems.' Grand Palm Hotel, Gaborone, 11 December.

Mmegi. 2002. 'Zim Govt Denies tension with Botswana.' 6–12 December.

Mogae, F. 1996. 'Budget speech.' Gaborone.

Mokopakgosi, B. and M. Molomo. 2000. 'Democracy in the face of a weak opposition in Botswana.' *Pula: Botswana Journal of African Studies*, 14(1).

Molomo, M. G. 2000a. 'Understanding government and opposition parties in Botswana.' *Commonwealth and Comparative Politics*, 38(1).

——. 2000b. 'Democracy under siege: The presidency and executive powers in Botswana.' *Pula: Botswana Journal of African Studies*, 14(1).

——. 2001. 'Civil–military relations in Botswana's developmental state.' *African Studies Quarterly*, 5(2). http://web.africa.ufi.edu/asq/v5/v5i2a3.htm.

Osei-Hwedie, B. Z. 1998. 'The role of Botswana in the liberation of Southern Africa since 1996.' In W. Edge and M. Lekorwe (eds), *Botswana Politics and Society*. Pretoria: Van Schaik.

——. 2001 'The political opposition in Botswana: The politics of factionalism and fragmentation.' *Transformation*, 45.

——. 2002. 'The quest for peace and security: The Southern African Development Community Organ on Politics, Defence and Security.' In D. Milazi, M. Mulinge, and E. Mukamaambo (eds), *Democracy, Human Rights and Regional Cooperation in Southern Africa*. Pretoria: Africa Institute of South Africa.

Picard, L. (ed). 1985. *The Evolution of Modern Botswana*. Lincoln: University of Nebraska Press.

——. 1987. *The Politics of Development in Botswana: A Model for Success?* Boulder: Lynne Rienner.

Republic of Botswana. 1977. Botswana Defence Force Act. Gaborone.

Samatar, A. 1999. *An African Miracle: State and Class Leadership and Colonial Legacy in Botswana's Development*. Portsmouth: Heinemann.

Selolwane, O. 2001. 'Monopoly politikos: How Botswana's opposition parties have helped sustain one-party dominance.' Paper presented to the Department of Sociology, University of Botswana, 27 September.

Shaw, T. 1994. 'The marginalization of Africa in the new world disorder.' In R. Stubbs and G. Underhill (eds), *The Political Economy and the Changing Global Order*. London: Macmillan.

Stedman, S. J. (ed). 1993. *Botswana: The Political Economy of Democratic Development*. Boulder: Lynne Rienner.

Sullivan, G. R. and A. B. Twomey. 1994. 'The challenges of peace.' *Parameters*, XXIV(3).

Swatuk, L. and A. Omari. 1997. 'Regional security: Southern Africa's mobile "front line".' In L. Swatuk and D. Black (eds), *Bridging the Rift*. Colorado: Westview Press.

Thumberg-Hartland, P. 1978. *Botswana: An African Growth Economy*. Boulder: Westview Press.

Uganda Ministry of Defence. *Uganda Defence Review*. 2002. Kampala: Intersoft Business Services.

Chapter 5: Lesotho

Ake, C. 1996. *Democracy and Development in Africa*. Washington, DC: Brookings Institution Press.

——. 2000. *The Feasibility of Democracy in Africa*. Dakar: CODESRIA Books.

Chabal, P. and J. Daloz. 1999. *Africa Works: Disorder as Political Instrument*. Oxford: James Currey.

Elklit, J. 2002. 'Lesotho 2002: Africa's first MMP election.' *Journal of African Elections*, 1(2).

Elman, M. 1997. *Paths to Peace: Is Democracy the Answer?* Cambridge, Mass.: MIT Press.

Fick, G., S. Meintjes and M. Simons (eds). 2002. *One Woman, One Vote: The Gender Politics of South African Elections*. Johannesburg: Electoral Institute of Southern Africa.

Hamman, H. 2001. *Days of the Generals: The Untold Story of South Africa's Apartheid-era Military Generals*. Cape Town: Zebra Press.

Harris, G. 1999. *Recovery from Armed Conflict in Developing Countries*. London: Routledge.

Huntington, S. 1968. *Political Order in Changing Societies*. New Haven: Yale University Press.

Hutchful, E. 1998. 'Introduction: Africa – Rethinking security.' *African Journal of Political Science*, 3(1).

IEC (Independent Electoral Commission). 2002. *Report on the 2002 General Election Held on 25 May 2002 for the National Assembly of the Kingdom of Lesotho*. Mimeo, Maseru.

Inter-parliamentary Union. 1997. *Men and Women in Politics: Democracy Still in the Making*. Report No. 28. Mimeo. Geneva: Inter-parliamentary Union.

IPA (International Peace Academy). 2002. *Peace-making in Southern Africa: The Role and Potential of the Southern African Development Community (SADC)*. Mimeo. New York: IPA.

Joseph, R. (ed). 1999. *State, Conflict and Democracy in Africa*. London: UCL Press.

Kingdom of Lesotho. 1997. 'A new partnership with the police: The Lesotho government strategy for policing.' Government white paper. Mimeo. Maseru.

——. 1998. Interim Political Authority Act. Maseru.

——. 2001. 'Agreement between the government of the Kingdom of Lesotho and the government of the Republic of South Africa on the establishment of a joint bilateral commission of co-operation.' Mimeo. Maseru.

——. 2002a. 'National budget.' Mimeo. Maseru.

——. 2002b. 'Budget speech to parliament for the fiscal year 2002/2003.' Maseru.

——. Ministry of Defence. 1998. *Annual Report of the Ministry of Defence*. Maseru.

Leon Commission. 2001. *Report of the Commission of Inquiry into the Events Leading to Political Disturbances, which Occurred in Lesotho during the Period between 1 July 1998 to 30 November 1998*. Mimeo. Maseru.

Letuka, P., K. Matashane, and B. Morolong. 1997. 'Beyond inequalities: Women in Lesotho.' Mimeo. Harare: Southern African Research and Documentation Centre.

LMPS (Lesotho Mounted Police Service). 1998. *Beyond 2000: A Development plan for the Lesotho Mounted Police Service, 1998–2003*. Mimeo. Maseru: LMPS.

Mandaza, I. 2000. 'Problems and prospects of governance in Africa.' In A. Sall (ed), *The Future Competitiveness of African Economies*. Abidjan: African Futures.

Matlosa, K. 1997. 'Political instability and elections: A case study of Lesotho.' *Lesotho Social Science Review*, 3(2).

——. 1998a. 'Democracy and conflict in post-apartheid Southern Africa: Dilemmas of social change in small states.' *International Affairs*, 74(2).

——. 1998b. 'Military rule and withdrawal from power: The case of Lesotho.' In E. Hutchful (ed), *The Military and Militarism in Africa*. Dakar: CODESRIA Books.

——. 1999. 'Conflict and conflict management: Lesotho after the 1998 election.' *Lesotho Social Science Review*, 5(1).

——. 2000. 'Aid, development and democracy in Lesotho, 1966–1996.' In L. Thompson (ed), *Development, Democracy and Aid in Southern Africa*. Centre for Southern African Studies Monograph Series. Cape Town: University of the Western Cape.

——. 2001. 'The dilemma of security in Southern Africa: The case of Lesotho.' In N. Poku (ed), *Security and Development in Southern Africa*. London: Praeger.

——. 2002a. 'Security sector reform in Lesotho, 1966–2002.' Mimeo. Accra: African Security Dialogue and Research.

——. 2002b. 'New regionalist impulses: Implications of the New Partnership for Africa's Development (NEPAD) for regional cooperation in Southern Africa.' Paper prepared for CODESRIA's 10th General Assembly, Kampala, Uganda, 8–12 December.

——. 2003a. 'Globalisation and regional security cooperation in Southern Africa.' In K. Matlosa (ed), *The Post-Cold War Regional Security Architecture in Southern Africa*. Harare: SAPES Books.

——. 2003b. 'Electoral system, constitutionalism and conflict management in Southern Africa.' *Africa Journal on Conflict Resolution*, 4(2).

—— and N. Pule. 2001. 'The military in Lesotho.' *African Security Review*, 10(2).

Meena, R. 1998. 'Conceptual issues of gender in Southern Africa.' Paper prepared for conference on Human Development in the SADC Region, Windhoek, Namibia, 10–12 June.

Molokomme, A. 2000. 'Building inclusiveness in SADC's democratic systems: The case of women's representation in leadership positions.' Paper prepared for the Southern African Elections Forum, Windhoek, Namibia, 11–14 June.

——. 2002. 'Gender equality and the new political culture in Southern Africa.' *Southern African Political and Economic Monthly*, 14(9).

Motebang, M. 1997. 'Women and politics: Prospects for the 1998 general election in Lesotho.' *Lesotho Social Science Review*, 3(2).

Mothibe, T. 1998. 'The military and the 1994 constitutional crisis: A question of trust.' *Review of Southern African Studies*, 2(1).

——. 1999. 'The military and democratisation in Lesotho.' *Lesotho Social Science Review*, 5(1).

Nabudere, D. 2003. 'African international relations after the events of September 11th.' In K. Matlosa (ed), *The Post-Cold War Regional Security Architecture in Southern Africa*. Harare: SAPES Books.

Nathan, L. 1994. *The Changing of the Guard: Armed Forces and Defence Policy in a Democratic South Africa*. Pretoria: Human Sciences Research Council.

——. 1998. 'Good governance, security and disarmament in Africa.' *African Journal of Political Science*, 3(2).

Ohlson, T. 1993. 'The end of the Cold War and conflict resolution in Southern Africa.' In R. Siddiqui (ed), *Sub-Saharan Africa: A Sub-continent in Transition*. Aldershot: Avebury.

—— and J. Stedman. 1994. *The New Is Not Yet Born: Conflict Resolution in Southern Africa*. Washington, DC: Brookings Institution Press.

Pule, N. and K. Matlosa. 1997. *The Impact of Retrenched Returnees on Gender Relations in Rural Lesotho*. OSSREA Research Report. Mimeo. Addis Ababa: OSSREA.

SADC (Southern African Development Community). 2001. *Report on the Review of Operations of SADC Institutions*. Mimeo. Gaborone: SADC Secretariat.

SAPES/UNDP/SADC. 2000. *Challenges and Opportunities for Regional Integration*. SADC Regional Human Development Report. Harare: SAPES Books.

Southall, R. and T. Petlane (eds). 1995. *Democratisation and Demilitarisation in Lesotho: The 1993 Election and Its Aftermath*. Pretoria: Africa Institute of South Africa.

Tamela, S. 1999. *When Hens Begin to Crow: Gender and Parliamentary Politics in Uganda*. Kampala: Fountain.

Thabane, M. 1998. 'The king in politics in Lesotho: Background to the 17th Aout of King Letsie III.' *Review of Southern African Studies*, 2(1).

UNDP (UN Development Programme). 2002. *Human Development Report 2002: Deepening Democracy in a Fragmented World*. New York: Oxford University Press.

World Bank. 2000. *Can Africa Claim the 21st Century?* Washington, DC: World Bank.

Chapter 6: Mauritius

Amnesty International. 2003. *Report 2003*. http://web.amnesty.org.report2003/mus.

Bastian, S. and R. Luckham (eds). 2003. *Can Democracy Be Designed?* London: Zed Books.

BBC (British Broadcasting Corporation). 2004. 'BBC News.' 9 July. news.bbc.co.uk/1/hi/uk/3879111.stm, accessed 24 October 2004.

——. n.d. Web site. http://news.bbc.co.uk./2/hi/uk_news/politics/1005064.stm, accessed 20 October 2004.

Brautigam, D. 1999. 'The "Mauritius Miracle": Democracy, institutions and economic policy.' In R. Joseph (ed), *State, Conflict and Democracy in Africa.* Boulder: Lynne Rienner.

Dassyne, Ishwarduth. 2004. Interview with the author, University of Mauritius. 19 March.

European Centre for Development Policy Management/IOC (Indian Ocean Commission). 1998. *The Future of the Indian Ocean Commission: Strategic Reflections on Regional Cooperation in the Next Ten Years.* Maastricht: European Centre for Development Policy Management.

Huntington, S. P. 1991. *The Third Wave: Democratisation in the Late Twentieth Century.* Norman: University of Oklahoma Press.

IRIN News. 2004. Web site. 11 October. http://www.irinnews.org.

Jaddoo, R. 2002. 'The challenges facing the security sector in Mauritius.' Unpublished paper.

Library of Congress. 2003. Web site. http://memory.loc.gov/cgi-bin/query/r?ftd/cstdy:@field(DOCID+mu0053/4.

Lodge, T., D. Kadima, and D. Pottie (eds). 2002. *Compendium of Elections in Southern Africa.* Johannesburg: Electoral Institute of Southern Africa.

Mauritius News (London). 2003. Web site. 24 October. http://www.mauritiusnews.co.uk/10/24/03.

Mauritius Police Force. 2003. Web site. 'Divisions and branches.' http://police.gov.mu.

Morvan, L. 2004. Interview with Lindsay Morvan, Southern Africa Human Rights NGO Network/ Mouvement pour le Progres de Roche Bois. 19 March.

Srebrnik, H. 2002. '"Full of sound and fury": Three decades of parliamentary politics in Mauritius.' *Journal of Southern African Studies,* 28(2).

UNDP (UN Development Programme). 2002. *Human Development Report 2002: Deepening Democracy in a Fragmented World.* New York and Oxford: Oxford University Press.

Chapter 7: Mozambique

Grobbelaar, Neuma and Anicia Lalá. 2003. *Managing Group Grievances and Internal Conflict: Mozambique Country Report.* Working Paper No. 12. Clingendael: Netherlands Institute of International Relations. June.

IRIN News. 2002. 'Mozambique focus on media freedom.' 13 November. http://www.irinnews.org.

Lalá, Anicia. 2002. 'Dez anos de paz em Moçambique: Da visão normativa a perspectiva realista.' *Estudos Moçambicanos,* 20. CEA-UEM. November.

Ostheimer, Andrea. 1999. 'Transforming peace into democracy: Democratic structures in Mozambique.' *African Security Review,* 8(6).

Pereira, Joao, Yul Davids, and Robert Mattes. 2002. *Mozambicans' Views of Democracy and Political Reform: A Comparative Perspective.* Afrobarometer Paper No. 22. November.

Ratilal, Prakash. 2002. 'Percepções sobre a economia.' In Brazão Mazula, *Moçambique:10 anos de paz,* vol. 1. Maputo: Imprensa Universitária.

Republic of Mozambique. 1990. Constituição da Republica de Moçambique (Constitution of the Republic of Mozambique). Maputo.

——. 1993. General Peace Agreement of Mozambique, 1992. Maputo: African European Institute.

——. 1997a. Lei da Política de Defesa e Segurança, in Boletim da Republica 40, Ia Serie, 3o Suplemento, 07/10/97 (Defence and Security Act 17 of 1997). Maputo.

——. 1997b. Lei das Defesa Nacional das Forças Armadas in Boletim da Republica 40, Ia Serie, 3o Suplemento, 07/10/97 (National Defence and Armed Forces Act 18 of 1997). Maputo.

——. 2001. Action Plan for the Reduction of Absolute Poverty, 2001–2005. Maputo.

——. 2002. Planos Operativos do Plano Estratégico Integrado do Sector da Justiça, 2002–2006. Maputo.

——. 2003. Plano Estratégico da Polícia da Republica de Moçambique, 2003–2012, vol. 1. Maputo. May.

Rocca, Roberto Morozzo della. 1998. *Moçambique da Guerra a Paz: Historia de Uma Mediação Insólita.* Maputo: UEM Livraria Universitaria.

Schneidman, Witney. 1991. 'Conflict resolution in Mozambique: A status report.' *Centre for Strategic and International Studies Africa Notes.* 28 February.

The Economist Intelligence Unit. 2003. *Mozambique Country Report.* London. April.

Tibana, Roberto. 2003 'Indicador composto da actividade económica em Moçambique.' *Economia e Negócios, Noticias.* 21 February.

UEM-CEP (Universidade Eduardo Mondlane, Centro de Estudos de População). 2002. *Inquérito Nacional de Opinião Publica 2001.* Maputo: UEM-CEP. January.

UN (United Nations). 2000. *Mozambique Common Country Assessment 2000.* Maputo: UN. November.

——/Republic of Mozambique. 2002. *Report on the Millennium Development Goals: Mozambique.* Maputo: UN System. August.

UNDP (UN Development Programme). 2000. *Mozambique: National Human Development Report, 1999.* Maputo: UNDP.

——. 2002. *Mozambique: National Human Development Report, 2001.* Maputo: UNDP.

US State Department. 2001. *Mozambique Country Report on Human Rights Practices 2000.* Washington, DC: US State Department. http://www.state.gov/g/drl/rls/hrrpt/2000/af/859.htm.

Chapter 8: Namibia

African Development Bank. 2002. *African Development Report 2001: Fostering Good Governance in Africa.* New York: Oxford University Press.

Afrobarometer. 2000. *Public Opinion and the Consolidation of Democracy in Southern Africa: An Initial Review of Key Findings of the Southern African Democracy Barometer,* vol. 1. July.

Arlinghaus, B. E. 1984. *Military Development in Africa: The Political and Economic Risks of Arms Transfer.* Boulder: Westview Press.

Bauer, G. 1999. 'Challenges to democratic consolidation in Namibia.' In R. Joseph (ed), *State, Conflict and Democracy in Africa.* Boulder: Lynne Rienner.

——. 2001. 'Namibia in the first decade of independence: How democratic?' *Journal of Southern African Studies,* 27(1).

Blaauw, L. 1995. 'Post-apartheid peace and security prospects in Southern Africa.' Unpublished honours research paper, Department of Political and International Studies, Rhodes University.

—— and P. Bischoff. 2001. 'Directing our future? Regionalism, developmental regionalism and SADC in Southern Africa.' *Africa Insight,* 30(3–4).

Brown, S. 1995. 'Diplomacy by other means: SWAPO's liberation war.' In C. Leys and J. S. Saul, *Namibia's Liberation Struggle: The Two Edged Sword.* London: James Currey.

Cawthra, G. 1986. *Brutal Force: The Apartheid War Machine.* London: IDAF.

Cilliers, J. 1996. 'Approaches to security in Southern Africa.' *Africa Insight,* 26(1).

Diamond, L. 1999. *Developing Democracy: Towards Consolidation.* London: Johns Hopkins University Press.

Du Pisani, A. 2000. 'Namibia's foreign policy: Transformation and emerging orders (1989–1999).' In C. Keulder (ed), *State, Society and Democracy.* Windhoek: Gamsberg Macmillan.

——. 2001/2. 'Peacemaking in southern and central Africa: Namibia's role.' *Namibia Yearbook,* 8.

ECA (Economic Commission for Africa). 2003. *Recent Economic Trends in Africa and Prospects for 2003.* Addis Ababa: ECA.

Forrest, J. 2000. 'Democracy and development in post-independence Namibia.' In Y. Bradshaw and S. Ndegwa (eds), *The Uncertain Promise of Southern Africa.* Bloomington: University of Indiana Press.

Frasier Institute. 2003. *Economic Freedom of the World: 2003 Annual Report.* http://www.frasierinstitute.org.ca.

Gordon, R. 1989. 'The praetorianization of Namibia.' *TransAfrica Forum*, 6(2).

Huntington, S. P. 1995. 'Reforming civil–military relations.' *Journal of Democracy*, 6(4).

IPPR (Institute for Public Policy Research). *Military Expenditure Database.* http://www.ippr.org.na/database.htm.

Keulder, C. 2002. *In Search of Democrats: Youth Attitudes towards Democracy and Non-democratic Alternatives*. IPPR Briefing No. 10. Windhoek: Institute for Public Policy Research. May.

——. 2003. *Conflict Vulnerability and Sources of Resilience Assessment for Namibia*. Unpublished report prepared for the US Agency for International Development.

Lamb, G. 2000. 'Civil supremacy in Namibia: A retrospective case study.' *Journal of Peace, Conflict and Military Studies*, 1(1).

Leys, C. and J. S. Saul. 1995. 'Introduction.' In C. Leys and J. S. Saul (eds), *Namibia's Liberation Struggle*. Athens, Ohio: Ohio University Press, and London: James Currey.

Mail and Guardian (Johannesburg). 2003. 28 March–3 April.

Malan, M. 1999. 'Can they do that? SADC, the DRC and Lesotho.' *Indicator SA*, 15(4).

McDonald, M. 2002. 'Security, sovereignty and identity.' Paper presented to the Jubilee Conference of the Australian Political Science Association, Canberra, October. http://arts.anu.edu.au/sss/apsa/Papers/mcdonald.pdf.

MISA (Media Institute of Southern Africa). 2002. *So This Is Democracy: The State of the Media in Southern Africa*. Windhoek: MISA.

Preston, R. 1993. 'Integrating fighters: The development brigade.' In R. Preston *et al.*, *The Integration of Returned Exiles, Former Combatants and Other War-affected Namibians.* Windhoek: NISER.

Republic of Namibia. 1990. The Constitution of the Republic of Namibia. Windhoek.

——. 1993. Statement on Defence Policy. Windhoek: Ministry of Defence. February.

——. n.d. 'Estimate of revenue and expenditure for the financial year 1 April 2002–31 March 2003.' Windhoek: Ministry of Finance.

——. Office of the Prime Minister. 2000. *A Decade of Peace, Democracy, and Prosperity 1990–2000.* Windhoek: Solitaire Press.

——. Ministry of Finance. 2004. 'Estimate of revenue and expenditure for the financial year 1 April 2004–31 March 2005.' Windhoek: Ministry of Finance.

Ruppel, H. 1987. 'Namibia: Security and its consequences.' In G. Totemeyer, V. B. Kandetu, and W. Werner (eds), *Namibia in Perspective*. Windhoek: Council of Churches in Namibia.

Sherbourne, R. 2001. *Defending the Indefensible? Namibia Defence Expenditure since 1990.* IPPR Briefing No. 1. Windhoek: Institute for Public Policy Research. April.

SADC (Southern African Development Community). 1992. Towards the Southern African Development Community: A Declaration by the Heads of State or Governments of Southern African States. Windhoek.

——. 2001. Protocol on Politics, Defence, and Security. Blantyre.

SWAPO Department of Information and Publicity. 1987. *To Be Born a Nation.* London: Zed Books.

Tsie, Balefi. 1998. 'Regional security in Southern Africa: Whither the SADC Organ on Politics, Defence and Security?' *Global Dialogue*, 3(3).

UN (United Nations). 2002. Charter of the United Nations and the Statute of the International Court of Justice. New York: UN Department of Public Information.

UNDP (UN Development Programme). 2002. *Human Development Report 2002: Deepening Democracy in a Fragmented World.* New York: Oxford University Press.

UN Office on Drugs and Crime, Regional Office for Southern Africa. 2003. *Strategic Programme Framework on Crime and Drugs for Southern Africa: 2003.* http://www.gov.za/, accessed 25 August 2003.

Van Aardt, M. 1996. 'Doing battle with security: A Southern African approach.' *South African Journal of International Affairs*, 3(2).

Windhoek Observer. 2003. 'Spy agency denies any link to Geingob dossier.' 18 June.

Wood, B. 1991. 'Preventing the vacuum: Determinants of the Namibian settlement.' *Journal of Southern African Studies*, 17.

——. 1984. 'The militarization of Namibia's economy.' *Review of African Political Economy*, 29.

Chapter 9: Seychelles

Arnold, G. 1995. *Wars in the Third World since 1945.* London: Cassell.

Baregu, M. 2002. 'Beyond September 11: Structural causes and behavioural consequences of international terrorism.' In C. Lee (ed), *Responding to Terrorism: What Role for the UN?* New York: International Peace Academy.

Bell, W. 2003. 'Seychelles and security in the Indian Ocean region.' Unpublished conference paper.

Bennett, G. 1993. 'Seychelles: Pressures achieve constitutional change.' In C. Legum (ed), *Africa Contemporary Record.* New York: Africana Publishing.

Botha, J. P. 1997. 'Security and co-operation in the Indian Ocean rim.' In *Diplomats and Defenders*. ISS Monograph No. 9. Pretoria: Institute for Security Studies.

Ellis, S. 1996. 'Africa and international corruption: The strange case of South Africa and Seychelles.' *African Affairs*, 95(379).

Fomunyoh, C. 2001. 'Francophone Africa in flux: Democratisation in fits and starts.' *Journal of Democracy*, 12(3).

Franda, M. 1982. *The Seychelles: Unquiet Islands*. Boulder: Westview Press.

Ostheimer, J. M. 1973. 'Independence politics in the Seychelles.' In J. M. Ostheimer (ed), *The Politics of the Western Indian Ocean Islands.* New York: Praeger.

Hatchard, J. 1993. 'Re-establishing a multi-party state: Some constitutional lessons from the Seychelles.' *Journal of Modern African Studies*, 31(4).

Lauseig, J. 1999. 'New security challenges in the Indian Ocean: Instigators, flows and factors of instability.' *African Security Review*, 8(1).

Lodge, T., D. Kadima, and D. Pottie (eds). 2002. *Compendium of Elections in Southern Africa.* Johannesburg: Electoral Institute of Southern Africa.

Mills, G. 1998. *South Africa and Security Building in the Indian Ocean Rim.* Johannesburg: South African Institute of International Affairs.

Singh, J. 1995. 'Towards durable peace and security in the Indian Ocean region.' *South African Journal of International Affairs*, 2(2).

Chapter 10: South Africa

Ayoob, M. 1995. *The Third World Security Predicament: State Making, Regional Conflict and the International System.* London: Lynne Rienner.

Beeld. 2005a. 'Verdediging laat Asmal rooi sien' (Defence makes Asmal see red). 16 March.

——. 2005b. 'Vredesmagte melk weermagbegroting' (Peacekeeping forces milk defence budget). 28 June.

——. 2005c. 'Soldate deel van staatsdiens se herskikkingsprogram sê minister' (Soldiers part of civil service transformation programme). 28 June.

Buzan, B. 1991. *People, States and Fear: An Agenda for International Security Studies in the Post-Cold War Era.* Hemel Hempstead: Harvester Wheatsheaf.

Geldenhuys, D. J. 1991. 'South Africa: From international isolation to reintegration.' *Strategic Review for Southern Africa,* XIII(1). May.

GCIS (Government Communication and Information System). 2005. *South Africa Yearbook 2004/5.* Pretoria.

Hough, M. and A. du Plessis (eds). 2000. *Selected Official South African Strategic and Security Perceptions: 1992–2000.* Pretoria: ISSUP.

IPA (International Peace Academy). 2001. *The Infrastructure of Peace in Africa: Assessing the Peacebuilding Capacity of African Institutions.* New York: IPA.

Job, B. L. (ed). 1992. *The Insecurity Dilemma.* London: Lynne Rienner.

Khanyile, M. (Defence Secretariat). 2003. Written comment. 15 September.

Le Pere, G. and B. Vickers. 2004. 'Civil society and foreign policy in South Africa.' In J. van der Westhuizen and P. Nel (eds), *Democratizing Foreign Policy? Lessons from South Africa.* New York: Lexington Books.

Mail & Guardian Online. 2003. 28 August.

Modise, J. 1999. 'Parliamentary briefing.' 9 February. http://www.gov.za/speeches/briefings99/defence.htm.

Motumi, N. 2003. Written comment. Received 4 September.

Ngoma, N. 2003. 'SADC: Towards a security community?' *African Security Review* 12(3). http://www.iss.org.za/Pubs/ASR, accessed 12 August 2005.

Republic of South Africa. DoD (Department of Defence). 2003. Strategic Business Plan. Pretoria: DoD.

Rotberg, R. and G. Mills (eds). *War and Peace in Southern Africa: Crime, Drugs, Armies, Trade.* Washington, DC: Brookings Institution Press.

SAIRR (South African Institute of Race Relations). 2002. *South Africa Survey 2001/2.* Johannesburg: SAIRR.

——. 2003. *South Africa Survey 2002/3.* Johannesburg: SAIRR.

——. 2005. *Fast Facts.* Johannesburg: SAIRR. March.

Solomon, H. 1998. 'From accommodation and control to control and intervention: Illegal population flows into South Africa.' In R. Rotberg and G. Mills (eds), *War and Peace in Southern Africa.* Washington, DC: Brookings Institution Press.

Chapter 11: Swaziland

Amato, P. 1997. 'African philosophy and modernity.' In C. Eze Emmanuel (ed), *Postcolonial African Philosophy: A Critical Reader.* Boston: Blackwell.

Baloro, John. 1991. 'The human right to free association and assembly and multi-party democracy: A study of the law and practice in Swaziland.' Paper presented at the 14th Southern African Universities Social Sciences Conference, University of Namibia, Windhoek, 11 October.

Booth, A. R. 1983. *Swaziland: Tradition and Change in a Southern African Kingdom.* Boulder: Westview Press.

Bujra, A. 2002. *African Conflicts: Their Causes and Their Political and Social Environment.* DPMF Occasional Paper No. 4. Addis Ababa: DPMF.

Davies, R. H. *et al.* 1985. *The Kingdom of Swaziland: A Profile.* London: Zed Books.

Du Pisani, A. 2002. 'State and society under South African rule.' In C. Keulder (ed), *State, Society and Democracy: A Reader in Namibian Politics.* Windhoek: Gamsberg Macmillan.

Geldenhuys, Deon. 1981. 'Some strategic implications of regional economic relationships for the Republic of South Africa.' *Strategic Review.* Pretoria: Institute for Strategic Studies. January.

Harding, S. (ed). 1976. *Can Theories Be Refuted? Essays on the Durkhem–Quine Thesis.* Reidel: Dordrecht.

Hlatshwayo, Nkonzo. 1992. 'The ideology of traditionalism and its implications for principles of constitutionalism: The case of Swaziland.' LLM dissertation, York University.

——. 1994. 'Constitution and Swazi culture: A recipe for harmony or disaster?' Paper presented at the IDEAL Conference, Manzini, 15 October.

Hobbes, Thomas. 1962. *Leviathan.* New York: Collier Macmillan.

ILO (International Labour Organisation). 1999. *Swaziland: A Report of the Committee of Experts.* Document 22/1999. Geneva: ILO.

Khumalo, B. 1996. 'The politics of constitution making and constitutional pluralism in Swaziland since 1973.' *UNISWA Research Journal,* 10.

Kingdom of Swaziland. 1968. Constitutional Law, Act 50/1968. Mbabane.

——. 1973a. The King's Proclamation to the Nation. Mbabane. 12 April.

——. 1973b. Legislative Procedure Order of 13 April. Mbabane.

——. 1978. The Establishment of the Parliament of Swaziland. Order No. 23/1978. Mbabane.

——. 1992a. Decree 1/1992. Mbabane.

—— 1992b. *Tinkhundla Review Commission Report.* Mbabane.

——. 1992c. Establishment of Parliament Order, 1992. Mbabane.

——. 1997. National Development Strategy: A Twenty-five Year Vision. Mbabane.

——. 2001. *The Constitutional Review Commission Report.* Mbabane.

——. 2005. The Constitution of the Kingdom of Swaziland. *Swaziland Government Gazette Extraordinary,* XLIII. Mbabane. 26 July.

Kuper, H. 1978. *Sobhuza II: Ngwenyama and King of Swaziland: The Story of an Hereditary Ruler and His Country.* New York: Africana Publishing Company.

Macmillan, H. 1985. 'Swaziland: Decolonisation and triumph of tradition.' *Journal of Modern African Studies,* 23(4).

Mazrui, A. 2001. 'Who killed democracy? Clues of the past and concerns of the future.' In *Proceedings of the Conference on Democracy, Sustainable Development and Poverty Reduction: Are They Compatible?* Addis Ababa: DPMF.

Mzizi, J. B. 1995. *Voices of the Voiceless: Toward a Theology of Liberation for Post-colonial Swaziland.* PhD thesis, Vanderbilt University, Nashville, Tennessee.

——. 2002. 'Leadership, civil society and democratisation in Swaziland.' In A. Bujra and S. Buthelezi (eds), *Leadership, Civil Society and Democratisation in Africa.* Addis Ababa: DPMF.

PUDEMO (People's United Democratic Movement). n.d. 'Towards a constituent assembly through a negotiation process.' Unpublished document.

——. 1994. Letter to His Majesty King Mswati III. July.

SFTU (Swaziland Federation of Trade Unions). 1994. Letter to the prime minister. February.

——. n.d. *Policies of the SFTU*. Mbabane.

Swazi Observer (Mbabane). 3 January 2003.

Van Wyk, A. J. 1965. *Swaziland: A Political Study*. Pretoria: Africa Institute of South Africa.

Wanda, B. P. 1990. 'The shaping of the modern constitution.' *Lesotho Law Journal*, 6(1).

Chapter 12: Tanzania

Bakari, M. A. 1999. *Democratization Process in Zanzibar: A Retarded Transition*. PhD thesis, Institute of Politics, University of Hamburg.

Baregu, M. 1993. 'Perception of threat and conception of defence before the mutiny.' In M. Baregu (ed), *Tanganyika Rifles Mutiny, January 1964*. Dar es Salaam: Dar es Salaam University Press.

Bienen, H. 1978. *Armies and Parties in Africa*. London: Africana Publishing Company.

Booth, K. 1994. 'A security regime in Southern Africa: Theoretical considerations.' *Southern African Perspectives*, 30. Centre for Southern African Studies, University of the Western Cape.

Breytenbach, W. 1995. *Conflict in Sub-Saharan Africa: From the Frontline States to Collective Security*. Arusha Papers: A Working Series on Southern African Security. Bellville: Centre for Southern African Studies and Centre for Foreign Relations.

Buzan, B., O. Waever, and J. de Wilde. 1998. *Security: A New Framework for Analysis*. Boulder: Lynne Rienner.

Chachage, S. 2000. *Environment, Aid and Politics in Zanzibar*. Dar es Salaam: Dar es Salaam University Press.

Commonwealth Expert Team. 2003. *Report of the Commonwealth Expert Team on the Pemba By-elections*. Zanzibar. 18 May.

Davies, R. 1992. 'Integration or co-operation in a post-apartheid Southern Africa: Some reflections on an emerging debate.' *Southern African Perspectives*, 18. Centre for Southern African Studies, University of Western Cape.

De Klerk, B. 2002. 'What makes democracy work?' *Conflict Trends: Special Issue on Democracy*, 4/2002.

Elman, M. 1997. *Paths to Peace: Is Democracy the Answer?* Cambridge, Mass.: MIT Press.

Geldenhuys, D. and D. Venter. 1979. 'Regional co-operation in Southern Africa: A constellation of states.' *International Affairs Bulletin*, 3(3).

The Guardian (Tanzania), various issues.

Huntington, S. 1991. *The Third Wave: Democratization in Late Twentieth Century*. Norman: University of Oklahoma Press.

Kaiser, P. J. 2003. 'Zanzibar: A multilevel analysis of conflict prevention.' In Chandra L. Sriram and Karin Wermester, (eds), *From Promise to Practice: Strengthening UN Capacities for the Prevention of Violent Conflict*. Boulder: Lynne Rienner.

Kassim, S. 2003. 'Women, democracy and political leadership.' In *Political Handbook and NGO Calendar*. Dar es Salaam: Friedrich Ebert Stiftung.

Kayode Fayemi, J. 2002. 'Framework for co-operative security in a region in transition: Challenges and prospects.' *Conflict Trends: Special Issue on Democracy*, 4/2002.

Maliyamkono, T. M. (ed). 2000. *The Political Plight of Zanzibar*. Dar es Salaam: TEMA.

Maundi, M. 2002a. 'Reconciliation and democratic consolidation in Zanzibar.' In *Political Handbook and NGO Calendar.* Dar es Salaam: Friedrich Ebert Stiftung.

——. 2002b. 'Addressing conflict in Tanzania.' In *Coping with Conflict: Agenda 2000 for Democratic Culture in Tanzania.* Dar es Salaam: Friedrich Ebert Stiftung.

——. 2002c. 'Tanzania's march towards democratic consolidation.' *Conflict Trends: Special Issue on Democracy*, 4/2002.

——. 2003. 'Democratic consolidation in Zanzibar: One year after MWAFAKA.' In *Political Handbook and NGO Calendar.* Dar es Salaam: Friedrich Ebert Stiftung.

Metz, S. 2002. 'A strategic approach to African security: Challenges and prospects.' *African Security Review.* Pretoria: Institute for Security Studies.

Mmuya, M. 2002. 'Milestones in the democratisation process in Tanzania.' In *Political Handbook and NGO Calendar.* Dar es Salaam: Friedrich Ebert Stiftung.

Nathan, L. and J. Honwana. 1994. *The Establishment of SADC Forums for Conflict Resolution and Security and Defence.* Discussion Paper. Centre for Conflict Resolution, University of Cape Town.

——. 1995. 'After the storm: Common security and conflict resolution in Southern Africa.' Arusha Papers No. 3. Bellville: Centre for Southern African Studies and Centre for Foreign Relations. February.

Nkiwane, T. 1999. 'Contested regionalism: Southern and Central Africa in the post-apartheid era.' *African Journal of Political Science*, 4(2).

Nyerere, J. 1966. *Freedom and Unity.* Dar es Salaam: Oxford University Press.

——. 1967. 'Tanzania policy on foreign affairs.' Address at the TANU National Conference, 16 October.

——. 2000. *Africa Today and Tomorrow.* Dar es Salaam: The Mwalimu Nyerere Foundation.

Okoh, P. 1989. 'Political strategies for the Frontline States.' *International Diplomatic Review*, 3, July. Dar es Salaam: Centre for Foreign Relations.

Omari, A. H. 1991. *The Rise and Fall of the Front Line States Alliance in Southern Africa: 1975–1995.* PhD thesis, Dalhousie University.

——. 2001. *Civil–military Relations in Tanzania.* Dar es Salaam: Centre for Foreign Relations.

SADC (Southern African Development Community). 1992. SADC Declaration and Treaty. Gaborone: SADC Secretariat.

——. 2001. Protocol on Politics, Defence, and Security Co-operation. Gaborone: SADC Secretariat.

Selebi, J. 1999. 'Building collaborative security in Southern Africa.' *African Security Review*, 8(5).

Sheriff, A. 1994. 'The union and the struggle for democracy in Zanzibar.' In Rwekaza Mukandala and Haroub Othman (eds), *Liberalisation and Politics: The 1990 Election in Tanzania.* Dar es Salaam: Dar es Salaam University Press.

Shivji, I. 1990. *Tanzania: The Legal Foundations of the Union.* Dar es Salaam: Dar es Salaam University Press.

Solomon, H. and J. Cilliers. 1996. *People, Poverty and Peace: Human Security in Southern Africa.* IDP Monograph Series No. 4.

TEMCO (Tanzania Election Monitoring Committee). *Report of the Tanzania Election Monitoring Committee on the Pemba By-elections.* Zanzibar. 18 May.

Zartman, I. William. 1992. 'Sources of conflict and institutions of conflict management in Southern Africa.' Paper presented at the Seventh International Conference on Peace and Security in Southern Africa, Centre for Foreign Relations, Dar es Salaam, Tanzania, July.

Chapter 13: Zambia

Ayoob, M. 1995. *The Third World Security Predicament: State Making, Regional Conflict and the International System*. London: Lynne Rienner.

Chisala, B. S. 1991. *Luchembe Coup Attempt*. Lusaka: Multimedia Publications.

Dube, T. J. 1998. 'Co-ordinating regional defence co-operation and structures for common security in Africa.' *African Armed Forces*, September.

Fisher, R. and William Ury. 1991. *Getting to Yes: Negotiating Agreement without Giving In*. New York: Penguin.

Haantobolo, Godfrey H. N. 2002. 'The role of the Zambian legislature in the transformation of the Zambia Defence Forces, 1964–2000.' The African Civil Military Relations Project, 2000–2002.

Habasonda, L. M. 2002. 'The military, civil society and democracy in Zambia.' *African Security Review*, 11(2).

Malan, M. and J. Cilliers. 1997. *SADC Organ on Politics, Defence and Security: Future Development*. ISS Occasional Paper No. 19. Pretoria: Institute of Security Studies. March.

Monitor (Lusaka). 2000. 7–14 April.

Mulikita, Njunga M. 1999. 'Democratisation and conflict resolution in Africa: The role of international election observers.' *Peace Keeping and International Relations*, 28(3), May–June.

——. 2002. 'Political parties and the unfinished quest for democratic governance in Zambia.' Paper presented to the ISS/OSSREA Workshop on the Sustainability of African Political Parties, Addis Ababa, Ethiopia, 6–10 May.

Mwanawasa, L. P. 2002. 'Speech by President Levy Patrick Mwanawasa, SC at the special meeting of parliament.' Lusaka. 11 July.

Ohlson, T. and Stephen Stedman. 1994. *The New Is Not Yet Born: Conflict in Southern Africa*. Washington, DC: Brookings Institution Press.

Olonisakin, F. 1998. 'Rethinking regional security in Africa: An analysis of ECOWAS and SADC.' *Strategic Review for Southern Africa*, 22(2), November.

Phiri, B. J. 2001. 'Civil control of the Zambian military since independence: Implications for democracy.' *African Security Review*, 10(4).

Pitso, G. L. 1999. 'Southern Africa regional security.' http:// www.mil.za/CSANDF/CJSuppl.

Republic of Zambia. 1964. Constitution of Zambia. Lusaka.

——. 1973. Constitution of Zambia 1973. Lusaka.

——. 2002. *The Report of the Committee on National Security and Foreign Affairs, the First Session of the Ninth National Assembly Appointed on 15th March 2002*. Lusaka: National Assembly of Zambia.

SACCORD (Southern African Centre for Constructive Resolution of Disputes). 2002. *Conflicts in Zambia and Beyond*. Lusaka: SACCORD.

Salih, Mohamed. 2001. *African Democracies and African Politics*. London: Pluto Press.

Saturday Post (Lusaka). 2003. No. 2278SA58.

Times of Zambia. 2000. 11 May.

World Bank. 1989. *Sub-Saharan Africa: From Crisis to Sustainable Growth*. Washington, DC: World Bank.

Chapter 14: Zimbabwe

Alao, A. 1995. 'The metamorphosis of the "unorthodox": The integration and early development of the Zimbabwean National Army.' In N. Bhebe and T. Ranger (eds), *Soldiers in Zimbabwe's Liberation War*. London: James Currey, and Portsmouth, New Hampshire: Heinemann.

Bhebe, N. and T. Ranger (eds). 1995. *Society in Zimbabwe's Liberation War*. Harare: University of Zimbabwe Publications.

Bond, P. and M. Manyanya. 2002. *Zimbabawe's Plunge*. Scottsville: Natal University Press.

CCJP (Catholic Commission for Justice and Peace). 1997. *Breaking the Silence, Building True Peace*. Report. Harare: Legal Resources Foundation.

Cilliers, J. 1996. *The SADC Organ for Defence, Politics and Security*. ISS Occasional Paper No. 10. Pretoria: Institute for Strategic Studies. October.

Copp, David, Jean Hampton and John Roemer (eds). 1993. *The Idea of Democracy*. Cambridge: Cambridge University Press.

EDC (Environment, Democracy and Challenges) News. 2002. Electronic newsletter edited by Leif Ohlsson under the Swedish International Development Agency (SIDA). No. 8, May.

Financial Gazette (Harare). 1999. 'Zimbabwe sinks 500 million dollars into DRC war.' 14 May.

Helen Suzman Foundation. 2000. 'Zimbabwe survey referendum and survey results. Democratic constitution for Zimbabwe.' http://news.bbc.co.uk/2/hi/africall 569284.stm.

Khapoya, V. B. 1994. *The African Experience*. London: Prentice Hall.

Krige, N. 1995. *Zimbabwe's Guerrilla War*. Harare: Baobab.

Mandaza I. 1998. *Governance and Human Development in Southern Africa*. Harare: SAPES.

Malan, M. and J. Cilliers. 1997. *SADC Organ on Politics, Defence and Security: Future Development*. Occasional Paper No. 19. Pretoria: Institute for Strategic Studies. March.

Manungo K. D. 1991. *The Role Peasants Played in the Zimbabwe War of Liberation, with Special Emphasis on Chiweshe District*. PhD thesis, Ohio University.

——. 1997. 'The plight of former migrant workers in Zimbabwe.' Paper presented at the Conference on Human Rights and Democracy, University of Zimbabwe. SAREC Project on Human Rights and Democracy in Zimbabwe.

Moyo, S. 1995. *The Land Question in Zimbabwe*. Harare: SAPES.

Republic of Zimbabwe. 1996. Constitution of Zimbabwe, rev. ed. Harare.

Shire, George. 2003. 'Robert Mugabe: Sinner or sinned against?' *African Business Magazine*. London. April.

Swartz, D. 1998. 'Political and democratic governance in South Africa in the context of Southern Africa.' In I. Mandaza (ed), *Governance and Human Development in Southern Africa*. Harare: SAPES.

Chapter 15: Conclusion

Baker, B. 1999. 'The quality of African democracy: Why and how it should be measured.' *Journal of Contemporary African Studies*, 17(2).

Burgess, J. P. and T. Owen (eds). 2004. 'Editor's note.' *Security Dialogue*, 35(3).

Buzan, B. 1991. *People, States and Fear: An Agenda for International Security Studies in a post-Cold War Era*. Hemel Hempstead: Harvester Wheatsheaf.

Cawthra, G. and R. Luckham. 2003. *Governing Insecurity: Democratic Control of the Military and Security Establishment in Transitional Democracies*. London: Zed Books.

Cheru, F. 2002. *African Renaissance: Roadmaps to the Challenges of Globalisation*. London: Zed Books.

De Coning, C. 1999. 'South African blue helmets in the Democratic Republic of Congo.' *Global Dialogue*, 4(2), August.

Edigheji, O. 2004. 'The African state and socio-economic development: An institutional perspective.' *African Journal of Political Science*, 9(1).

Elklit, J. 2002. 'Lesotho 2002: Africa's first MMP election.' *Journal of African Elections*, 1(2).

Ellis, S. and D. Killingray. 2002. 'Africa after 11 September 2001.' *African Affairs*, 101(402).

Hughes, C. 2000. 'Globalisation and security in the Asia-Pacific: An initial investigation.' Paper presented at the 8th meeting of the CSCAP Working Group on Comprehensive and Co-operative Security, Kaula Lumpur, Malaysia, 19–21 October.

Landsberg, C. 2003. 'Building sustainable peace requires democratic governance.' Synopsis. *Newsletter of the CPS Governance Programme*, 7(1), April.

Lodge, T. 1999. *Consolidating Democracy: South Africa's Second Popular Election*. Johannesburg: Witwatersrand University Press and Electoral Institute of Southern Africa.

Luckham, R. 2003. 'Democratic strategies for security in transition and conflict.' In G. Cawthra and R. Luckham, *Governing Insecurity: Democratic Control of the Military and Security Establishment in Transitional Democracies*. London: Zed Books.

Mandaza, I. and D. Nabudere (eds). 2002. *Pan-Africanism and Integration in Africa*. Harare: SAPES Books.

Mansfield, E. D. and J. Snyder. 1995. 'Democratisation and war.' *Foreign Affairs*, May–June.

Matlosa, K. 2001. 'Dilemmas of security in Southern Africa: Problems and prospects for security co-operation.' In E. Maloka (ed), *A United States of Africa*. Pretoria: Africa Institute of South Africa.

Mhone, G. and O. Edigheji (eds). 2003. *Governance in the New South Africa: The Challenges of Globalisation*. Cape Town: University of Cape Town Press.

Nabudere, D. (ed). 2000. *Globalisation and the African Post-colonial State*. Harare: African Association of Political Science.

Regan, P. M. and E. A. Henderson. 2002. 'Democracy, threats and political repression in developing countries: Are democracies internally less violent?' *Third World Quarterly*, 23(1).

SAPES/UNDP/SADC. 2000. *SADC Regional Human Development Report*. Harare: SAPES Books.

Schedler, A. 2001. 'Measuring democratic consolidation.' *Studies in Comparative International Development*, 36(1).

Southall, R. 2003. 'Democracy in Southern Africa: Moving beyond a difficult legacy.' *Review of African Political Economy*, 96.

Smith, M. E. 2004. *Europe's Foreign and Security Policy: The Institutionalisation of Co-operation*. Cambridge: Cambridge University Press.

UN Commission on Human Security. 2003. *Human Security Now*. New York: UN.

Vale, P. 2003. *Security and Politics in South Africa: The Regional Dimension*. Boulder: Lynne Rienner.

Van Nieuwkerk, A. 1999. 'Promoting peace and security in Southern Africa: Is SADC the appropriate vehicle?' *Global Dialogue*, 4(3), December.

Zacharias, A. 1999. *Security and the State in Southern Africa*. London: Tauris Academic Studies.

Zeleza, P. 2003. *Rethinking Africa's Globalisation: The Intellectual Challenge*, vol. 1. New Jersey: Africa World Press.

Index